Making Sense of Experiential Learning

Diversity in Theory and Practice

Other titles recently published under the SRHE/Open University Press imprint.

Michael Allen: *The Goals of Universities*
Tony Becher: *Academic Tribes and Territories*
William Birch: *The Challenge to Higher Education*
David Boud *et al.*: *Teaching in Laboratories*
Heather Eggins: *Restructuring Higher Education*
Colin Evans: *Language People*
Derek Gardiner: *The Anatomy of Supervision*
Gunnar Handal and Per Lauvås: *Promoting Reflective Teaching*
Vivien Hodgson *et al.*: *Beyond Distance Teaching, Towards Open Learning*
Peter Linklater: *Education and the World of Work*
John Pratt and Suzanne Silverman: *Responding to Constraint*
Marjorie E. Reeves: *The Crisis in Higher Education*
John T. E. Richardson *et al.*; *Student Learning*
Derek Robbins: *The Rise of Independent Study*
Gordon Taylor *et al.*: *Literacy by Degrees*
Malcolm Tight: *Academic Freedom and Responsibility*
David Watson: *Managing the Modular Course*
Alan Woodley *et al.*: *Choosing to Learn*

Making Sense of Experiential Learning

Diversity in
Theory and Practice

Edited by
Susan Warner Weil
and Ian McGill

The Society for Research into Higher Education
& Open University Press

Published by SRHE and
Open University Press
12 Cofferidge Close
Stony Stratford
Milton Keynes MK11 1BY

and
242 Cherry Street
Philadelphia, PA 19106, USA

First Published 1989

British Library Cataloguing in Publication Data

Making sense of experiential learning: diversity
 in theory and practice.
 1. Experiential learning by students
 I. Weil, Susan Warner   II. McGill, Ian
370.15'23

ISBN 0-335-09549-6

Library of Congress Cataloging in Publication Data

Making sense of experiential learning: diversity in theory and
 practice/[edited] by Susan Warner Weil and Ian McGill.
   p. cm.
   Papers from the First International Conference on Experiential
Learning held in London, England in the summer of 1987.
   Includes bibliographies and index.
   1. Experiential learning—Congresses.   I. Weil, Susan Warner.
II. McGill, Ian.   III. International Conference on Experiential
Learning (1st: 1987: London, England)   IV. Society for Research
into Higher Education.
BF318.5.D57   1989
153.1'5—dc19
                                                88-39511
                                                    CIP

 ISBN 0-335-09549-6 (Open University Press)

Typeset by Rowland Phototypesetting Limited
Bury St Edmunds, Suffolk
Printed in Great Britain by St Edmundsbury Press Limited
Bury St Edmunds, Suffolk

Contents

List of Contributors

Susan Warner Weil develops and facilitates strategies to help individuals and organizations become more effective in reflecting and building upon experience as the basis for continuous learning and change. Her PhD research focuses on the experiences of adults, as they learn – and come to terms with – formal education at different stages in their lives. She is presently Associate Director of Higher Education for Capability at the Royal Society of Arts and Visiting Lecturer/Consultant to the Centre for Higher Education Studies at the University of London.

Ian McGill works experientially on personal and management development programmes in organizations with an emphasis upon self-development, and action learning and where the organization is seen as a learning community. Ian is also a consultant to government agencies concerned with organizational and social change. Ian is Principal Lecturer at the Business School, Brighton Polytechnic, where his recent work has been on the development of courses and programmes with an experiential and action learning base as well as having a related staff development role.

This book builds on the authors' many years of experience in staff, management, organizational development and social change initiatives in a variety of learning sectors including higher education, trainer training, industry, public and voluntary organizations and the community.

Dr Amina Barkatoolah works as a Researcher at the Lifelong Education Section of the University of Paris VIII and is a consultant for UNESCO, Paris.

Avtar Brah is a Lecturer in the Centre for Extra-Mural Studies, Birkbeck College, University of London, England.

Dr David Boud is Acting Director of the Tertiary Education Research Centre at the University of New South Wales, Australia.

Dr Richard Bawden is Dean of the Faculty of Agriculture at Hawkesbury, Australia.

Tom Bourner works in the Department of Business Management at Brighton Polytechnic, England, undertaking research and introducing experiential approaches into higher education.

Costas Criticos is a Lecturer in Educational Technology at the University of Natal, Durban, South Africa.

Dr Paul Frost is a Senior Lecturer in the Centre for Business Research in Industrial Relations at the Brighton Polytechnic, England.

Dr Dwight E. Giles, Jr is Senior Lecturer and Director of the Field and International Study Program in the New York State College of Human Ecology at Cornell University, USA.

Jane Henry is a Lecturer in Educational Technology at the Open University, England.

Dr Lucy Horwitz teaches mathematics to adults at the College of Public and Community Service of the University of Massachusetts, USA.

Jane Hoy is Course Organizer for Social Science and Women's Studies in the Centre for Extra-Mural Studies, Birkbeck College, University of London, England.

Dr Miriam Hutton teaches at the School of Social Work at the University of Manitoba, Canada.

Dr Annikki Järvinen is a Senior Lecturer in Educational Sciences at Tampere University, Finland.

Dr Phyllis Marie Jensen is a consultant researcher in Canada specializing in work related to the victimization of women and children.

Dr Jackson B. Keregero is Associate Professor of Extension Education and Director of the Institute of Continuing Education at Sokoine University of Agriculture in Morogoro, Tanzania.

Dr Mary K. St. John Nelson is Associate Professor in the Science Business and Mathematics Division of the General College at the University of Minnesota, USA.

Dave O'Reilly tutors in the School for Independent Study at North East London Polytechnic, England.

Dr Roger Packham is Principal Lecturer/Reader in Agriculture in the Faculty of Agriculture at Hawkesbury Agricultural College, Australia.

Shari L. Peterson is an Assistant Professor in the General College at the University of Minnesota, USA.

Dr Marie Redwine is Director of the Adult Degree Program at South Western Adventist College, USA.

Roger Roberts is a Lecturer at Hawkesbury Agricultural College, Australia.

Dr Phillida Salmon is a Visiting Fellow in Psychology at the University of London Institute of Education, England.

Susan Segal-Horn, previously at Brighton, is now a Lecturer in Strategic Management at Cranfield School of Management, England.

Tara Serrao is a Development Worker with Christa Sharan Social Development Society in Chikmagular District, Karnataka, India.

Timothy K. Stanton is Associate Director and Co-ordinator of Action Research and Internships at Stanford University's Public Service Center, USA.

Dr Danny Wildemeersch is a Lecturer at the Unit of Social Pedagogy (Department of Educational Sciences) of the Catholic University of Leuven, Belgium.

Julie Wylde is currently a Consultant to a training and development organization working in India and Africa.

Foreword

This book deals with the most pervasive form of learning in society: that which comes by and from experience. From the discovery of how to exploit the potential of fire to the ability of different cultural and linguistic groups to communicate with each other, most of the significant steps in human development can be associated with some form of experiential learning.

Although experiential, or experience-based, learning can be regarded as the earliest approach to learning for the human race, the significance and potential of it has not been fully recognized until relatively recently. In the formal educational system it has tended to be devalued and regarded as somehow fundamentally inferior to those organized forms of knowledge which have been constructed as subjects or disciplines. The practical and the applied do not tend to have the same status in educational institutions as the academic and the abstract. Academic rigour is a commonplace of classroom discourse, that education should be true to the lived experience of learners is an alien idea. The heritage of Aristotle and Descartes still reigns supreme.

Luckily, times are changing and there is a dawning recognition of the importance and centrality of learning from experience in the academy as well as the community in which it was always secure. Increasing numbers of teachers and practitioners of all kinds are realizing that the polarity between the intellectual and the practical is an absurdity which can no longer be supported and that we can only progress if we accept that thinking and action are entirely complementary. Case study, simulation and practical work are vital for more than particular forms of professional education; learning need not be bound by the limits of the classroom or the walls of the institution; attention to values, feelings and emotions can enhance learning rather than detract from it; people can learn without the presence of a teacher!

Great progress has been made throughout this century in the development of particular forms of experiential learning. The transformation of the primary school classroom is but one example. However, developments have often taken place in isolation from each other, with separation of levels of education, of subject areas and of national boundaries. I am continually struck by the lack of awareness of important educational developments which take place somewhere else, even when that somewhere else is in the same institution.

Similarly, in the area of conceptualizing experiential learning, we find the same pattern. The influence of John Dewey, and of misinterpretations of his work, cannot be underestimated, even though his name is probably not known to most of those who have been affected. Indeed, the whole area of experiential learning is sorely in need of clear thinking and useful theory. It is not a straightforward matter to articulate what is good practice and how it can be conceived.

Into this arena entered Ed Rosen who saw the need for a forum to bring together what he had sensed was emerging in the field. Experiential learning, without fanfare and without the benefit of academic respectability, is in the vanguard of educational development and those who are struggling with its implementation, often in isolation, can find strength in meeting each other and communicating their experience. Thus was born the First International Conference on Experiential Learning in London in June 1987.

The conference brought together an extraordinary range of people. No one who was there would have failed to have had their awareness of new ideas and new practices extended. Among the sometimes chaotic programme, people from different countries who engaged in many different experience-based learning practices, met, exchanged meanings and were personally challenged. From this forum two things became clear. First, there was a need to continue dialogue about very important ideas; and second, it was necessary to transcend the barriers of time and place and involve others in the debate.

At this point the initiative was taken by Susan Warner Weil and Ian McGill who took on the task of making sense of the conference and providing a stimulus for this further dialogue.

The outcome is not a collection of papers presented at the conference, in fact very few papers as such were presented. It is the endpoint of a process of inviting contributors to the conference to develop their ideas and inviting others to do the same. No pretence is made in the book that there is a common message or that a common framework is shared: different authors describe their practice and the ways in which they think about experiential learning.

This book is significant in the development of ideas in experiential learning. For the first time in a single volume some of the very different perspectives and applications of experiential learning are discussed. Susan and Ian perceptively describe the different 'villages' of experiential learning. Each village represents a common interest within the state of learning from experience as a whole. Within each, people talk and write, to a greater or lesser extent, with shared values and assumptions. People within each village have been communicating with each other and developing their own characteristic flavour of experiential learning. Rarely in the past has there been commerce between the villages; villagers have used their own language and concepts often in ignorance of the practices of those in neighbouring villages. As they communicate they find that their neighbours have good advice to offer and that there are practices from which they can learn.

While the metaphor of villages should not be taken too far, we see in this book the beginnings of a vigorous debate about what is experiential learning and how it can help to promote active learners who take responsibility for their learning. The goal for some is access to education or change in educational institutions, for others it is personal transformation, and for yet others it is social and political change. Many would not subscribe to, and perhaps they would even reject, the goals of others, but all would recognize that they have much to learn from them.

Part of the excitement of involvement in this area is the contact between different countries, different cultures and different ethnic groups. Although the settings in which we work vary enormously, we share a common human enterprise: to understand ourselves and others as we learn from experience. It might be hard to see what management training in Britain or social action in Africa have in common, but, when they are using experiential learning strategies, each can learn from the other and we can learn from both.

You can take the chance to do this for yourself here. Experiential learning is flourishing and extending its influence. Here we see that there is strength in diversity.

David Boud

Preface

The idea of a publication that aims to capture the sheer diversity and complexity of experiential learning derived originally from the First International Conference on Experiential Learning held in London, in the summer of 1987. Over 100 people gathered from all over the world to focus on experiential learning from a wide number of perspectives. The contributors to this book were participants at the Conference. However, all their contributions, while deriving from the Conference, were specifically written with the intention of cohering round the major themes we have identified as significant at this stage in the development of experiential learning. The conference was a very creative resource.

The perspective quotations which we used to introduce each Part were drawn from many hours of video- and sound-tapes made at the conference. They were a collective product. The dialogues which we have drawn upon are intended to represent the essence of what was said, not an exact replication. They are drawn upon here with permission of the producers, Jini Rawlings and Ed Rosen.

Acknowledgements

We would like first to acknowledge our debt to the organizers of the Conference whose inspiration and much agony and toil resulted in people from all over the world coming together around the theme of experiential learning. Colin Mably, David O'Reilly, Susan Warner Weil, Dain Trafton and Eric Willcocks all put in much effort to make it happen. Particular thanks are due to Ed Rosen, who first conceived the idea and took the main brunt of the organizing as conference convener. We would like to thank all the participants we met with whom we shared much. They gave us many ideas that are represented in the themes of this book.

Our decision to publish Chapter 19 is based on its critical reflection on experiential learning in Apartheid South Africa. We are supported in our decision by the appropriate anti-apartheid organizations in this country and in South Africa.

Thanks to Ettore Gelpi of Unesco for his particular contribution to our 'perspectives'.

We thank the contributors for their patience with our requests for changes to chapters, often at the last minute.

We should like to thank those who came for a one-day session in London in February 1988 to enable us to sound out with them our 'sense' of the issues and themes that had emerged at the Conference: Carol Baume, Mike Jarrett, Colin Mably, Jini Rawlings, David O'Reilly, and Ed Rosen. Again our thanks to Ed and Jini and their colleagues who made the videos and for access to this excellent material.

To Cheryl Anderson, a special thanks for the support she gave us in getting all the administrative tasks completed within our deadline, and to everyone at the Learning Experience Trust, for their assistance in locating relevant sources.

We are grateful to our colleagues at the Centre for Higher Education Studies in the Institute of Education and Brighton Polytechnic who were tolerant of the time it took and the pressures on us. Our appreciation to Noreen O'Conner for her listening and facilitating skills at just the right time. Our thanks to David Boud, Carlis Douglas, Tim Kemp, Robert Murray, Bob Sang, Malcolm Tight and Lorna Unwin for reading, commenting and offering insights into our drafts of the first and final chapters. We take full responsibility for the outcomes!

Also, our personal thanks to Hannah and Tim for their continuous support.

Finally, we are grateful to Phillida Salmon, for allowing us to borrow the title of her book for Part 2: 'Coming to Know' (Salmon, P., 1980, *Coming to Know*. London: Routledge, Kegan and Paul). Before being substantially modified, Chapter 12 originally appeared in Mead (1987, Vol. 18, Part 4, pp. 277–86) as 'Non-facilitated Action Learning'.

Susan Warner Weil
and Ian McGill,
London.

Introduction

Origins

As people from all over the world gathered for the first international conference on experiential learning, many of us soon realized that the very term experiential learning meant different things to different people and that no one had actually sat down and attempted to embrace the diversity of meanings and practice that the term connoted. We also realized that not only did the term experiential learning have different meanings, but that people also represented very different 'constituencies' and had very different values about experiential learning.

We have identified four distinct 'villages' within the global village of experiential learning. One village is clearly identified round the assessment and accreditation of prior experiential learning as a means of gaining access and recognition in relation to educational institutions, employment and professional bodies. A second village is the place for those who centre their activities on changing the practice, structures and purposes of post-school education. Another village can be identified among those who place learning from experience as the core of education for social change mainly outside educational institutions. Finally, there is the village where there is a focus on the potential and practice of personal growth and development. There are undoubtedly overlaps between these 'villages' and nuances of difference within the villages. We have found the metaphor valuable for conveying sense and meaning both within the villages and for extending our understanding of experiential learning through dialogue across the four villages. We take these issues and ideas further in the first and final chapters.

Style, stance and process

We have asked authors to speak about theory and practice related to experiential learning from their own position, in the first person, in specific rather than generalized contexts. In our view one of the strengths of experiential learning in practice is the meaning that we give our actions and therefore our thinking. They are not separate entities. Meaning is not 'out there'; we are part of that meaning and we can therefore convey it personally.

Moreover, we as editors do not assume one truth, one reality, one body of knowledge to be associated with 'experiential learning'. Nor have we attempted a 'neutral' interpretation of experiential learning. We are also white, Western and would be ascribed middle class. A glance at the titles for each part, the quotations that introduce them and our opening paragraphs for each chapter will show that we are concerned with particular issues and values. These have evolved out of our own experiential learning, including our work in education, training and development, and social change in this country and the USA. We trust our approach will enable readers to relate to us and to appraise their own starting point. Indeed, it is our intention to challenge the view that experiential learning is value-free or neutral and can be divorced from its context. Thus we convey our own personal stance in our chapters and opening paragraphs while also offering readers multiple realities that do exist in this developing area.

The central focus of the book is on post-initial education, within and outside formal systems of education. Some 'villages' are better represented than others. For example, we did not consider it necessary to duplicate the substantial practice and documentation on the accreditation and assessment of experiential learning. We have thus included only two chapters on this, although issues relating to this village are dealt with through our own contributions.

We would like to emphasize that the sexist language which appears in quotations from other authors has been retained only in the interests of maintaining the veracity of the original.

Organization of the book

A word about the structure of the book. The first chapter sets out our framework for making sense of experiential learning and its meanings and applications. This acts as a detailed introduction to many of the contributions. In the final chapter we explore the possibilities resulting from integrating ideas across the four villages. The book is divided into five parts which are intended to provide coherence and structure. The chapters are grouped within these parts to reflect their primary emphasis.

At the beginning of each chapter we have written 'opening paragraphs' which introduce the chapter and make links with other chapters and parts. These links are intended to suggest ways in which the authors' approach and values are affirmed, elaborated and indeed challenged in other chapters. We also underline connections with and build on ideas we introduce in the first and final chapters. These opening paragraphs are intended to signpost readers towards different paths through the book. These paragraphs are not value-free, but rather reflect our own issues and our own concerns as identified in Chapter 1. We try to be visible as people throughout the book and to make our own struggles visible.

We introduce each part with 'perspectives' which have been drawn from many hours of video- and sound-tapes made at the conference. Our purpose in including these has been to convey those moments of dialogue which often capture the essence of the major critical issues, conflicts and questions we need to ask about experiential learning. The perspectives also show the many different starting points that we come from as practitioners. The perspectives, therefore, provide an alternative 'entry' point with which you may engage.

Part 1, 'Making Sense', provides conceptual frameworks to account for the diversity of theory and practice associated with different meanings and purposes of experiential learning. This part conveys multiple meanings and purposes, which influence practitioners' 'ways of seeing' the world.

Part 2, 'Coming To Know', deals with the processes of coming to know oneself as a person and in relation to others. The contributors concentrate upon the ways in which as individuals, and as practitioners in and outside educational institutions, we can 'come to know', to use Salmon's (1980) phrase, ourselves in relation to our worlds and in the process create and extend learner autonomy.

Part 3, 'Creating New Possibilities for Learning', conveys developments in post-school education settings. There readers will find accounts of current practice in a number of countries in relation to course programme modes, access, professional education and institutional change. Critical issues are also raised in respect of the assessment and accreditation of prior learning.

In Part 4, 'Transforming and Empowering', contributors record and develop ways in which experiential learning can be used as a transformative force in society, particularly in overcoming forms of oppression whether from the state, institutions within it, or forms of social oppression. The authors critically reflect on the means by which experiential learning can contribute to social change and how the very process of experiential learning itself can be an engine or means of enabling liberation by virtue of its potential democratic and participative approach.

In Part 5 we conclude by appraising the possibilities for experiential learning that may emerge as a result of dialogues across the villages.

Experiential learning, whether personal, in use in formal institutions or in the community, is usually concerned with swimming against the mainstream to bring about change. This inevitably involves struggle, which contributors have been asked to convey in their chapters.

As co-editors, we hope that our own and others' explorations of this developing field will engage a wide range of readers – whatever their degree of familiarity with experiential learning. We look forward to the dialogue that is certain to emerge from engagements with this book.

Reference

Salmon, P. (1980). *Coming To Know*. London: Routledge, Kegan and Paul.

Part 1

Making Sense

1. Perspectives

Everybody is talking about what experiential learning means to them. Sometimes it seems as if people are ignoring the different issues that people are expressing. But if we look at those differences, maybe we can build a meaning for experiential learning that incorporates *all* of us.

For those of us from Third World countries, experiential learning is not about picking up credits and bits of knowledge. It is about survival. It means life and death situations and it's about working with young children as well as adults and women as well. It's almost as if the West is teaching the rest. They're saying, '*This* is what experiential learning is.' But then, can we possibly be talking about validating peoples' experiences, in the ways that they keep saying they are? For us, experiential learning is not a methodology; it is not a technique. It *is* education.

There seem to be two different ways of looking at experiential education: one in terms of challenging the traditional structures of education and in some cases even moving forward and thinking about challenging traditional structures of societies. Alternatively, people are talking about fitting the non-traditional or experiential learning that people do as individuals back into a very rigid structure, in which the traditionalists decide which bits of that learning are valid . . .

What we are actually doing in our own work is trying to empower people and be involved in educating in the community, and so when people talk about experiential learning only in terms of traditional institutions, the connection between what I am doing and what they say they are trying to do just isn't there. Meeting with people working in institutions, though, opens my eyes; it gives me a broader definition of experiential learning. I just hope I do the same for them.

Experiential learning means to me several kinds of learning: not just within education institutions or at work but learning outside education institutions and outside productive systems in the community, I think it is very important to keep a very broad interpretation of experiential learning. It's amazing how many people only think about experiential learning in relation to their job or training. Our society needs skills that go beyond what are currently seen as educational or relevant for employment. Skills of cultural development and of social life and of challenging inequality. Vocational or educational experts often have too narrow a perspective of the future and future production.

1

A Framework for Making Sense of Experiential Learning

Susan Warner Weil and Ian McGill

Introduction

'Experiential learning' refers to a spectrum of meanings, practices and ideologies which emerge out of the work and commitments of policy makers, educators, trainers, change agents, and 'ordinary' people all over the world. They see 'experiential learning' – with different meanings – as relevant to the challenges they currently face: in their personal lives, in education, in institutions, in commerce and industry, in communities, and in society as a whole. Across such diversity, however, we discern four emphases for experiential learning. Each emphasis forms the basis for a cluster of interrelated ideas and concerns about experiential learning. Associated with each cluster are people who share aims and values that are more common than different. We have chosen to refer to these clusters of people and ideas as 'villages'.

In this chapter, we describe these four villages, and some of the practices, assumptions, challenges and influences we see associated with each. This 'making sense framework' is intended to complement other chapters in Part 1, and in turn provide a foundation for the remainder of the book.

In summary, we see the four villages as follows:

1. *Village One* is concerned particularly with assessing and accrediting learning from life and work experience as the basis for creating new routes into higher education, employment and training opportunities, and professional bodies.
2. *Village Two* focuses on experiential learning as the basis for bringing about change in the structures, purposes and curricula of post-school education.
3. *Village Three* emphasizes experiential learning as the basis for group consciousness raising, community action and social change.
4. *Village Four* is concerned with personal growth and development and experiential learning approaches that increase self-awareness and group effectiveness.

The essence of our personal stance in our chapters, and the book as a whole, is that:

> A person who knows only his own village will not understand it; only by seeing what is familiar in the light of what is the norm elsewhere will we be enabled to think afresh about what we know too well (source unknown).

By 'locking into' one village, we may, without intending it, limit and inhibit the realization of our basic ideals and values. We may lose out on the richness that can emerge from engaging with different meanings and purposes for experiential learning. Through dialogue across the villages, we are enabled to consider what we intend, and what we do, from new perspectives. Contradictions can become clearer. Such dialogue affords opportunities to participate in conceptualizing and enacting new possibilities for experiential learning. (In Chapter 22, we consider some of these new possibilities.)

The four 'villages' of experiential learning

Below, we illustrate and characterize each of the four villages, highlighting its key assumptions, influences and challenges. Although each village emphasizes different meanings and purposes for experiential learning, we do not mean to imply that people necessarily identify exclusively with any one of these groups, or that these 'broad brush' categorizations do justice to differences within the villages themselves. From the perspective of any one village, alternative interpretations of experiential learning may be seen as more or less acceptable. In our own experience, however, people tend to use the term 'experiential learning' as if no differences existed. For this reason, more than any other, we hope that our 'four village analysis' will provide a useful introduction to the field, while also contributing to further dialogue and debate.

Village one: The assessment and accreditation of 'prior' experiential learning

In this village, for which we use the acronym APEL, the concern is with assessing and accrediting learning outcomes resulting from life and work experiences as a basis for creating new routes into higher education, employment and training opportunities, and achieving professional status. Experiential learning refers to learning which has not been validated previously within an educational or professional system of accreditation. As Evans (1983) explains further, it can include:

> . . . instruction based learning, provided by any institution, which has not been examined in any of the public examination systems. It can include those undervalued elements of formally provided education which are not encompassed by current examinations . . . It does not refer therefore to any form of experiential learning which comes from planned experience and is

somehow assessed as part of a course by an education institution. It is not concerned with opportunities for using experience for participatory learning. It is concerned with opportunities for entering courses, and for gaining remission of study to shorten a course.

A frequently stated aim of APEL is to reduce inequalities in society and create new opportunities for so-called 'disadvantaged groups'. APEL is seen as an important means of widening access to higher and continuing education for people who, by virtue of their age, gender, race, socioeconomic background and/or prior educational qualifications, have traditionally been under-represented. For example, Lambert speaks of the value of assessing prior learning for 'women returners' to formal education, who have worked largely inside the home since leaving school as a means of:

. . . confirming the value of life experience and the learning within it, by emphasising the value of learning which may be underrated in our educational establishments (Lambert, 1987).

People in this village are concerned with how to make judgements about 'prior experiential learning', in ways that will be regarded as valid and reliable by academics, employers, professional and training bodies. Developments relating to APEL have stemmed from initiatives in the United States and, more recently, in Britain. To the best of our knowledge, the originators of this interpretation of experiential learning were the Council for the Advancement of Experiential Learning (now the Council for Adult and Experiential Learning) in the US, under the leadership of people such as Arthur Chickering, Morris Keeton, and Pamela Tate. In Britain, the lead in these areas has been taken by Norman Evans, now Director of the Learning from Experience Trust, the Council for National Academic Awards and, increasingly, the Training Agency (formerly the Manpower Services Commission) and the National Council for Vocational Qualifications. A perspective from France on such developments, as well as some of the critical issues arising from them, is provided by Barkatoolah (Ch. 14, this volume).

More recently, in the US and UK, APEL has come to be seen as not just providing alternative routes of entry to, and exemption from certain courses in, higher education, but it is also being seen as a means of gaining entry to professions, to jobs and employment progression, and to training and development opportunities sponsored by employers. It is increasingly associated with notions of economic regeneration and retraining, as well as the need for continuing education to cope with technological change and the 'knowledge explosion' (see, e.g. Chickering, 1983).

With regard to practice, this village emphasizes the responsibility of the student to support her or his claim to knowledge and skills derived through experiential learning with appropriate evidence. The focus of APEL is on the *outcomes* of learning that has taken place prior to the point of assessment and accreditation; learning experiences are regarded merely as the means through which specific knowledge and skills were acquired:

It is not important where, why or how learning is achieved but rather to identify what has been learnt and can be assessed (CNAA, 1988).

The use of some kind of portfolio as a means of documenting learning outcomes is common:

. . . usually but not exclusively in written form, which gives an account of the source and nature of the learning, and evidence of its acquisition (Hinman, 1987).

One example of how autobiographical reflection and the development of portfolios can promote confidence and commitment to further study, while also serving as a means of accrediting prior experiential learning, is offered by Redwine (Ch. 8, this volume).

Processes associated with good practice in APEL are summarized by Mansell (1987) as including systematic reflection, the identification of significant learning, synthesis of evidence, and assessment of accreditation. Strange (1980) likens the entire process to a petition:

From statements defining their degree program and requirements, students determine what learning outcomes fit the program and requirements. They then assemble a petition-like document or portfolio descriptions of the evidence they can present in an attempt to meet requirements for identified parts of their degree requirements. From these petitions are developed the actual evidence judged for credit in faculty evaluations.

Students are supported in these processes through, for example, groupwork or formal classes, tutorials, the use of tailor-made instruments and manuals, and interviews (Evans, 1988). The responsibility for assessment rests with academic staff, who can use conventional as well as more innovative procedures to assure themselves that the student can indeed demonstrate the learning said to have been derived from experience. Chickering (1986) stresses the importance of tailoring the assessment to the individual student. Learner-centred, rather than academic, or curriculum-centred approaches to APEL, can help to challenge extant assumptions about how knowledge is 'packaged' in higher education.

There are some people in this village who stress that APEL processes and procedures are relevant at a number of points in the educational experience of the learner, and that therefore they should not be restricted to one-off exercises at entry, but rather, 'right across the curriculum and at all points of assessment' (e.g. Storan, 1987; Keeton, 1981).

People who identify with this grouping tend to believe that issues raised by the consideration of giving credit for experiential learning go to the heart of the 'aims of education, and . . . the functions of assessment and credentialing' (Keeton, 1981). This work has done a great deal to stimulate wide-ranging debate about quality, cost-effectiveness, outcomes and purposes in higher education, and associated concerns with academic and institutional performance (e.g. Keeton, 1980). APEL advocates tend to see themselves as engaged in changing the traditional power relationship between learners and formal educational institutions. As Evans (1985) argues:

> To empower individuals to take charge of their own study through basing facilities for learning on the principles of recognition, of accumulation and progression, means individual choice is assured . . . And it seems reasonable to claim that it could produce a democracy of learners.

Summary

In summary, approaches within this village emphasize experiential learning as a basis for identifying individual learning outcomes. The processes associated with APEL, therefore, are seen less as an end and valuable in themselves, and more as a means to an end. This 'village' has given rise to the considerable debate about outcomes of education, and the most efficient and effective ways these might be achieved. Employers and academic institutions still tend to play a dominant role in determining what kinds of evidence and assessment procedures, and what knowledge and skills, or competencies, are considered to be valid outcomes of prior learning. How broadly or narrowly the latter are defined vary considerably. In our experience, awareness of self and self-in-relation to others, is not a dominant preoccupation within this village. The importance, however, of APEL in boosting self-esteem and confidence is often asserted, since it provides a means of emphasizing adult learners' strengths, rather than their weaknesses. This is seen as particularly crucial for learners whose previous experience in formal education has been largely negative. An underlying assumption in this village is that experiential learning is neutral, and that particular experiences can be selected, interpreted and evaluated without considering the influence of the social context on such processes. Finally, social change is assumed to be achievable through creating opportunities for individuals to progress, be it into education, employment or training.

Village two: *Experiential learning and change in higher and continuing education*

This village incorporates a wide range of people in post-school education whose emphasis for experiential learning may span from the use of a technique in teaching to a philosophy for justifying learner-centred and indeed learner-controlled learning as the basis for an entire course, department or institution. The different ways in which experiential learning is interpreted and applied in post-school education can be limited by demands and restrictions in the organization; the boundaries of the professional staff's own understanding of its possibilities; and the extent to which the 'subject experts' are able and indeed willing to relinquish their traditional roles and power.

Whatever the degree to which people in this village are involved in experiential learning approaches, they tend to share two main concerns: that the prior experience of learners, and particularly adult learners, is valued and used as resource for further learning; and that learning is active, meaningful and relevant to 'real life' agendas.

Within this village, there are those who stress the importance of experiential learning techniques or methods (such as structured exercises, role plays, simulations, field trips and visits, project work and laboratory or field research). These approaches might be used within a largely traditional degree course or, alternatively, they may serve as the predominant means for working with ideas, research and theory. The emphasis for others may be on work and field placements, service internships, cooperative (or sandwich) education, action learning within work organizations, and cross-cultural experiences as significant and assessed components in a course of study. Still others may stress the value of outdoor activities; the opportunities to shadow, or be apprenticed to, someone in a community or profession, or to be mentored. Here also will be those who are concerned that post-school education involve more personal and group development activities, such as those which predominate in Village Four. Still others would be concerned with developing independent and contract-based learning (see Ch. 2, this volume, for a further analysis of experiential learning approaches; and Keeton and Tate, 1978).

Boud and Pascoe (1978) identify what they consider to be the most important characteristics of experiential education:

1. The involvement of each individual student in his or her own learning (learning activities need to engage the full attention of a student).
2. The correspondence of the learning activity to the world outside the classroom or educational institution (the emphasis being on the quality of the experience, not its location).
3. Learner control over the learning experience (learners themselves need to have control over the experience in which they are engaged so that they can integrate it with their own mode of operation in the world and can experience the results of their own decisions).

These dimensions are further elaborated by Boud (Ch. 3, this volume).

Kolb (1984) points out that in the USA, such learning '. . . is on the increase in higher education . . . [and] . . . in the curricula of undergraduate and professional programs'.

Whatever the form of experiential learning, some of the specific objectives that people identify with their use of these approaches in higher and continuing education include, for example:

*   A better understanding of what theory from reading or lectures might mean in actual practice.
*   Reflection on prior experience in relation to new ideas and information.
*   An active consideration of the implications of research in the context of a real-life situation.
*   The assimilation and application of intellectual understandings to actual problems.
*   The consideration of a particular constellation of professional assumptions from the perspective of a specific social or occupational group.

- The integration of a variety of disciplinary or meaning perspectives in relation to a real-life problem.
- Reframing the ways in which we perceive and respond to particular situations.
- Reflection upon and appraisal of personal and occupational goals from alternative vantage points.
- A more self-aware approach to one's own professional practice.
- A deeper understanding of how we feel in certain situations, and of the limitations of our understanding and practice.
- A recognition of how institutional, social and cultural factors may cause individuals to act in ways that contradict personal and professional intentions.
- An awareness of how personal values and meanings influence our perceptions and choices of action.
- Actual experience of, for example, industry and commerce, or social change groups, and how they operate.
- Opportunities to experience different kinds of values and assumptions in action, in relation to particular activities and enterprises.

Kolb, whose work is cited in a number of chapters in this book, sees experiential learning as, 'the process that links education, work, and personal development'. Working from Lewin's original experiential learning model, as discussed by Henry in Chapter 2, he stresses the need for learning environments to foster opportunities for learning that enable students to work with, and build upon, learning experiences in a variety of ways. Kolb's cycle can be summarized as follows: experience serves as the basis for reflection and observation; conceptualization and analysis; the testing and application of ideas. Each cycle gives rise to yet another cycle (Kolb, 1984).

Kolb (1981) argues that development is attained through 'higher-level integration and expression of nondominant modes of dealing with the world'. This involves not only grasping knowledge, at experiential and intellectual levels, but it also involves actively transforming it. He argues that the four modes of operating identified in his learning cycle each foster different capacities: affective, perceptual, symbolic and behavioural (Kolb, 1984). He criticizes the tendency of academic environments to 'over-emphasize' symbolic learning and early specialization, and to fail to provide sufficient opportunities for development and integration. These entail:

> learning how to learn, and . . . appreciation of and competence in diverse approaches to creating, manipulating, and communicating knowledge. (Kolb, 1981).

For an example of ways in which Kolb's analysis has been combined with other theoretical contributions, as the basis for profound change in an entire institution of higher education, and all aspects of its curriculum, see Packham *et al.* (Ch. 13, this volume).

People such as Catherine Marienau, Rita Weathersby and Arthur Chickering are concerned with making the values and aims of human development the 'unifying purpose or idea' for higher education (Chickering, 1981). They and others suggest that traditional approaches put 'ceilings on development' (e.g.

Weathersby, 1981). They stress the relevance of experiential learning approaches and philosophies to developing people who cannot just cope with change, but can challenge and question the status quo (see Chickering and Marienau, 1982).

People who operate within this village and are involved in curricula that are largely experientially based often stress learner centredness or learner control. This notion is significant in decisions about what to learn, how and where to learn it, and about the criteria by which learning might be assessed. It is actively acknowledged that initial learning objectives (negotiated, for instance, through 'learning contracts' with individuals and groups as suggested by Knowles, 1986) will be influenced by the processes and experience of learning itself. Continual opportunities for review and reflection are seen as essential. As Stephenson (1988) argues, such programmes:

> . . . 'reach the parts of the person that other courses miss.' It puts the development of personal qualities and attributes on to centre stage, rather than being something to be picked up on the side.

Learner-centred or learner-controlled experientially based programmes in post-school education have been significantly influenced by goals derived from personal growth and development approaches. Carl Rogers (1983b), as much an influence in this village as in Village Four, summarizes these educational aims as being concerned with:

> . . . a climate of trust in the classroom in which curiosity and the natural desire to learn can be nourished and enhanced.

> . . . a participatory mode of decision-making in all aspects of learning in which students, teachers, and administrators each have a part.

> . . . helping students to prize themselves, to build their confidence and self-esteem.

> . . . uncovering the excitement in intellectual and emotional discovery, which leads students to become life-long learners.

> . . . developing in teachers the attitudes that research has shown to be most effective in facilitating learning.

> . . . helping teachers to grow as persons, finding rich satisfaction in their interaction with learners.

> . . . an awareness that, for all of us, the good life is within, not something which is dependent on outside sources (Rogers, 1983, p. 3).

Cowan and Garry (1986) contrast the role of educators who operate within more traditional pedagogic frameworks:

- They do not actively set out to relate that which is learnt to that which is already understood (this is particularly true beyond the specific bounds of the topic being covered).

- No serious attempt is made within the programme to identify or to resolve the *total* relevant needs of learners in that participant group.
- Nothing is or can be done to identify or build on relevant experiential learning.
- All participants are treated similarly; and there is a presumption that their learning is, or should be, of a similar nature.
- Motivation is, by implication, extrinsic rather than intrinsic, and hence encourages superficial learning

People who are concerned that experiential learning becomes more widespread in higher and continuing education see themselves as grappling with issues that, according to Chickering (1977, in Kolb, 1984, p. 7) go to the 'heart of the academic enterprise'. They regard themselves as concerned with bringing about 'major changes in the current structures, processes, and content of higher education' (ibid.). These changes are seen as essential to preparing learners for 'learning to learn' in a changing society, widening access to higher education, developing relevant and meaningful continuing education programmes, and building partnerships between higher education and others, such as employers.

Summary
In summary, people in this village tend to stress the process of learning, in ways that can entail everything from a technique to a total educational philosophy, the latter involving a fundamental change in the role of the teacher and her relationship with students. For this group, experiential learning is seen as an integrative process synonymous with quality post-school education itself. This entails opportunities to develop different kinds of capabilities (e.g. perceptual, affective, behavioural and analytical) and to 'make sense' of theory, research and information on a variety of levels in many different learning situations (within and outside the classroom, individually and in groups). Process and outcomes are therefore inextricably related. The emphasis in this village is on individual development, and the pursuit of personal and occupational goals, although collaborative working in groups is often a feature of courses which are based on an experiential learning philosophy. The social context, as the mediator of individual development and group experience, is a lesser concern, except in particular disciplines and professions. Some approaches in this village, however, work from the assumption that experiential learning approaches will enhance learners' capacity to see knowledge as contextual and relativistic (Perry, 1970, 1981; and see Ch. 16, this volume). Although self-awareness may be a stated aim in this village, the learner's emotional and social development may still be seen as secondary to the development of the intellect and skills of application.

The use of APEL procedures and practices, through which new students can gain access to further, higher and continuing education, combined with experiential learning approaches that encourage the development and integration of different kinds of capabilities throughout in higher and continuing education programmes, are together seen to hold immense potential for radically transforming the higher education system from how we currently know it.

Village three: Experiential learning and social change

This village is concerned with using learning from experience as the basis for group consciousness raising, community action and social change. The distinction between learning from experience and 'experiential learning' is elaborated upon by Brah and Hoy (Ch. 6, this volume) who stress that in the former approach, individual experience is not seen as:

> . . . independent of power relations in society. Instead, individuals are enabled to make sense of their personal stories by making links between autobiography, group history and social and political processes.

In this village, therefore, a particular concern is how internalized dominant assumptions or ideologies in the wider society are recognized. Reflection on prior learning in this village is seen as a means towards personal and collective empowerment:

> This is the process whereby people become aware that the meaning system that they have imposed upon their life world is not the only system and that there are alternative systems of meaning. Having become aware that their original system is not necessarily the only one, or the best one for them, they might rethink their position and then try to act upon the world in order to transform it (Jarvis, 1987).

Rich (1972) speaks of 're-vision' when she refers to reflection upon prior experience as a basis for new learning, and for acting back upon the world in new ways:

> Re-vision – the act of looking back, of seeing with fresh eyes, of entering an old text from a new critical direction – is for us more than a chapter in cultural history; it is an act of survival. Until we can understand the assumptions in which we are drenched we cannot know ourselves. And this drive to self-knowledge, for woman, is more than a search for identity: it is part of her refusal of the self-destructiveness of the male-dominated society.

In other words, re-vision is an experiential learning process, whereby experience can be reclaimed and alternative interpretations of prior learning can emerge, based on new understandings of how such learning may have been moulded by unseen forces. An example of this kind of experiential learning based on re-vision is provided by Wylde (Ch. 11, this volume).

Within this village, there are many who argue that perception, language and the development and application of knowledge cannot be divorced from its social context. There is an emphasis on developing knowledge that goes 'beyond appearances', and on grasping the 'essential structure of reality' (Youngman, 1986). The argument is that, when experience is taken out of context and viewed as if in a vacuum, commonality in the 'human race' tends to be emphasized, and the social meanings and consequences of certain social positionings become submerged. For example, there are many in this village who would see the difficulties encountered by particular social groups not as a function of merely individual prejudice, but rather as more directly linked to institutionalized ideologies, social mechanisms (such as institutional practices) and the ways in which certain groups implement and maintain systems of privilege or deprivation (Douglas, 1988).

This village includes many different kinds of groups, each of which brings different emphases and ideologies to their interpretations and purposes for experiential learning. Some are involved in community action and mutual support networks that do not necessarily challenge or transform social structures, but rather transform the group's relationship to them. For them, the concern is to evolve new meanings and forms of knowledge that have relevance to the complexities of their own lived experience. This changed relationship provides a basis for using expertise within dominant social structures in ways that have personal and collective validity and are relevant to the challenges being faced. In this part of the village are groups who are validating their own understandings and skills, such as in relation to their health and their bodies, such as within the fields of alternative medicine and women's health care in all parts of the world. It includes community action groups, who are concerned to take control of their own learning. There are groups of individuals who share a common background, such as with regard to their race, gender, disability or socioeconomic class, whose access to opportunities and power is unequal, as compared with other groups in that society. These groups are increasingly involved in challenging academic or other kinds of 'received' interpretations of their own experience, through trying to understand how both these accounts and their own understandings of them have been influenced by particular social, historical and economic conditions (see Chs 6 and 20, this volume).

Others in this village may be concerned not just with liberation from dominant meaning systems and structures, but also with challenging and changing these, through personal and collective action (see Chs 18 and 19, this volume).

Whatever the aims, such kinds of learning from experience are seen to be valid in themselves. They have emerged from a perception or analysis of the inadequacies, biases and oppression of formal structures and systems. To many in this village, it would be anathema to have such learning assessed and accredited by a formal institution. Learning is borne out of a struggle to examine experience from new perspectives – *not* those embodied in dominant values, structures and institutions of societies. Reclaiming one's own experience has its own validity. Others would question the extent to which learning outcomes resulting from these processes could possibly be assessed and accredited, since they inevitably challenge status quo conceptions of knowledge and experience.

From the perspective of this village, post-school, education is seen to emphasize transmission at the expense of transformation:

> Education as transmission presupposes an intact past which can be handed over to the next generation; education as transformation demands that the future re-order the past, and the *a priori* handed to us. Education as transmission presupposes that our historical experience may be reduced to the level of fact; but education as transformation takes hold of historical experience at the level of event, thus emphasizing its uniqueness, and not the repetitiveness of mere fact (Boston, 1972).

There will also be those within this village who are concerned with the growing emphasis on education as an:

> . . . apolitical, acurricular, reactive and consumer-oriented enterprise which casts the educator in the role of marketing expert and technician of the teaching–learning machine (Wildemeersch, Ch. 5, this volume).

There are people in this village who are critical of experiential learning approaches that foster self-fulfilment, a heightened sense of personal authority or self-direction, and individual achievement; and social adjustment at the expense of consciousness raising, collective empowerment and community or social action. These more individualistic kinds of approaches can be seen by some people in this village as perpetuating the illusions which obscure the realities of the wider social condition, and continue to benefit those in power. Overall, people in this village are more likely to scrutinize taken-for-granted assumptions such as: 'Technological advances benefit society'; 'science means progress'; 'a democracy ensures equality of opportunity for all'.

Theoretical underpinnings for experiential learning practice within this 'village' come largely from educators and theorists from a range of backgrounds, such as Paolo Freire, Antonio Gramsci, Karl Marx, Ivan Illich, Henry Giroux and Julius Nyerere, as well as from specifically feminist, anti-racist, or class-based critiques of education (see, e.g. Thompson, 1983; Brandt, 1986; Keddie, 1980).

The notions of dialogue and participation are critical in this village, but their meanings are imbued with nuances that are not evident in other villages. As Freire (1972, pp. 63–4) says:

> Dialogue . . . requires an intense faith in man, faith in his power to make and remake, to create and re-create, faith in his vocation to be more fully human which is not the privilege of an elite, but the birthright of all men . . . The 'dialogical man' is critical and knows that although it is within the power of men to create and transform in a concrete situation of alienation, men may be impaired in the use of that power . . . Without this faith in man, dialogue is a farce which inevitably degenerates into paternalistic manipulation.

In this village, there can be a tension between 'top down' and 'bottom up' interpretations of experiential learning. For example, some believe that a dialogue aimed at transformation must be guided by a radical critique offered by a particular theory. For others, it must remain grounded in experience itself. For some groups in this village, the 'songs of collectivity' and the critique of theory and experience can become an end in itself – resulting in, so to speak, a 'paralysis of analysis'. For others, the critique is valuable only in so far as its outcomes are translated into specific personal and collective action.

Examples of how people differentially interpret experiential learning in the 'social change village' are offered in Chapters 5 and 6 in Part 1 and Chapters 18–21 in Part 4. Through our introductory paragraphs, we cite some of the wider issues about experiential learning that arise for us out of their particular understandings and interpretations of experiential learning.

Summary

To summarize, in this village, there is a commitment to understanding patterns that cut across individual experience. This understanding becomes the basis for seeing ways in which individual interpretations of experience may be as much a function of human diversity as of power dynamics operating in the social context. For example, something that an individual has interpreted as a personal failing in her life may not be that at all, but rather a function of how she is perceived and positioned in that society, and of the structures which reinforce those perceptions and that social positioning. Reflections on experience from a wider social perspective in groups can help people to decide what action they wish to take in relation to themselves, and their role in society, and indeed society itself. There will be differences within this village, however, in what is constituted as the priorities for, and nature of, collective and personal action.

The context (i.e. economic, political, historical) within which experience occurs, and is understood, is the content for learning. The process of learning, within any kind of group, can also be seen as content, in so far as it perpetuates particular perceptions and power relationships that restrict individual choice and action. Personal empowerment and group empowerment are often seen as integral to each other.

As Cunningham (1983) argues, empowerment educators would consider it essential to engage with the question of 'what one learns from experience and who judges its worth'. Experience itself is viewed as anything but a context-free concept, and education cannot be neutral, given that both take place in a particular social context (see Chs 6 and 19, this volume). In this village, there will be those who are critical of experiential learning approaches that encourage individualism and narrowly defined economic objectives.

The process of reflecting is considered best done in groups, where there is a commitment to critiquing 'commonsense assumptions' or 'taken-for-granted experiences' from different perspectives. Such groups can form initially in relation to some form of common experience, although the impact of consciousness raising can spread to groups in any of the four villages. Although social change may be identified as a common end, the meanings this has will differ within this village. For some, this may entail groups taking responsibility for themselves and taking action, but in ways that do not fundamentally affect social structures, but change their relationship to them; for others, social change entails a direct challenge to social structures and systems, to dominant assumptions and values. The notions of participation, 'dialogue' and 'empowerment' are critical in this village, although what these mean in practice can vary considerably.

Village four: Personal growth and development

In this village the emphasis is largely on personal and interpersonal experiencing, as a basis for personal growth and development. For some, experiential learning is understood in the context of therapeutic goals, such as how to increase an individual's insight into the ways in which past experience has given rise to attitudes and behaviours that diminish personal effectiveness. For others, the emphasis is on increasing awareness of how we relate to others in groups, and increasing peoples' emotional, cognitive and behavioural understanding of influences on group functioning. There is an overall concern with increasing personal and group effectiveness, autonomy, choice, and self-fulfilment (see, e.g. Boydell, 1976; Heron, 1982; Kilty, 1982; Smith, 1980).

Reason and Marshall (1987, p. 114) suggest that personal development can be interpreted from three interrelated perspectives:

> . . . firstly, from an existential perspective as the here-and-now struggle with one's being-in-the-world; secondly, from a psychodynamic perspective which views current patterns of experience and behaviour as rooted in unresolved distress from earlier (often childhood) experiences; and thirdly, from a transpersonal perspective which views individual experience as a reflection of archetypal patterns of the collective unconscious.

Personal development is seen by this village as providing opportunities to explore new ways of being in the world; to recognize unproductive patterns in our ways of responding; to learn how what we say we do may be contradicted by our behaviour; to change old ways of responding to interpersonal situations; and to affirm aspects of ourselves which we have perhaps undervalued. These aims are usually pursued in a group, or a one-to-one counselling relationship, where there is a shared commitment to these meanings for personal development and growth. Empathy, risk-taking, constructive feedback, creative and cooperative problem solving, and support are key concerns in such encounters. Reflection on prior experience, as well as 'here and now experience' within the group or relationship itself, provides the basis for insight and change.

The example of 'communication skills' (building on the analysis offered by Harrison and Hopkins, 1969) enables us to consider some of the different forms and purposes associated with experiential learning in this village as compared with, for example, the post-school education village. In the latter, 'communication skills' might be seen as associated with fluency in using the written word, and in verbal exchange; with the capacity to abstract and generalize; and with the ability to reason and generate ideas, based on sound argument and evidence. Whereas here, greater emphasis would be laid upon reducing the gap between what we intend to communicate and what we actually communicate in gesture, word and deed; developing and communicating empathy; and being open to a language of feelings, attitudes, desires and fears, within oneself and others.

Such an aim can be approached in a whole variety of ways within a group committed to personal growth and development, with each having slightly different implications for the role of the group facilitator. For example, in a work-based team, concerned to learn about communication, the facilitator might find a way of meeting personal development needs, but in ways that are acceptable within that organizational culture. For example, after some form of needs assessment either before or at the beginning of the group, she might ask team members to 'brainstorm' all the kinds of communication problems that confront them in their work situation. After group discussion and analysis of this list, the group might then decide to focus on a particular aspect, in relation to certain kinds of work situations. Group members may then be asked to work in small groups, and reflect on, for example, recent relevant situations in which they felt that they did not communicate what they intended to communicate. The task in the small groups might be to identify common elements in such experience, and guidelines for practice. Individuals may also be asked to record for themselves any feelings, attitudes, fears and desires which they believed blocked them in that situation, and some ways they might work on these through other development options, such as counselling, supervision or the use of a diary. Following group feedback on the task, there might be some input from the facilitator at this stage on theory or research relevant to the topic at hand.

Group members might then do some role-play work in groups of three, using pre-given situations or ones they set themselves, which are problematic in terms of communication within the team and will allow them to apply in practice some of the ideas discussed so far. The facilitator would clarify the structure and process for this group's work. For example, each person in turn role-plays a relevant situation with another, and one person functions as an observer. The first person might then share what feelings arose for him in that role, and how effectively he believed that he communicated what he intended. The second person would then do the same, giving feedback in ways that is constructive and conducive to learning (which in itself affords further practice in communication). Finally, the observer would share what she noticed and felt during the role play. After each person has had a turn, the group might spend some time recording the key issues that came out of the experience for them, both individually and as a threesome. In the large group, the facilitator might then guide a large group discussion, processing issues as they arise, suggesting how these may link with other observations and insights within the group and any outcomes of previous activity. She may also encourage people to identify (privately and publicly) goals for further learning and action.

Thus, in this example, the facilitator is guiding, supporting, encouraging challenge and risk taking, and creating a climate conducive to learning. The focus here is on the individual within the group, and the effectiveness of the group itself. Experiential learning becomes the basis for cognitive, perceptual, affective and behavioural learning, and for exploring ways in which these can be integrated in the work situation and beyond. Content learning (e.g. about 'communication') is not at the expense of learning also about oneself, or the personal and interpersonal meanings that particular information, theory or research may have in actual practice.

Alternatively, similar aims might be pursued through an encounter group, or in a group therapy setting, which would ordinarily take place outside formal education or work settings. Here, individuals may be encouraged to become more open about their feelings and anxieties within the group, and to explore some of the origins of these in their past experiences. This can entail risk taking of a different sort. The facilitator will usually take less responsibility for structure and direction within this approach to personal growth and development. He may, however, take primary responsibility for helping individuals and the group as a whole to interpret their 'here and now' and past experience, by sharing observations and suggesting 'hypotheses' which individuals and the group may wish to consider, in order to learn more about what is happening. He is also likely to play a key role in maintaining a climate in which risk taking and support are balanced, a situation conducive to learning and change, although his aim would be to do so in ways that promote group accountability and responsibility. In some settings, the facilitator may also bring a particular expertise to working with experience using particular approaches such as psychodrama or Gestalt methods.

Rogers (1983a) describes the stages of such a group as: 'milling around'; resistance to personal expression or exploration; description of past feelings; expression of negative feelings; expression and exploration of personally meaningful material; the expression of immediate interpersonal feelings in the group; the development of a healing capacity within the group; self-acceptance and the beginning of change; the cracking of facades; the individual receives feedback; confrontation; the development of helping relationships outside the group; the basic encounter; the expression of positive feelings and closeness; behaviour changes in the group. Rogers suggests that such phases are relevant to thinking about other kinds of groups. However, it is our own view that the feelings associated with the various stages in a group's development, and how the group's dynamics are both interpreted and dealt with will depend upon a variety of factors; for instance, the context within which the group occurs; what is considered 'legitimate' and 'illegitimate' within that group culture; the ways in which power is exercised within the group; and the dominant assumptions which mediate how group and individual responses are perceived.

Within this village, it is intended that such approaches will lead to some form of change within personal, interpersonal or organizational spheres. Some within this village speak also of 'social change' (e.g. Walter and Marks, 1981), but in ways that assume experience to be value-free, and individuals to be accountable and largely in control of their destiny. Self-awareness and personal effectiveness are seen as the key to autonomy and choice:

> The inner world of the individual appears to have more significant influence upon his behavior than does the external environmental stimulus (Rogers, 1983b).

For example, race and gender may be seen as only 'differences' within 'one race, the human race'. Difficulties experienced by black people and women may be interpreted by those with more status or power as due to individual prejudice (on their part or on others); individual shortcomings; a lack of motivation; or as rooted in insufficient personal autonomy and interpersonal skill. In this village, the processing of experience, such as in the above examples, is likely to be influenced by these assumptions, in contrast to those operating in the previous village.

This village is strongly influenced by the ideas of people associated with humanistic psychology, such as Carl Rogers, Abraham Maslow and Rollo May, and theories of psychotherapy and psychoanalysis, such as those developed by Carl Jung, Jacob Moreno (who developed psychodrama and sociodrama) and Fritz Perls (who developed Gestalt therapy). Kurt Lewin has also been influential in this area, particularly in that his work provided a theoretical rationale for encounter and sensitivity groups in the US during the 1950s and 1960s.

Summary
The emphasis in this village is on individual and interpersonal experiencing. Experience tends to be treated as neutral and value-free with regard to the wider social context, but not with regard to individual experience. Approaches in this village span from therapeutic and counselling approaches in which inner and past experiencing is the primary concern to development approaches where awareness provides the basis for understanding oneself as well as improving group functioning. In more structured approaches (usually regarded as more appropriate to educational or work settings), experiential learning includes the development of understanding of how emotions, fears, anxieties, defences, values and attitudes influence behaviour, but in ways which respect privacy and the boundary between therapy and educational or work-based development. The process of individual and interpersonal experiencing, in all its complexity and with all its shades of joy and despair, is of central concern in this village. What a facilitator does and how she does it may vary according to the context for personal growth and development approaches. There is, however, an overall emphasis on creating a climate conducive to risk taking, support and challenge. People who think of experiential learning in the context of this village are concerned with change, but in ways that stress personal autonomy, choice and self-fulfilment, and interpersonal effectiveness. Approaches identified with this village tend to operate largely on the assumption that social change will result from increased opportunities for people to become more self-aware, more genuine, more understanding of others' perspectives and experiences, and more attuned to factors influencing group and interpersonal effectiveness.

Dialogue and diversity: Some implications

In our experience, when we enter into encounters characterized by diversity, we tend initially to assert our commonalities and deny our differences. For example, when we meet across the villages, a common assumption operates about what we mean by 'experiential learning', e.g. 'learning which arises from the first hand experience of the learner' (Boud and Pascoe, 1978) or something to do with the notion of 'direct encounter' (Keeton and Tate, 1978). We may all speak about experiential learning as a vehicle for change. We resonate to words like 'involvement' or 'relevance'. We discuss our commitment to increasing institutional responsiveness to the variety of experiences represented in the lives of different people in a society. We are likely to convey to each other some dissatisfaction with the status quo, and we may refer to our efforts to challenge or change it in some way.

However, despite this commonality, there may be profound differences in the means, ends and ideologies we consciously or unconsciously ascribe to experiential learning. When we examine our particular notions of change in a wider context, we begin to realize ways in which our current understandings of experiential learning might be not just enriched, but transformed. We may also become better attuned to differences in our own villages.

In our experience, those who would regard themselves as committed to experiential learning – as leaders of educational institutions, as policy makers, as change agents, as practitioners in various learning or social change contexts, and increasingly, trainers and people in industry – tend to emphasize the norms and assumptions of one village often at the expense of another. Critical debate and discussion regarding experiential learning becomes confined to one village alone. This may be a common feature of evolving 'movements', but in our view there is the risk that we curtail our own opportunities to learn from experience and realize our basic ideals and values more effectively.

For example, those involved in initiatives aimed at assessing and accrediting prior experiential learning seldom speak to those groups who are learning from experience outside the formal system – the very people whom the APEL village says it wants to bring into post-school education. Policy makers seldom speak to those lecturers in higher education who dare to swim against the mainstream. Those who are concerned with process-centred training and personal growth outside the system seldom speak to those in formal education who are trying to put process issues on the agenda of courses where content-based syllabi, transmission methods, and traditional assessment procedures still predominate. Those who make social change a priority, those who emphasize personal growth and autonomy, and those who are concerned with widening access, can all too easily dismiss each others' values and aims as irrelevant to their own.

O'Reilly (1987) captures the true nature of the challenge when we bring together an international group representing each of these four villages:

> . . . what might an educator working in a rural village in Asia or Africa have in common with someone developing innovative forms of education for non-traditional learners in the cities of North America, Australia and Europe? Or what basis for concerted action might there be between those working within academic institutions to open access to learning and those who wish to realise fully the educational dimension of their work in community groups and the voluntary sector? What might there be in common between new approaches to management education and concepts emerging from complementary medicine and holistic paradigms?

Each of us who are concerned with experiential learning bring individual commitments shaped by personal biographies, and by particular institutional, economic and social contexts. We each tend to identify with one, maybe two villages in particular. Each of the four emphases we have suggested for the villages stem from a different analysis of how best to bring about development and change through experiential learning. Each of these will now be reviewed.

In the APEL village, it is believed that by providing opportunities for systematic reflection on experience, the self-esteem and confidence of adult learners, particularly those who have been disenfranchised from educational and job opportunities, can be boosted. APEL seeks to create new routes of access to higher education, employment and training opportunities and professional recognition.

In the post-school education village, it is assumed that experiential learning approaches will make higher education more responsive to a broader band of society. As a philosophy of education, it seeks to promote the development and integration of a wider range of capabilities, and a greater sense of personal commitment to and responsibility for righting what is wrong in the world around us.

In the village concerned with social change, it is assumed that by critiquing 'taken-for-granted' assumptions about our experiential learning, we shall be sufficiently enlightened and empowered to know how to bring about personal and social change in our lives and the society in which we live.

In the personal growth and development village, individual and social change is assumed to come through increased awareness of self and others, and through improved capacities to learn from prior, and 'here-and-now' experience.

Within and across each of these villages, people are struggling to make sense of what experiential learning means in practice. What are the actual challenges arising from these analyses and commitments to change (whatever that may mean?) – engaging in dialogue; empowerment; autonomy; surviving or transforming; generating involvement in relevant learning; generating commitment; creating personal meaning; making sense of experience. These notions come up repeatedly in the chapters which follow.

In the paragraphs with which we introduce each chapter, and through the 'perspectives' that are intended to serve as introductory 'triggers' for each of the five parts of the book, we invite readers to examine their own meanings and purposes for experiential learning. Our hope is that the diversity of vantage points will enable readers to make sense of theory and practice in some new ways, and to look afresh at what they know so well within their own village.

In conclusion, we should like to pose some questions as 'springboards' for whatever path readers choose to take through this book.

- When we emphasize one dimension of experiential learning at the expense of others in our theories and our practice, what do we put at risk, if our aims are genuinely to bring about change and development – be it at personal, institutional or social levels?
- For example, if in APEL we validate individuals' previous uncertificated learning gained through life and work experience, to what extent does that experience remain validated and become integrated in the subsequent educational experience to which access has been gained?
- In post-school education, to what extent can experiential learning approaches be identified with capacities to engage proactively in change if the boundaries of experience remain strictly determined by teachers and subjects, and status quo assumptions?
- If our emphasis is on social change, at what cost do we deny the importance of our personal awareness as a basis for changing behaviour and the functioning of institutions and society in the direction of equality?

- If our concern is with experiential learning as a route to self-awareness and improving group effectiveness, at what cost do we consider such experiencing as neutral, and somehow separated from its social context?

We are all concerned with change in some form – but what forces operate so that one emphasis for experiential learning predominates at the expense of others in any one village? Who decides which aspects of experiential learning are valid and which are not? Why are some experiences seen as normative and others as 'deviant' or 'problematic'?

We believe that there is now considerable potential for an 'experiential learning movement', but any such movement is dependent upon our active engagement with such questions. We may each perceive our commitments as 'transformational' within our own particular context. But until we subject them to scrutiny by others coming to experiential learning from different villages or, indeed, to people representing a wider band of social backgrounds within each village, we may remain unaware of contradictions between our beliefs and values, and how these are experienced by others in actual practice.

There is an old saying that a fish does not know water until it is out of it. Salmon (1988) says, 'the joy, the excitement, the sense of personal freedom, which can arise when people extend the horizons of their understanding', has been stressed by people such as Carl Rogers. However, Salmon (1988) suggests that this is a gross oversimplification of our actual experience of significant learning:

> . . . learning is not always like this. New understanding is potentially threatening . . . Where what is presented seems to bear no relation to any of one's ways of making sense of things, there is no possibility of grasping it, no sense of its connotations.

Salmon argues that to genuinely move forward, and reconstruct the basis of our knowing, represents 'the deepest kind of learning' (1988, p. 29).

In the final chapter, we examine some of the implications of differences across the villages and pose questions for each village from the perspective of other villages. We explore how dialogue can help us both to extend the boundaries of our own experience, and to confront assumptions about experiential learning in each village. We consider what possibilities might emerge when we integrate a wider range of emphases into our theory and practice. In Chapter 22, we also offer some of our own meanings for experiential learning. But, meanwhile, we invite readers to find their own points of departure within this book.

References

Boston, B. O. (1972). Paulo Freire: Notes of a loving critic. In Grabowski, S. (Ed.), *Paulo Freire: A Revolutionary Dilemma for the Adult Educator*. Syracuse, N.Y.: Publications in Continuing Education and ERIC Clearinghouse for Adult Education.

Boud, D. and Pascoe, J. (1978). *Experiential Learning: Developments in Australian Post-secondary Education*. Sydney: Australian Consortium on Experiential Education.

Boydell, T. (1976). *Experiential Learning*. Manchester: University of Manchester Department of Adult and Higher Education.

Brandt, G. (1986). *The Realization of Anti-racist Teaching*. Brighton: Falmer Press.

Chickering, A. W. (1977). *Experience and Learning: An Introduction to Experiential Learning*. New Rochelle, N.Y.: Change Magazine Press.

Chickering, A. W. (Ed.) (1981). *The Modern American College*. San Francisco: Jossey Bass.

Chickering, A. W. (1983). *Education, Work and Human Development: Making Sponsored Experiential Learning Standard Practice*. New Directions for Experiential Learning, No. 20. San Francisco: Jossey Bass and CAEL.

Chickering, A. W. (1986). *Principles of Good Practice in Assessing Experiential Learning*. Columbia, Md.: CAEL.

Chickering, A. W. and Marienau, C. (1982). Adult development and learning. In Menson, B. (Ed.), *Building on Experience in Adult Development*. New Directions for Experiential Learning, No. 10 San Francisco: Jossey Bass and CAEL.

CNAA (1988). Credit accumulation and transfer. *Information Services Digest*, 1(1), 6.

Cowan, J. and Garry, A. (1986). *Learning from Experience*. London: Further Education Unit.

Cunningham, P. (1983). Helping students extract meaning from experience. In Smith, R. M. (Ed.), *Helping Adults Learn how to Learn*. New Directions for Continuing Education, No. 19. San Francisco: Jossey Bass.

Douglas, C. (1988). Equal Opportunities and Organisational Change. Unpublished paper.

Evans, N. (1983). *Curriculum Opportunity*. London: DES/Further Education Unit.

Evans, N. (1985). *Post-education Society: Recognising Adults as Learners*. London: Croom Helm.

Evans, N. (1988). *The Assessment of Prior Experiential Learning*. Development Services Publication 17. London: Council for National Academic Awards.

Freire, P. (1972). *Pedagogy of the Oppressed*. Harmondsworth: Penguin.

Harrison, R. and Hopkins, R. L. (1969). The design of cross-cultural training: An alternative to the university model. *Journal of Applied Behavioral Science*, 3(4), 431–59.

Heron, J. (1982). Experiential Training Techniques. Guildford: University of Surrey, Human Potential Research Project.

Hinman, J. (1987). From assessment to accreditation: Reflections on the use of prior learning in further education. Griffin, C. (Ed.), *Assessing Prior Learning: Progress and Practices*. Conference Report, June 1987. London: Learning from Experience Trust.

Jarvis, P. (1987). *Adult Learning in the Social Context*. London: Croom Helm.

Keddie, N. (1980). Adult education: An ideology of individualism. In Thompson, J. (Ed.), *Adult Education for a Change*. London: Hutchinson.

Keeton, M. T. (1980). Editor's notes: Enhancing quality in higher education. In Keeton, M. T. (Ed.), *Defining and Assuring Quality in Experiential Learning*. New Directions for Experiential Learning, No. 9. San Francisco: Jossey Bass and CAEL.

Keeton, M. (1981). Assessing and credentialing prior experience. In Chickering, A. W. (Ed.), *The Modern American College*, pp. 631–41. San Francisco: Jossey Bass.

Keeton, M. T. and Tate, P. J. (1978). The boom in experiential learning. In Keeton, M. T. and Tate, P. J. (Eds), *Learning by Experience – What, Why, How?* New Directions for Continuing Education, No. 1. San Francisco: Jossey Bass and CAEL.

Kilty, J. (1982). Experiential Learning, Guildford: University of Surrey, Human Potential Research Project.

Knowles, M. S. (1986). *Using Learning Contracts*. San Francisco: Jossey Bass.

Kolb, D. (1981). Learning styles and disciplinary differences. In Chickering, A. W. (Ed.), *The Modern American College*. San Francisco: Jossey Bass.

Kolb, D. (1984). Experiential Learning. Englewood Cliffs, N.J.: Prentice-Hall.

Lambert, P. (1987). The assessment of prior learning: Curriculum Duplication. In Griffin, C. (Ed.), *Assessing Prior Learning: Progress and Practices*. Conference Report, June 1987. London: Learning from Experience Trust.

Mansell, J. (1987). The way ahead: Priorities for the future. In Griffin, C. (Ed.), *Assessing Prior Learning: Progress and Practices*. Conference. Report, June 1987. London: Learning from Experience Trust.

O'Reilly, D. (1987). *Conference Report of the First International Conference on Experiential Learning*. London: Regents College.

Perry, W. G. (1970). *Forms of Intellectual and Ethical Development During the College Years: A Scheme*. New York: Holt, Rinehart and Winston.

Perry, W. G. (1981). Cognitive and ethical growth: The making of meaning. In Chickering, A. W. (Ed.), *The Modern American College*. San Francisco: Jossey Bass.

Reason, P. and Marshall, J. (1987). Research as personal process. In Boud, D. and Griffin, B. (Eds), *Appreciating Adults Learning: From the Learner's Perspective*. London: Kogan Page.

Rich, A. (1972). When we dead awaken. Writing as revision. *College English*, **34**(1), 18–25.

Rogers, C. (1983a). The process of the encounter group. In Tight, M. (Ed.), *Adult Learning and Education*. Milton Keynes: Open University Press.

Rogers, C. (1983b). *Freedom to Learn for the 80's*. Columbus, Ohio: Charles E. Merrill.

Salmon, P. (1988). *Psychology for Teachers: An Alternative View*. London: Hutchinson.

Smith, P. (1980). *Group Processes and Personal Change*. London: Harper and Row.

Stephenson, J. (1988). The experience of independent study at North East London Polytechnic. In Boud, D. (Ed.), *Developing Student Autonomy in Learning*. London: Kogan Page.

Storan, J. (1987). *Making Experience Count*. London: Learning from Experience Trust.

Strange, J. (1980). Credit for learning gained in life and work experience. In Moon, T. G., Jr. and Hawes, G. R. (Eds), *Developing New Adult Clienteles by Recognising Prior Learning*. New Directions for Experiential Learning, No. 7. San Francisco: Jossey Bass and CAEL.

Thompson, J. (1983). *Learning Liberation: Women's Response to Men's Education*. London: Croom Helm.

Walters, G. A. and Marks, S. E. (1981). *Experiential Learning and Change: Theory, Design and Practice*. New York: John Wiley.

Weathersby, R. (1981). Ego development. In Chickering, A. W. (Ed.), *The Modern American College*. San Francisco: Jossey Bass.

Youngman, F. (1986). *Adult Education and Socialist Pedagogy*. London: Croom Helm.

2

Meaning and Practice in Experiential Learning

Jane Henry

Henry has undertaken an investigation into just what do people mean when they talk of and 'do' experiential learning. The chapter is based on qualitative research among a sample of people engaged in the field into the meanings applied to experiential learning. The term is often used to convey different meanings, purposes and practice. She provides a catalogue of approaches based on two dimensions. The first stresses the 'applications' versus personal and/or social meanings, the second polarizes autonomy and choice versus the needs of the environment. This issue is further extended by Boud in Chapter 3. Whether we are engaged in the assessment and accreditation of prior learning, experiential learning for change in communities or higher education, or social change or personal growth Henry makes a contribution to the identification of issues and the search for a common language across the four villages of experiential learning discussed in Chapter 1. She concludes that amidst the wide range of meanings and usages are vantage points from which to make sense of the diversity. But she identifies the need for a wider story, which we address in our Conclusion in Chapter 22.

Introduction

The term experiential learning often produces the blankest of looks on the faces of those not already familiar with the term. This is largely because experience is such a broad term that the phrase experiential learning does not obviously suggest any particular type of learning experience to an unschooled ear. Indeed, many people argue that all learning is experiential.

Even advocates of this mode of learning are often hard put to define what they mean by experiential learning or use the term to refer to very different kinds of learning goals, experiences and outcomes. In an attempt to sort out the confusion of usage I sent out a short questionnaire to members of the First International Conference on Experiential Learning. The questionnaire asked participants to offer their explanation of experiential learning along with an example of experiential learning they personally were associated with.

I received 52 replies, which seems to me to illustrate the confusion well. Of these responses, 7 were from the Americas, 29 from Europe including Israel, 13 from Australasia and 3 from Africa; most of these were from people attached to colleges or universities. They included those engaged in teaching agriculture, nursing, business, art, language, education and other fields. In this chapter I have simplified and drawn out general trends from the many considered responses I received.

Meaning

Theory

First, let us consider briefly some of the theories of experiential learning that have been offered. Kolb's (1984) description of the learning cycle is by far the most popular. This theory posits four stages of experiential learning – concrete experience, observation and reflection, abstract conceptualization and generalization, and active experimentation (summarized in Fig. 2.1). This cycle appears to have validity and offer a plausible and appealing theory of experiential learning to many people; Kolb is often the main or only theorist quoted in papers on experiential learning. Awareness of this model clearly influenced some of the experiential learning definitions sent to me which featured several stages (see pp. 27–8).

A possible disadvantage of Kolb's model is that it can be used as a description of the learning process in general and overlaps with various other attempts to define the learning cycle, for instance Dewey's (1916) process of problem selection, observation, design, development and testing, or Carkhuff's (1969) model of understanding, exploration and action (for other examples, see Boydell, 1976). This makes it difficult for the outsider to register how experiential learning is different from any other kind of learning.

Kolb's descriptions of each stage are general and abstract. Further confusion arises as proponents of experiential learning often use different keywords to summarize their understanding of the Kolb cycle and experiential learning process. For example, stage three may emerge as conceptualization (Gibbs,

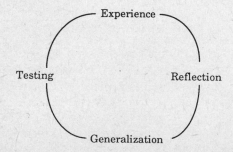

Figure 2.1 The Kolb Learning Cycle (after Kolb and Fry, 1975).

1987), generalization (Boud and Pascoe, 1978), sorting things out (Boydell, 1976), or puzzle out (Kilty, 1982). Stage four may emerge as experimentation, testing implications in new situations, action plans or planning for the future. One could argue that planning for the future, experimenting and testing new situations all relate to trying out in some way. Similarly, puzzling out and making sense of experience relate to a personal sense of meaning, but conceptualizing and generalizing probably refer to a rather different kind of abstract thinking.

What is needed is an attempt to relate the activities, goals and outcomes of the various experiential learning approaches to these different stages. For example, Gibbs (1987) relates Kolb's cycle to educational practice by placing common experiential methods within a particular sequence in Kolb's model. He distinguishes four types of activities: planning for experience, increasing awareness, reviewing and reflecting on experience and providing substitute experiences. He lists a series of methods under each: for instance, under 'planning for experience' (a stage spanning the conceptualization and experimentation stages), he includes action plans and learning contracts. Under 'increasing awareness' (which spans experimentation and experience), he suggests listening exercises and questions. Packham *et al.* (Ch. 13, this volume) offer an alternative elaboration of this cycle.

Another way of classifying experiential learning is not to describe the sequence of learning that is entailed, but to pull out the dimensions that are characteristic of this particular approach. A hallmark that tends to separate experiential learning theorists from the rest is their determination not to neglect the human side of learning and to acknowledge the role of affect and conation, alongside cognition. Boud and Pascoe (1978) suggests student involvement, learner control and the correspondence of the learning task to activities outside the classroom are central to any experiential learning activity. This stress on autonomy and learner control on the one hand, and relevance to activities in the 'real world' on the other, seems central to experiential learning (this is developed further by Boud, Ch. 3, this volume).

So much for the educational theorist. What of the experiential practitioner? Looking at individuals' definitions of the term and comparing this to an example of their mode of teaching and learning given in response to my questionnaire, it becomes clear that many of the differences in usage are conditioned by differences in the kind of learning experiences and situations people are in. It is an examination of the relationship between these differences and use of the term that forms the subject matter of the remainder of this chapter.

Definitions

Both the experiential theorist and educational practitioner seem to agree on what experiential learning is not. It is definitely not the mere memorizing of abstract theoretical knowledge, especially if taught by traditional formal methods of instruction such as lecturing and reading from books. Indeed it is extreme disaffection with these traditional modes of teaching and learning that seems to unite exponents of experiential learning. There is less agreement on an appropriate positive definition of the term.

There were two broad classes of definition offered by my respondents:

1. *All learning is experiential.* This was a minority definition, and one favoured by those who were involved in radical personal politics or a practical attempt at a future utopia. This group often explicitly stated that experiential learning was as much to do with learning in everyday life as learning in educational institutions.

2. *Experiential learning is a sequence of stages.* The particular sequence cited varied, but all stressed that an experience alone was not enough to count as experiential learning: the 'experiencer' had to consciously realize the *value* of that experience. Patterns in the responses giving rise to this definition took two forms:

   (a) Experience→ Reflection
       For those of a human potential movement persuasion, practising group or pair-based awareness, a two-stage model of experience followed by discussion was enough. Here the participant was expected to articulate an experience and then discuss the meaning of that experience for them with others.

   (b) Experience→ Reflect→ Act
       For those teaching in a problem-solving mode a three-stage model was common. A number of respondents seemed to have spent a good deal of time working out in their own mind what they meant by experiential learning. The naming of these three stages varied, for example:

   Experience→ Reflect, Analyse→ Act, Action, Test-out, Synthesize

Others listed four stages or made explicit the character of operations which make up each stage. Though there is overlap, different respondents chose to highlight different aspects of this cycle of stages. Three composite examples follow:

Theory→ Experience→ Reflect→ (Generalize→ Decide)→ Understand
Reflect (Diverge)→ Conceptualize→ Decide→ Act
Goal→ Generalize→ New insight→ Plan

Purpose

People seem to agree that experiential learning is about ensuring that people can 'do' rather than merely 'know', but differ in their emphasis on what skills enable the desired quality of 'do-ability'. Most stressed one or both of two distinct aspects – to involve the student personally and/or practically.

Personal involvement
This involvement has several aspects. Above all, the learning experience is

intended to be meaningful to the student, but meaning is of course a very broad and vague term. Certainly, a large part of the meaningfulness referred to seems to be concerned with with personal development.

On an individual level, personal development involves students becoming conscious of their own *needs* and desires and, therefore, ultimately gaining a wider agency through the capacity to exercise conscious choice effectively, i.e knowing what you want, and going for it in a constructive way. For some, personal development includes the development of *higher cognitive* goals like analytical, evaluative and synthesizing skills.

Part of the goal of personal development seems to be concerned with affective goals like 'understanding oneself', along with an *empowerment* that allows the student to be assertive enough to ask questions and challenge received knowledge. For some respondents, empowerment has more to do with social consciousness raising with a view to enhancing interpersonal understanding and tolerance and/or global cooperation and harmony. For others, empowerment is more closely allied to direct participation in some kind of political action (see Ch. 1, this volume).

Practical involvement
There seem to be three clusters of concern here: one stressing application, another the benefits of giving the student control of learning, and a third stressing the benefits of active learning for the learning process itself.

Respondents taking a firm stance on this line felt the term 'experiential learning' should only be used where the outcome was some *new* understanding, skill or approach. Others felt that an *applied* component relating theory to practice and reality was enough.

Again, the motivation for ensuring 'practical involvement' could be very different. At one extreme there were those who wished to give the learner *control* of the learning process, generally assuming this would produce a more socially responsible and autonomous human being. Another group advocated experiential learning because they believed it to be a more *effective* form of learning, seeing the active involvement as demanding higher-order skills that are generalizable and lead to a greater transfer of learning. At the same time it was commonly believed that experiential learning was more motivating for the students, which was perceived to produce more involvement by the student and so greater learning. Finally, because the learning was based on real needs it was perceived to be concerned with more useful topics.

Practice

Types of activity

Experiential learning is a broad church encompassing a number of different traditions. The type of learning experiences sent to me were so diverse I found it necessary to categorize them as follows (see Figs 2.2 and 2.3):

● Independent learning.

- Personal development.
- Social change.
- Non-traditional learning.
- Prior learning.
- Work experience.
- Learning by doing.
- Problem-based learning.

1. *Independent learning* offers students control of the learning process, typically by a learning contract which offers participants a chance to opt to study situations of interest to them. It often uses problem-solving and project-based methods.
2. *Personal development* work focuses on affective learning. The usual method employed centres around group discussion and/or pair work (e.g. co-counselling), but may employ other techniques from the human potential armoury such as drama, guided imaging, narrative exercises, using diaries or autobiographies, bodywork and creative arts approaches (such as meditation, dance or drawing).
3. Adherents to what I termed *social change* were more diverse, but shared a common, relatively radical philosophy committed to building what they referred to as a more harmonious world for all, including the disadvantaged. In settings where participants were from radically different backgrounds, group discussion was used successfully. The differing backgrounds offered a sufficient variety of views to stimulate understanding, empathy and fundamental attitude changes. Another case involved offering resources to those

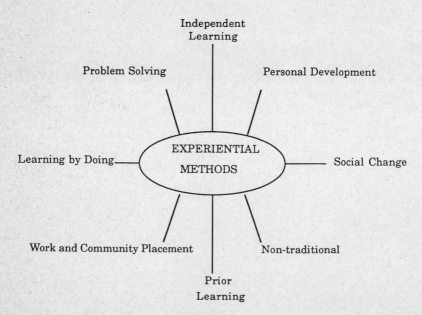

Figure 2.2   Forms of experiential learning.

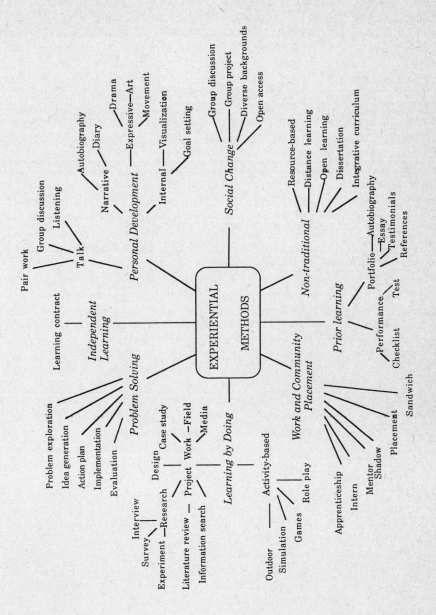

Figure 2.3　Experiential learning methods.

who would not traditionally get this opportunity, enabling them to use these resources to produce something for the community.

4. *Non-traditional* education may include a combination of independent study, prior learning, and open learning or distance study methods. I have included in this group some activities that did not strike me as obviously experiential. For instance, one academic viewed an integrative curriculum in higher education (e.g. considering different models of human beings) as experiential. Equally, basic literacy and numeracy courses were perceived by someone in a developing country to be experiential, in that they offered the possibility of gaining a much needed skill to equip the student to operate in daily life more effectively, and so improve their quality of life. These examples illustrate clearly that what is seen as experiential is relative to the constraints under which the learning is offered. Most of the examples related to work with mature students.

5. *Prior learning* involves the assessment of previously completed work for accreditation towards an educational qualification. Typically, the student submits a portfolio demonstrating competencies arising from past work and life experience. This may include essays, an autobiography, testimonials and references. Alternative procedures include performance measures, such as competency checklists, tests, discussion, extended papers, or an examination of any relevant evidence for the learning outcomes claimed.

6. *Work and community placements* take various forms: the classic apprenticeship with an individual 'master' who has the skills to be acquired; attachment to a mentor; shadowing one or more individuals, or working in a relevant environment. The latter may involve the student in a particular role (e.g. a trainee nurse), undertaking a particular project (e.g. as part of a sandwich course), simply being in a particular environment observing and taking part in day-to-day activities on a work attachment, or an internship where the student is shown how the work or community environment operates.

7. *Learning by doing* falls into two categories: *project-based* learning and *activity-based* learning. Structured learning experiences of this kind are generally offered by an educational institution or other formal learning environment. Project work refers to an extended piece of work in which the student (or group of students) is required to select a topic, collect relevant information and organize this material into a presentation. This term covers diverse activities such as research, an information search or design. Research projects may be based around qualitative or quantitative methods involving surveys, interviews or experiments. Information searches include literature reviews, and work with primary documents or secondary sources. Design projects may involve building a tangible product or just producing plans which would enable one to do so (Henry, 1977). The case study approach is an allied method. Activity-based learning includes practicals, simulations, games, role plays or expressive approaches like drama, art, and imaginative activities (e.g. visualization).

8. *Problem-based* learning has been conceptualized in various ways, but the essence of the procedure is to start with a problem, explore it, generate possible solutions, select one, implement it and revise as necessary. It

therefore entails design, experience, evaluation and feedback procedures and offers scope for extensive involvement and decision making.

Figure 2.4 provides a model of the key dimensions on which these different approaches are focused. The horizontal axis stresses applications in the 'real world' (especially work and community) versus a concern with meaning. The vertical access polarizes a focus on student autonomy and choice versus the needs of the environment in which the student finds herself. The methods on the left of the diagram – problem solving, learning by doing and work placement – all emphasize applications of learning; those on the right are concerned with personal and social values. Arguably, the methods at the top of the diagram – independent learning, problem solving and personal development – offer most autonomy (or, in the case of personal development, are concerned with developing that quality). Likewise, those methods in the lower half of the diagram – work placement, prior learning and non-traditional learning – respond in particular to needs in the environment.

Each quadrant also illustrates a particular concern. Thus, a personal focus is of central concern in independent learning, personal development and social change activities. Social issues are central to social change, nontraditional and prior learning. Prior learning, work placement and learning by doing are all practically oriented, and what we might term the full or staged experiential learning approaches of independent learning, problem solving and project work are relevant on several counts: they allow the student choice and control, and offer a sequence of practically relevant learning that will stretch the student (for a fuller account, see Henry, 1988).

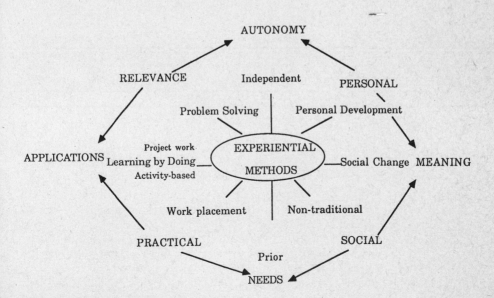

Figure 2.4 Experiential learning approaches.

Features

Discipline, duration and location

It is not just abstract ideals or theoretical dimensions that distinguish these various approaches to experiential learning. There are some very fundamental differences in the amount of time allowed, where the activity is offered, by whom, in which area and how it is assessed.

1. *Discipline.* Certain of these activities are more common in some disciplines than others. Work placements, activity-based learning and problem-solving approaches are found in the teaching of applied subjects especially (e.g. agriculture, nursing, engineering and business). Prior learning and non-traditional learning are typically available to mature students and, though theoretically of use to everyone, personal development features are more common in training for the service professions (e.g. teachers, the police and psychologists).

2. *Duration.* The amount of *time* allowed for these activities also varies enormously. The personal development activities described were all relatively short, lasting anything from 12 hours to 2 weeks. However, most were of 2 days duration or a series of between 5 and 30 one-and-a-half-hour sessions. Problem-solving and project work activities were often allocated larger chunks of time, ranging from weeks in schools to months in higher education. This allowed the student considerable flexibility as to how to order, and when to do, the work. Work placements tended to be shorter for school-age students (perhaps a few days a week), and often much longer for undergraduates (e.g. 4–12 months). Work placement, problem-solving and project-based learning were more common in the latter stages of courses, whether at school or in further education.

3. *Location.* It is also interesting to note which of these approaches occurs most often in the community and which in formal educational and training centres. In so far as it is possible to generalize at all, it seems prior learning or at least the work leading to the assessment of it, was often home-based; non-traditional learning often occurred in community centres other than educational institutions; activity-based learning, problem solving and work placements were directed from school, college or university. Project work could take students off campus, and in one case a problem-solving approach was run from an off-campus location. Personal development activities happened in educational institutions, the community, or indeed anywhere with an appropriate room.

Assessment

The assessment methods used in experiential learning are as diverse as the activities. Personal development tends to use informal self-assessment and peer feedback. Where formal assessment is required, academics sometimes resort to setting conventional assignments (such as a literature review), which may be unrelated to the affective learning that forms the major part of the course. Work placements are often assessed by academics or work supervisors; sometimes the student is required to complete a project as well. Projects are often assessed by written assignments or portfolios. Many shorter activities are not formally assessed. A problem-solving approach may require a written and oral presentation. Assessment in independent learning can be student-initiated, and can take the form of the student presenting an oral case for their graduation backed up by a presentation of their written work, and written comments on their performance by their supervisor. Prior learning is often assessed via a portfolio, documenting outcomes of past experience and, in some cases, by dissertations and written papers.

Outcome
This brief overview would not be complete without a consideration of the outcomes claimed for the experiences offered. Once again, both the personal development side of experiential learning and the practical relevance of the learning were apparent in the outcomes mentioned.

1. *Personal development.* A common outcome claimed for these experiential learning activities was *awareness*, often self-awareness (obviously so in the case of personal development). In the socal change approach, attention was drawn to the awareness of others. In work placement, awareness of self, and above all the realities of the work environment, was said to be fostered. If the activity was of a longer rather than a short duration, it appeared to develop a quality of *confidence* that was not there before. This seemed to be so whether the task was knowledge-based, such as in some non-traditional approaches to basic skills (like learning to read and write), or the self-respect that comes from accomplishing a difficult task. Where the student truly 'owned' the task as a result of choosing it in the first place (e.g. large projects or independent learning), liberation in the form of personal *empowerment* was claimed.
2. *Competencies.* Experiential approaches also teach *useful skills.* For example, problem-solving courses often claim improved *communication* skills as an outcome and project courses improved *decision-making* skills; work placement sometimes provides a useful *network* of contacts. Engaging in processes related to the assessment and accreditation of prior learning seemed to combine most of these virtues. Self-awareness, *new skills* and a qualification, with a saving in time and money by avoiding the duplication of previously covered territory, were all said to result. (Surprising as it may seem, virtually no one volunteered fun or enjoyment as an outcome.)

Conclusion

One has to ask after reading through this catalogue of learning methods, whether it is useful for people engaged in such widely different activities to think of themselves as a coherent professional group. There are groups concerned specifically with a particular type of experiential learning, such as prior learning, problem-based learning, personal development, independent learning and project work. Is it an advantage for these groups to attempt to develop a common language?

What emerged from the questionnaires was how strongly people felt about the importance of the balance of education switching to more experiential activities, whether they were teaching language, educating their children out of school, involving those who do not traditionally receive education, or trying to offer those with which to do something more relevant with their lives. Most of these experiential approaches not only share an underlying philosophy but face common problems, such as being accepted in traditional institutions and developing appropriate alternative assessment methods to those normally used in formal education. Partly for these reasons, I believe it is useful for the field to go forward as a whole.

The current shift from the industrial to the information age will also affect education. It is predicted that four or five different jobs per lifetime will be the norm, so the impetus to provide more training grows. The pace of change is such that educators have to face the problem of knowledge obsolescence, e.g. science graduates may find their undergraduate studies outdated by the time they complete their doctorates. The increasing availability of on-line data and knowledge on tap also shifts the educational emphasis from retaining knowledge to developing the 'knower'. The challenge is to develop competent individuals who have initiative, sensitivity to others and awareness of practical realities, along with sufficient confidence, insight, skill and flexibility to act effectively in a changing world.

Experiential learning methods are designed to provide just such self-motivated, assertive, adaptable, able situation improvers and communicators who know how to find relevant information and apply it. Indeed, they are arguably better placed to do so than those trained by the traditional 'chalk and talk' emphasis on analytic cognitive skills and discipline-based knowledge, at the expense of affective, conative, synthesizing, integrative and practical skills. Experiential learning actively recognizes these educationally neglected sides of humanity which encourage the learner to perceive the relationship between different aspects of their lives, different disciplines and viewpoints and to take responsibility for their actions.

If we just had a story that was easier for others to grasp, experiential learning methods might be in much more widespread use than they currently are.

Acknowledgements

I should like to thank all those who sent replies to my questionnaire and/or additional relevant material.

References

Boud, D. and Pascoe, J. (1978). *Experiential Learning: Developments in Australian Post-Secondary Education*. Sydney: Australian Consortium on Experiential Education.
Boydell, T. (1976). *Experiential Learning*. Manchester: Department of Adult and Higher Education, University of Manchester.

Carkhuff, R. R. (1969). *Helping and Human Relations*, Vol. 1: *Selection and Training*; Vol. 2: *Theory and Research*. New York: Holt, Rinehart and Winston.

Dewey, J. (1916). *Democracy and Education*. New York: Macmillan.

Gibbs, G. (1988). *Learning by Doing*. London: Further Education Unit.

Henry, J. (1977). *The Course Tutor and Project Work*. Teaching at a Distance, No. 9. Milton Keynes: Open University.

Henry, J. (1988). *Variety in Experiential Learning*. Project Memo. 15, IET. Milton Keynes: Open University Press.

Kilty, J. (1982). *Experiential Learning*. Guildford: Human Potential Research Unit, University of Surrey.

Kolb, D. and Fry, R. (1975). Towards an applied theory of experiential learning. In Cooper, C. L. (Ed.), *Theories of Group Process*, pp. 33–56. Chichester: John Wiley.

Kolb, D. (1984). *Experiential Learning*. Englewood Cliffs, NJ: Prentice-Hall.

3

Some Competing Traditions in Experiential Learning

David Boud

Boud extends our understanding of experiential learning across the spectrum of the 'four villages' (Chapter 1). He reflects in particular on different assumptions associated with the notions of 'adult learning' and 'autonomy in learning'. With the former, Boud categorizes four main traditions of adult education that have influence across all four 'villages' of the experiential learning movement. He characterizes these as freedom from distraction, freedom as learners, freedom to learn and freedom through learning. Each of these has its own core values and purposes. As practitioners we are challenged to consider whether we fall into one tradition or are more eclectic in our use of the traditions. On autonomy and self-direction in learning his purpose is to disentangle some of the ideas that are linked to these concepts. Boud distinguishes autonomy as a goal for personal development and for becoming effective in a knowledge or skill area, from autonomy as in approaches to learning which he categorizes as individual-, group- or project-centred. The chapter provides a clarity of definition with which we can distinguish other contributors' points of departure. A valuable parallel can be made with Wildemeersch (Chapter 5) and with Chapter 1 in terms of the individual and societal implications of experiential learning in practice. At the acquisition of disciplines level Boud provides a framework in which to set Horwitz (Chapter 7) and the struggle of her learners to become autonomous learners.

About 10 years ago a colleague and I attempted to portray in a simple fashion what we saw to be the characteristics of experiential learning (Boud and Pascoe, 1978). We looked at a variety of programmes operating mainly in Australia and sought to distil the chief educational features. Of particular concern to us was how we could marry the European and American notions of experiential learning, both of which had taken root in Australia. At that time, European use of the term focused mainly on group-based human relations-type activities, whereas Americans frequently used it to describe work and field-based placements outside educational institutions.

We found that each of the programmes we examined had, in different combinations, a mix of three features. We present these visually in Fig. 3.1. We argued then that there was no absolute feature which meant that a particular activity could be described as experiential learning, but that there was a spectrum of more or less experiential activities along three main dimensions. A programme could be legitimately described as experiential if it showed significant characteristics of at least one of these dimensions. Commonly, experiential learning activities showed a mix of all three.

During the past 10 years, I have become aware of a great deal more work about experiential learning and I have seen many more programmes in action. I have been prompted to think of ways of conceptualizing what is sometimes an elusive notion. I have found it useful to distinguish between two aspects. First are those descriptions of what people do which they label 'experiential learning', which is what Fig. 3.1 portrays; these focus on goals, purposes and sometimes content. Second are the processes in which teachers and learners engage when they are involved in experiential learning.

There is a great deal of work taking place in this latter area and it seems to be of more immediate importance than the attempt to map the field. Work of this kind seeks to make sense of what occurs in experiential learning and draws from the practice of excellent proponents ideas and models which are helpful to those who are involved in planning and implementing projects and programmes. Probably the most significant work of this type has been directed to an understanding of the cycles of learning activity in experience-based learning and the role of reflection in it – starting with Dewey (1938) and Lewin, and moving on to Kolb (1984) and Schön (1983). Reflection has emerged as the key concept and my colleagues and I have been guilty of coining a slogan in the title of a book, *Reflection: Turning Experience into Learning* (Boud *et al.*, 1985). This aims

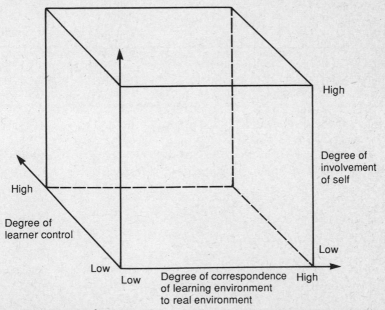

Figure 3.1 Dimensions of experiential education (from Boud and Pascoe, 1978).

to explore some of the approaches which can be used in experiential learning to promote reflection. There is much fruitful work occurring in this area generally, and as some of it is described elsewhere in this book, I will not dwell on it here.

It is impossible to discuss experiential learning without bringing in many ideas and issues from closely related aspects of education, training and learning. Experiential learning is not a realm of activity which can be divorced from other educational practices. It may be less controllable and more context-related, but it is no less in need of clear thinking which builds upon useful concepts from elsewhere. Indeed, its very characteristics make it an important arena for the development of ideas which can be applied in more conventional settings.

The two areas which I believe have much to offer to an understanding of experiential learning are those of adult learning and autonomy in learning as it has been applied in higher education. The rest of this chapter will concentrate on these aspects and examine their implications for experiential learning practices.

Main traditions in adult learning

There are many ways in which we could classify the traditions of adult learning. One of the simplest ways of doing this is to take four themes which are influential in current theory and practice. Each one of these holds sway over a different domain of post-secondary education and training and has grown up in response to the particular demands of these domains.

By characterizing them as four traditions, I do not wish to imply that there has not been some cross-fertilization or that there are not hybrids of one kind or another. In particular, I believe that there are a number of earlier traditions than those I list (Houle, 1977), an example of which is based on the ancient tradition of an individual passing on his or her expertise to the next generation. In the area of practical learning this has been called 'sitting by Nellie' and more formally it has given rise to the apprenticeship system in which young people learn to become skilled by watching and working under the supervision of older, skilled practitioners. Today this is not regarded as particularly educationally effective and most countries have sought to reform the apprenticeship system, but it is an extraordinarily powerful form of socialization for work.

To simplify discussion, I will present a fairly idealized version of each approach (based on Boud, 1987) and briefly discuss the implications for teachers or facilitators.

Training and efficiency in learning

The tradition of adult learning which has the strongest conventional research base is that which treats teaching and learning as though they comprised only a technology. The aim of this approach is to make learning tasks as straight-forward as possible to ensure that all learning is directed efficiently towards a given purpose. Goals are made explicit and they are broken down into operational objectives which can determine whether they have or have not been achieved.

Learning goals are derived from analyses of the kinds of tasks learners will be expected to perform and the competencies successful learners should exhibit. The characteristics and prior skills of the learners are assessed; programmes are systematically designed to take account of the structure of knowledge and skills in the area and the motivation and conceptual framework of the expected learners. These programmes are tested on representative groups of the population of learners and subsequently modified in the light of the feedback obtained to improve effectiveness. Attempts are made to allow learners as much flexibility as possible and respond to individual differences, but constraints of time and cost often limit this aspect. I have described this as *freedom from distraction* in learning (Boud, 1987).

Not all programmes which aspire to the goals of this tradition are developed as systematically as the description above suggests, but the criteria for effective learning outlined are those to which many programme developers aspire.

Effective facilitation in this tradition means being able to predict and respond to the full range of possible responses of learners. Feedback from trainers to learners and from learners to trainers is a central feature.

Self-directed learning and the andragogy school

This is the tradition which has made the most impact in recent years on formal post-secondary courses. It has been promoted by Malcolm Knowles (1984) and Knowles and Associates (1985) using the term andragogy – the art and science of teaching adults. It has been enormously successful in giving teachers of adults the confidence that comes from having a territory which is uniquely their own.

It draws attention to the unique goals and interests of individual learners and places these as central in the teaching and learning process. The role of the facilitator is to assist the learner to meet these goals by providing a helpful structure which enables learners to clarify their expectations, plan programmes which meet the goals they have specified, draw on the resources which are available, obtain evidence of the success of their endeavours and make judgements about the outcomes of their self-directed programme. The most common device used to support this process is the learning contract which records and formalizes the intended learning. It is proposed by the learner and negotiated with and approved by the facilitator. This I have characterized as freedom from the restrictions of teaching or as *freedom as learners*.

Learner-centred education and the humanistic educators

While the self-directed learning tradition has emphasized the individual learner, a related approach has placed the individual learner within a group setting and has given great attention to an individual's personal, as distinct from professional, or task, needs. The most influential person in this area was Carl Rogers (1983), with his learner-centred education deriving from his earlier experiences in client-centred therapy. Many of the figures in this tradition have been influenced by therapeutic processes and have sought to bring the insights of psychotherapy and group dynamics to mainstream educational settings.

Workers in this tradition recognize that it is often difficult for learners to acknowledge and express their needs. Learners may be constrained by their own early negative experiences of learning and they need the context of a highly supportive and respectful environment to be able to recognize their needs and begin to explore them. It is important for them to value learners and respond uniquely to them. Learning must involve the whole person, not just the intellect. Emotions and feelings can severely inhibit learning of all kinds. Practitioners aim to liberate learners from their inner compulsions and inappropriate behaviour. They allow them, in Rogers' famous phrase, *freedom to learn*.

Critical pedagogy and social action

The three approaches listed above all focus on learning as a phenomenon of individuals, which in its most fundamental sense it must be. However, all learning occurs in a particular social, cultural and political context and this influences what is learned and the ways in which it is learned. Proponents of critical pedagogy would claim that theirs is not simply another perspective on adult learning, but a shift in ideology away from one based on functionalism and the importance of the individual to one based on dialectics and collective action. Learners must seek to understand their world and transcend the constraints it places on them in order to liberate themselves and their fellow learners. Learning can never be value-free, it must either work to change the world or to reinforce the status quo. Educators in the critical tradition are pursuing *freedom through learning*.

Facilitators within this tradition need to understand the context-specific nature of knowledge and the values which impinge on learners and assist them to appreciate their position in society and how this constrains their goals and the ways in which they learn.

Freire (1973; Freire and Shor, 1987) argues that the most important thing for facilitators to do is to enter into dialogue with learners and promote dialogue among them. Such a dialogue involves more than simply listening and responding; it involves a checking of understanding, allowing one's ideas to be criticized by others, exploring one's appreciations of the limitations placed on one's consciousness by historical and social circumstances, and being prepared to change one's approach as such awareness creates a new framework within which to act. Learning is necessarily a phenomenon of both teachers and learners. Teachers should not expect to remain unaffected by what they do. The recent development of forms of critical action research (e.g. Carr and Kemmis, 1983) has enhanced work in this tradition.

Although it is possible to identify these traditions, and arguably there are many more than those I have outlined, it is often easy when discussing learning with someone from within one of them to gain the impression that what falls outside their domain is in some sense not legitimate. Most practitioners, not surprisingly, have been raised with one approach and it is a difficult transition to make to acknowledge the value and worth of others. But, if we are to be effective in developing experiential learning, I believe that we must at least have an awareness of the richness of the varying approaches, if not a sympathy towards each.

Some of these traditions are harder to put into practice than others and require the development of quite particular expertise. Each also has strong ideological ties – whether acknowledged or not – and attitudinal aspects which place some limits on transferability.

Three aspects of autonomy

A common feature of most forms of experiential learning is that they pursue some notion of freedom and autonomy for the learner, though they define this in different ways: from the drudgery of organizing complicated bodies of knowledge; from dependence on the teacher; from their own self-imposed constraints; and from the limitations of one's social context. Autonomy and self-direction are central concepts in experiential learning. It may be helpful to disentangle some of the ideas which are linked to these, often vaguely expressed concepts. There seems to be three separate ideas concerning autonomy which are often confounded.

1. *Autonomy as a goal.* Here the aim of educators is to foster the development of autonomous persons, i.e. people who will reach their own understandings and make their own decisions without being unduly influenced by others. The literature in the philosophy of education which discusses the characteristics of an educated person is primarily concerned with this aspect of autonomy, and the goals of educational institutions draw heavily on this rhetoric of autonomy.
2. *Autonomy as an approach to teaching and learning.* Here autonomy (or self-direction) is a name given to a range of teaching methods. Students engage in 'self-directed learning' or some other teaching/learning strategy. There is a substantial literature describing various practices which are intended to promote autonomy or self-direction through particular methods. The first edition of my book *Developing Student Autonomy in Learning* was almost entirely devoted to this aspect of autonomy.
3. *Autonomy as a necessary element in learning.* An important goal of much learning is that students become autonomous with respect to a given body of knowledge and skills, i.e. they are able to make their own judgements about facts and opinions and they can appreciate and apply criteria for assessment of what is and is not appropriate in the given area. This is the ultimate goal of

all subject teachers. They aspire to produce individuals who are not dependent on others for making judgements about a particular body of knowledge. Candy (1988) has termed this aspect epistemological autonomy.

One of the great confusions in discussions of autonomy is that autonomy (in the sense of definitions 1 and 3 above) does not necessarily develop through the application of autonomous methods. There is no causal link between the teaching methods used and the desired outcome. Students may be given considerable freedom in designing and planning their own programmes, but they may still suffer from debilitating dependencies on others in so far as they can understand and use the knowledge they are working with. However, while we must be cautious about claiming too much for autonomous methods, it is unlikely that teaching approaches which encourage dependency on teachers will be more successful in pursuing these goals. What we seek are autonomous approaches which also promote epistemological autonomy.

Brookfield (1985, pp. 14–15) has made the point well, that self-directed methods do not necessarily lead to liberated learners:

> we should distinguish between the techniques of self-direction and the internal change in consciousness that we can call self-directed learning . . . It is quite feasible, then, to exhibit the methodological attributes of self-directed learning within a framework of assumptions, expectations, allowable goals, and possible alternatives that is narrow and unchallenged. Learning to be a good disciple, an efficient bureaucratic functionary, or an exemplary political party member are all projects where the techniques of self-directed learning are evident. At the same time, none of these projects exhibits autonomous critical thought concerning alternatives, options, or possibilities.

We must be clear though on what we are doing when we select a particular approach. Learners need to engage with what it is they are learning in meaningful ways, and these meaningful ways might vary greatly depending on the kinds of knowledge which are being pursued. Very different activities are required for developing expertise in, say, mathematics compared to welfare work. Approaches to the development of autonomy are subject-dependent and, I believe, context-dependent. While there are some robust approaches, they cannot be selected uncritically.

Teaching approaches for the development of autonomy

Although many names have been used to describe approaches which teachers can use to promote autonomous learning there are three main classes of approach which have been adopted. Each has a particular emphasis and has characteristic methods associated with it (the following is taken from Boud, 1988).

The individual-centred approach

This is characterized by a focus on individual learners and their needs. Teachers, co-learners and other resources for learning are enlisted to facilitate the attainment of the goals of the individual as defined by the individual. Groups of learners may provide encouragement but they do not generally have a specific role of commitment to any project other than their own.

A typical example of an approach in this category is using a learning contract. In the first part of a course, by using learning contracts students are first introduced to the idea and learn something about how they can draw upon the resources of others. They then prepare individual contracts which specify learning goals, activities in which they will engage, criteria for judging their performance and how the contract will be assessed. These draft contracts are negotiated with a teacher and, after modification, the agreed contract provides the specification for learning. Many other people may be involved in the learning activities, but they are usually contacted by the particular learner in response to a particular need they have identified.

The use of learning contracts has been extensively discussed by Knowles (1975) and Knowles and Associates (1986), and the important role of negotiation and the need for flexibility is further examined by Tompkins and McGraw (1988).

The group-centred approach

This cluster of approaches is characterized by a focus on the needs of a particular group of learners and a strong commitment to group learning, and group processes. Individuals pursue their own learning needs within the context of the group, referring to others for support and feedback and for validation of the enterprise. Much learning occurs from interactions between group members. There is usually an emphasis on democratic decision making and the consideration of different points of view within the group. The development of the group itself is often a focus for learning with the aim being for the group to strive towards a relationship among its members that allows individuals to engage in their own learning with the tangible support of others. Interdependence is highly valued. One example of a group-centred approach is Heron's peer learning community:

> A peer learning community is based on two fundamental principles of parity: equality of consideration and equality of opportunity. First, the needs and interests, skills and resources which each person – whether staff or student – brings to the community are equally worthy of consideration. Second, it is equally open to anyone – whether staff or student – to contribute to or intervene in the course process at any time in any manner which he [sic] judges to be appropriate (Heron, 1974, p. 2).

Heron points out that these principles do not imply that all contributions made by individuals, or that the skills and resources which each brings, are of equal value from the point of view of fulfilling course objectives. However, equal attention must be given to a consideration of what different individuals want to get from the course and bring to the course; and that equal opportunity must be given to different individuals to make their needs felt, to exercise their judgement on course events and to exercise whatever skills and resources they do bring to the course.

Another example of a group-centred approach which uses a peer learning community approach, within the constraints of one subject in a formal postgraduate programme in science education, is described by Boud and Prosser (1980). In this course, aims, activities and assessment procedures were all negotiated between staff and students and the course was conducted cooperatively, drawing upon the skills and expertise of both groups. It is a variation of this approach which I currently use in my own teaching.

Curriculum negotiation is a common theme in group-centred approaches and two examples of how this works in practice are given by Miller *et al.* (1986) in the training of adult educators and Harber and Meighan (1986; Meighan and Harber 1986) in teacher training.

The project-centred approach

In this group of approaches the particular learning project and its outcome is often as important or more important than the individuals or the group which is working on it. The project gives meaning to and characterizes the enterprise. The goals of the particular learning situation are central and often override the special interests of individuals or groups. There is typically a strong practical or relevance orientation defined in terms external to the learners directly involved. The needs and interests of this group are considered, but these influence the details of the enterprise rather than the main activities. In practice, elements of both the first two classes of approach may be included.

Learning through projects is one of the most common activities in courses of all kinds. Morgan (1983, p. 66) defines such a form of learning as:

> an activity in which students develop an understanding of a topic through some kind of involvement in an actual (or simulated) real-life problem or issue and in which they have some degree of responsibility in designing their learning activities.

Problem-based learning is an example of a project-centred approach which is gaining considerable ground in courses which train students for the professions. The basic idea which underlies problem-based learning is that:

> the starting point for learning should be a problem, a query or a puzzle that the learner wishes to solve. Organized forms of knowledge, academic disciplines, are only introduced when the demands of the problem require them (Boud, 1985, p. 13).

A typical series of stages in a problem-based learning approach is given by Barrows and Tamblyn (1980):

1. The problem is encountered first in the learning sequence, before any preparation or study has occurred.
2. The problem situation is presented to the student in the same way it would present itself in reality.
3. The student works with the problem in a manner that permits his [sic] ability to reason and apply knowledge to be challenged and evaluated, appropriate to his level of learning.
4. Needed areas of learning are identified in the process of work with the problem and used as a guide to individualised study.
5. The skills and knowledge acquired by this study are applied back to the problem, to evaluate the effectiveness of learning and to reinforce learning.
6. The learning that has occurred in work with the problem and in individualised study is summarised and integrated into the student's existing knowledge and skills.

Students exercise considerable initiative and engage in individual learning in association with the problem, but it is the problem itself which ultimately defines the area of learning.

It is important to stress that the individual-centred, group-centred and project-centred approaches are three general ways of viewing the promotion of autonomy and any particular approach may involve a combination of the others. These are not rigid distinctions but they do provide the characteristic flavour to a particular learning experience.

Issues in applying these ideas in practice

It is one thing to have a clear view of some of the main traditions which have influenced experiential learning, the role of autonomy and the variety of approaches which might be adopted to promote autonomous learning; it is quite another to apply these ideas in any given context. There are major implications for the training of experiential educators and the design of courses.

One of the questions which arises is how sophisticated should training be? Too often those working in experiential education are simply doing what they have picked up as an adjunct to their normal work. They have learned from experience, but their experience is limited. There is little training available and, sometimes, desired. However, unless we are challenged to move beyond our existing practices then experiential education will remain forever peripheral to mainstream education and promise more than it can deliver.

The training of those who will be responsible for organizing, supervising and conducting experiential learning activities needs to take account of the competing traditions of experiential education and the practices which are associated with them. It is easy to become constrained by a particular way of operating which blinds us to the opportunities offered by alternatives. It is not a simple matter of picking and mixing from different approaches though.

Not all combinations are possible or desirable. Some demand a commitment to a particular view of education or how people should interact with each other, all are influenced by their own ideology. However, it is not possible to make a decision without a good appreciation of what is involved in each tradition and each approach. The training of experiential educators might therefore profit from a focus on providing experiences of different approaches upon which participants might critically reflect before planning for their own practice. Through this they might be able to test the realms of applicability of each strategy, clarify their own personal preferences and make judgements about what is needed in their own situation.

Experiential learning is an area of rapid development. Governments and institutions are discovering the potential for dealing with complex problems by the use of new forms of learning through experience. This provides considerable opportunities, but also great dangers. There is the opportunity to innovate and to tackle previously neglected problems, but there is a danger of experiential learning becoming a fashion which is dismissed when it becomes familiar. The danger exists only if practitioners become wedded to a particular approach which meets their present needs, but do not change with circumstances. Through an awareness of the competing traditions of experiential learning and the importance of making creative responses to unique situations, experiential learning can be a potent influence for human development and social change.

References

Barrows, H. S. and Tamblyn, R. (1980). *Problem-based Learning: An Approach to Medical Education*. New York: Springer.

Boud, D. J. (1985). Problem-based learning in perspective. In Boud, D. J. (Ed.), *Problem-based Learning in Education for the Professions*, pp. 13–18. Sydney: Higher Education Research and Development Society of Australasia.

Boud, D. J. (1987). A facilitator's view of adult learning. In Boud, D. J. and Griffin, V. R. (Eds), *Appreciating Adults Learning: From the Learner's Perspective*, pp. 222–39. London: Kogan Page.

Boud, D. J. (1988). Moving towards autonomy. In Boud, D. J. (Ed.), *Developing Student Autonomy in Learning*, pp. 17–39, 2nd edition. London: Kogan Page.

Boud, D. J. and Pascoe, J. (1978). Conceptualising experiential education. In Boud, D. J. and Pascoe, J. (Eds), *Experiential Learning: Developments in Australian Post-secondary Education*, pp. 61–6. Sydney: Australian Consortium on Experiential Education.

Boud, D. J. and Prosser, M. T. (1980). Sharing responsibility: Staff–student cooperation in learning. *British Journal of Educational Technology*, **11**(1), 24–35.

Boud, D. J., Keogh, R. and Walker, D. (Eds) (1985). *Reflection: Turning Experience into Learning*. London: Kogan Page.

Brookfield, S. (1985). Self-directed learning: A critical review of research. In Brookfield, S. (Ed.), *Self-directed Learning: From Theory to Practice*, pp. 5–16. New Directions for Continuing Education, No. 25. San Francisco: Jossey-Bass.

Candy, P. (1988). On the attainment of subject-matter autonomy. In Boud, D. J. (Ed.),

Developing Student Autonomy in Learning, pp. 59–76; 2nd edition. London: Kogan Page.

Carr, W. and Kemmis, S. (1983). *Becoming Critical: Knowing Through Action Research.* Geelong: Deakin University Press.

Dewey, J. (1938). *Experience and Education.* New York: Collier Macmillan.

Freire, P. (1973). *Education for Critical Consciousness.* London: Sheed and Ward.

Freire, P. and Shor, I. (1987). *A Pedagogy for Liberation: Dialogues on Transforming Education.* London: Macmillan.

Harber C. and Meighan, R. (1986). A case study of democratic learning in teacher education. *Educational Review*, **38**(3), 273–82.

Heron, J. (1974). *The Concept of a Peer Learning Community.* Guildford: Human Potential Research Project, University of Surrey.

Houle, C. O. (1977). Deep traditions of experiential learning. In Keeton, M. T. and Associates (Eds), *Experiential Learning: Rationale, Characteristics and Assessment*, pp. 19–33. San Francisco: Jossey-Bass.

Knowles, M. S. (1975). *Self-directed Learning: A Guide for Learners and Teachers.* New York: Association Press.

Knowles, M. S. (1984). *The Adult Learner: A Neglected Species*, 3rd edition Houston: Gulf Publishing.

Knowles, M. S. and Associates (1985). *Andragogy in Action.* San Francisco: Jossey-Bass.

Knowles, M. S. and Associates (1986). *Using Learning Contracts.* San Francisco: Jossey-Bass.

Kolb, D. A. (1984). *Experiential Learning: Experience as the Source of Learning and Development.* Englewood Cliffs, N.J. Prentice-Hall.

Meighan, R. and Harber, C. (1986). Democratic learning in teacher education: A review of experience at one institution. *Journal of Education for Teaching*, **12**(2), 163–72.

Millar, C., Morphet, T. and Saddington, T. (1986). Curriculum negotiation in professional adult education. *Journal of Curriculum Studies*, **18**(4), 429–43.

Morgan, A. (1983). Theoretical aspects of project-based learning in higher education. *British Journal of Educational Technology*, **14**(1), 66–78.

Rogers, C.R. (1983). *Freedom to Learn in the 80's.* Columbus, Ohio: Charles E. Merrill.

Schön, D. A. (1983). *The Reflective Practitioner: How Professionals Think in Action.* New York: Basic Books.

Tompkins, C. and McGraw, M. J. (1988). The negotiated learning contract. In Boud, D. J. (Ed.), *Developing Student Autonomy in Learning*, pp. 172–91, 2nd edition. London: Kogan Page.

4

Learning from Action:
A Conceptual Framework

Miriam Hutton

*Hutton enters experiential learning at the point where both learning and action are required –
a situation increasingly pertinent for effective experiential learning. Her focus is 'on
knowledge for use and learning from doing'. She is critical of the traditional scientific method
in the approach to solving problems. She prefers to involve learners in engaging with 'issues' or
'a focus of concern'; these lend themselves less easily to tidy, straightforward or 'one-best'
solutions. Drawing upon Schön's (1971, 1983) work she is concerned to recognize the
complexity of situations in which the outcomes are not clear. She explores a model for more
flexible learning that acknowledges complexity and that can help practitioners to make
decisions when the outcomes of their own actions are not clear. The key is the process by which
we undertake the approach to decision making which she elaborates in the text. Hutton is also
critical of another derivative of the traditional scientific method applied in complex situations
– objective setting. She reminds us once again that the greatest resistance to shedding
traditional approaches tends to come from Western institutional settings.*

*Readers of Chapter 1 will recognize the new 'ways of seeing', and the post-positivist
paradigm story we discuss in Chapter 22, underlying experiential learning in Hutton's
framework. This chapter also links up with Salmon (Chapter 21) on personal stance and
McGill et al. (Chapter 12) on action learning.*

Introduction

The framework which follows has evolved out of my experience as an educator
over many years. At the Canadian university where I teach I have had
particular responsibility for helping social work students to integrate theory and
practice. This involves teaching students how to do social work and how to learn
from their practice experience. I have also carried responsibility for designing
programmes and teaching a variety of people from different cultures who were
working in the human services. Many of these people have had considerable
experience but limited formal education. Thus the focus for my teaching has
always been on knowledge for use, and learning from doing.

My undergraduate degree is in science, and I carried my conviction about the advantages of the scientific method and the problem-solving approach into my practice and teaching. Gradually, however, I found that the students I taught were not necessarily satisfied. Sometimes they were bored and sometimes they felt that their experience and knowledge were being denied. Often the practice situations that they were dealing with were far too complex for the linear and reductionist approach of the problem-solving method. Sometimes situations required immediate action and the student could not wait for the careful collection of data and a delineation of goals and objectives.

For a long time I thought that the route to better teaching lay in clearer objectives, and more precision. But the sheer volume of objectives drove me to look for simpler and more elegant abstractions which could be remembered, and used in a variety of ways.

As I struggled to teach people how to bring about change, or how to prepare themselves for future action, I found the scientific problem-solving method, as it is frequently used, to be limited in a number of ways. First, there is an underlying assumption that knowledge precedes action. This focuses the learner's attention on a specific body of knowledge, and reduces the expectation to 'what is' rather than including 'what might be'. Second, there is an assumption that problems can be limited, and that there can be closure: indeed, a solution infers closure. Third, there is too often an expectation that there is a single best solution. In reality there may be many alternatives not one of which is clearly the best. Fourth, previous experiences and the relationships among the people who are involved are often ignored or undervalued. And, finally, complexity is handled by partialization and reduction which limits the validity for practical application.

I began to look for an approach to learning and acting which could accommodate what people brought, and the relationships among people and elements; which would be able to accommodate ongoing change over time; which would enable students to be able to order complexity, and to begin to act constructively with whatever they had at a given moment in time; and, finally, which could facilitate students' ongoing learning. In short, I wanted an approach to learning which could enable people to act and to learn at the same time.

My search for ordering social complexity and social learning was helped by finding Donald Schön's books, *Beyond the Stable State* (1971), and *The Reflective Practitioner* (1983). Much of what follows has grown out of my reading of Schön's work.

I have chosen not to use the term 'problem' because of its common association with the scientific method and those limitations mentioned, and because the word 'problem' tends to invite a 'solution', which is too often assumed to be singular. In addition, the idea of 'problem' carries a pejorative connotation. Instead, I try to use such terms as 'issue' (which suggests resolution or ordering), 'situation', or 'focus of concern'.

For me, experiential learning is learning which is rooted in our doing and our experience. It is learning which illuminates that experience and provides direction for the making of a judgement as a guide to choice or action.

The framework

The framework that I am presenting for experiential learning is deceptively simple. It consists of identifying a process for the making of a judgement or decision, rather than focusing upon the outcome expected.

Normally, many decisions are made on the basis of habit, or common sense, and many are made unconsciously. The use of habitual patterns provides a considerable measure of efficiency and enables us to do far more than would be possible if we made every decision with a conscious mind. Familiar situations and straightforward problems may likewise be dealt with using habitual responses or scientific problem-solving approaches. But when the situation is 'not so simple' or 'new' we need something more.

In conventional problem solving, action is determined by a goal or objective. When we know where we are going it seems relatively straightforward to plan actions that will take us toward our goal. Evaluation is usually tied to measuring how closely we have achieved the stated goal. If we do not achieve the goal there may be a loss of confidence which may engender puzzlement, anger, or a sense of failure. The more attached one is to the expected outcome the greater the likelihood that one will have some sense of failure, disbelief, or anger.

A belief that one is doing the 'right thing' may be helpful in motivating or generating action. If one is unsure one may find it difficult to act or follow through, or one may find that much energy is consumed in the process of living with competing perspectives. Recognizing the differences and choosing to act may require considerable self-confidence, perhaps even courage. When one is under the stress of many changes the making of such decisions may be particularly difficult.

Initially, the framework being suggested may feel uncomfortable, and threatening. Ultimately, the framework may contribute to confidence because self-esteem is not tied to outcome. Rather, every action is an opportunity for new learning and new growth.

Making complex decisions involves judgement, which I define as the considered weighing of factors and their relationship to each other, as a guide to choice or action. In my view, learning to make sound judgements is one of the major tasks for professional education; or of living in modern society. Indeed, I have come to view the process of making a judgement as also being a key in learning how to learn.

Since decisions are made at a variety of points for most social situations (or for learning activities) the making of choices can become quite complex. When we are attempting to make decisions or judgements as guides for choice or action we are often in the 'middle of the muddle'. Our usual way of working may not seem to be effective; the situation may be in flux; the need to act may be immediate; or we may no longer be clear about where we are going. The problem-solving approach would suggest the gathering of facts and information and establishing a new goal based on these. But sometimes there is no time, or we have too much information rather than too little. In any case, most situations which involve human beings may be changing continuously. How do we make a decision, which implies closure, and yet which is flexible enough to allow us to adapt to ongoing changes?

People and organizations resist change. The resistance may be particularly great when people feel that they have some investment in the original design, or when their response has become a habit. Schön (1971) has called this resistance 'dynamic conservatism', and he suggests that it will be particularly strong when a change is perceived to threaten a 'stable state'. One's stable state is an important factor in shaping and maintaining identity. Schön suggests that organizations and institutions, as well as individuals, have a sense of 'stable state'.

We all need to have a sense of stability in our lives. At the same time we need to be able to adapt to change: growth is change; the seasons change; children grow older; our own needs and expectations change; the society around us is changing continually. Without enough change we become bored or ineffective. But change has also been defined as 'stress'. In a world where change seems to be exponential, we may find that we are needing new ways to adapt.

Schön suggests that the traditional problem-solving approach and the scientific method may no longer meet our needs. As these are usually developed, one tries to determine outcome and goal and to see these as the fixed points to work toward. The intent of scientific problem solving is to order and reduce the variables so that one can in the future find a way of replicating or controlling outcome. The intent is to be able to predict accurately and with some consistency. But when the variables cannot be controlled for, one needs an alternative approach. For this Schön suggests that we need to have a stable *process* rather than a fixed *outcome*. The stable state is maintained in the situation not by controlling the outcome but by using a process.

Schön suggests that what can be fixed is the knowledge that one has about conditions and stance. *Conditions* are those facts which may be known, such as physical characteristics, history, culture, resources available, structure, relationships, and so on. *Stance* includes attitudes, values, beliefs, expectations, and assumptions.

While both conditions and stance will change over time, we can identify them at the point in time when we are making a judgement or decision. The conditions and stance are the knowledge we have and which we draw upon as we proceed. They provide us with some basis for making our choice. Choice implies some alternatives. Sometimes people come to a decision making without recognizing that alternatives exist.

If we generate a range of alternatives, and reflect upon the possible and probable outcomes for each of these alternatives, we may make a *tentative* judgement. Because of the tentative nature of our judgements, we remain open to new information which can help confirm or deny the validity of our judgement. While the choice is tentative we must begin to act as if it was fixed. But we must be prepared to learn as we go and to be able to adapt to the new information which will be generated by the action itself. The value of a list of alternatives becomes apparent if we have to modify our plan. Because we have already generated some other possible ways of acting we are more easily able to respond. We are not surprised and thrown off stride by the need to adapt our planning, and we have some alternatives 'ready' to explore and to use.

Evaluation is built in from the beginning. One is always ready to learn and to modify as one goes along. An unanticipated outcome is not necessarily a failure, but there are always some intended or expected outcomes and/or some un-intended or unexpected outcomes. Both provide the basis for new learning, and new action.

What we have then is a stable process for ordering decisions. We are not concerned about the predictable outcome. Rather, we begin where we are, and learn as we act.

Social situations, of course, usually involve a series of judgements and actions, each of which may contribute to new learning. In addition, there is frequently more than one actor involved. These add to the complexity of the process as well. The use of theoretical knowledge may compound or reduce the factors which need to be included in the judgement process. I have tried to provide a diagramatic representation of the framework to assist in ordering this complexity (see Fig. 4.1).

In order to implement this framework one would ask a number of questions. In a given situation we can begin by asking what do we know and what do we need to know? Probably 'the need to know' list will be more than one item and will generate some alternative courses of action. For example, if I want more information about a community, where will I look for that information? From a book, from individuals who live there, or from other people who have expertise? Each of these choices will have a consequence and will generate new knowledge.

For example, if I choose to ask residents about their community I may anticipate a change of attitude toward the ownership of their particular situation, or I may recognize that I may also generate a sense of fear or puzzlement. As I weigh these possibilities my knowledge about some of my own assumptions may grow and, with that, new questions or insights about what I am working toward.

Perhaps the new knowledge does not emerge until I have actually sought some answers. Perhaps I am surprised by the anxiety and fear of residents; such a response might then send me back to ask questions of others who are experts, or to ask additional questions of one or two residents. If I had had a very clear expectation to achieve a particular outcome I might be tempted to push on anyway and ignore the anxiety level of residents. But if my purpose is to learn from my actions and adapt to new learning, I will more easily adapt to the emerging reality.

As one begins to ask 'what do we need to know?' one may find that there is a need to go back and rethink the original starting point. As one proceeds one may find that one needs some additional structure. One may begin to look for 'the pattern that connects'. Differences and similarities become useful, as does the unexpected response or finding. Contradictions to one's tentative hypotheses push one to examine alternatives: what might be some probable (based on past or present) outcomes, or what might be some possible (ideal) outcomes?

In this process we gradually come to identify more of the conditions and the stance that we are working with. Often the stance and conditions are inter-

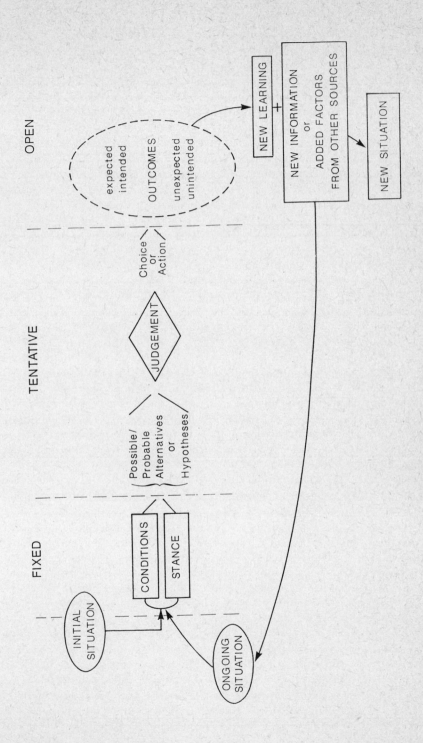

Figure 4.1 A reflective framework for learning from action.

twined. Assumptions and values are taken for granted and may not be conscious, but may be very powerful none the less. I have sometimes found it helpful to have people begin with the conditions, and then to look for the linking assumptions, or stance, that relate to a particular condition.

When I am working with people of other cultures, I do not want to impose my cultural bias on them any more than I can help. I also assume that they bring to any situation some knowledge and life experience. Much of that is likely to be useful, even though some new learning may also be needed. So I like to begin by asking them: 'What would they probably do in such a situation, who would be involved, and who would be likely to be helpful?' I try to have people identify what they already know. Sometimes this requires some drawing out to get at the information that they have not yet made conscious, or information which they have not thought of as appropriate to this particular situation.

In teaching Inuit (Canadian Eskimos), for example, I was particularly concerned about their cultural values. As I prepared to teach them something about counselling, I recognized that nearly everything which I knew had been learned in my own cultural context, and so might be inappropriate. I decided to have them teach me what they needed to know.

I asked them to begin by identifying examples of situations where they might be expected to help. Then I asked them 'what would you do?' This would produce some ideas but then they might say 'I don't know'. I realized that they were screening out information that it was not polite to know. So then I would ask: 'Who would usually be expected to help?' Often their reply would include 'the priest', 'the brother', or 'a friend'. If I then asked them 'What would the priest, or the friend do?', they would know. Speaking together, sometimes in Inuktitut and sometimes in English, they would put together an appropriate way of helping for that situation. Asking 'What do you know?' and 'What do you need to know?' generated enough material to begin. Together we were able to speculate about alternatives, and I was able to provide additional insight or understanding about particular aspects.

As they explored these situations further, they developed a sense of their own culture and way of working. They were also learning how to learn in new situations. They developed skills in asking good questions, and in taking their own thinking further. And to my great delight they continued to do this after I had returned home.

The process which I used with the Inuit was not dependent upon a single right answer. The process assumed that we could learn as we went along, and that the collective input of several people or a variety of ideas would be helpful.

This brings me to another aspect of decision making. When we make decisions there are often a number of people involved or affected. We need a process which can accommodate the multiplicity of actors. Sometimes we bring together an array of people who are representative of different perspectives. The dialogue among actors is assumed to be an aid to decision making. Such collective decision making, while ideal, is time-consuming and may not always be practical. The decision process can accommodate the perspectives of different actors without necessarily being a group process. For example, I may be able to identify something about the conditions and stance of each of the major actors as a result of my previous experience or knowledge. By comparing the similarities and differences between actors I can start to speculate about the possible outcomes of particular alternatives. Where change or intervention is being considered, differing sets of assumptions (stance) can be very significant and, if ignored, may well upset even the most careful planning.

For example, in a community project the project co-ordinator may assume that political empowerment is the most important goal, whereas the local community members might view community harmony as essential, and government sponsors anticipate increased economic benefits. The project may well flounder unless these underlying assumptions are brought into the open and dealt with. Uncovering assumptions is not an easy task. Often these are unconscious or taken for granted. They may need to be teased out of actions or statements and verified. This process may need to accompany action. The value of a tentative choice becomes apparent.

In teaching this approach I have found that people sometimes encounter difficulties, such as:

1. People are often locked into a habitual expectation, and find it difficult to modify this. Particularly common is the expectation that one has not enough resources, or control, and that someone else should be doing something. It seems difficult to recognize that there are always some choices.
2. People may need help in articulating the elements that they take for granted. These might include ways of perceiving the situation, or the expected outcome, or what they already know.
3. Underlying assumptions and expectations (stance) are particularly difficult for people to identify, and may require an outside facilitator or some practice.
4. The number of decisions which are made in planning and carrying out a learning project or activity are not always recognized. Many decisions are made at the unconscious level or are taken for granted. For example, in the process of teaching a class, one makes a decision about when to start teaching; what to do or say while you are waiting to begin; what to do to gain the attention of the class; whether or not the seating or other physical arrangements are suitable; what to do if they are not; when to hand out resource materials or assignments; and when to stop for questions, or to verify that one is being heard. These decisions all contribute to the effectiveness of the interaction but will be largely taken for granted unless something goes awry.
5. Those who are steeped in the scientific method may find the identification of tentative assumptions based on inference to be very unsatisfactory! Some people have a great need to be grounded in verifiable facts. This approach with its open-endedness may leave such people feeling uncomfortable.
6. Conversely, some people will be overwhelmed with the detail that this process can generate.
7. Finding the balance between how much to include, or what might provide clues to be followed up further (more judgements) seems to require some practice for most people.

Some students seem to grasp this approach very quickly, and some seem to have considerable difficulty. I am not sure why, or quite what constitutes the block for some people. Students from other cultural backgrounds, or with less formal education, seem to learn this approach and use it most easily; students who have learned the conventional academic way of going about things seem to have the most difficulty. Perhaps this approach to learning is closer to the way in which we process new learning in our informal learning activities. When we reflect on our learning and try to make the unconscious conscious, of course, we find ourselves struggling, and awkward. I have found Bateson's (1972, 1979) work particularly helpful, and also comforting, for Bateson has articulated his own process in trying to understand the experience of adaptation and learning used by all living organisms.

Conclusion

The problem-solving approach based on the scientific method is frequently taken for granted in learning and work with humans and social situations. In reality, the difficulties facing people do not always lend themselves to singular tidy solutions. Often the future is not known and the complexity of interdependent factors compounds our learning and action. Nor is the Western scientific problem-solving approach necessarily compatible with other cultural traditions for learning.

The proposed framework provides an alternative for guiding decision making when the nature of the outcome is not necessarily clear. The framework provides a process which facilitates both learning and action. The process illuminates the making of a judgement without predetermining an outcome. Action can begin and new learning is anticipated from both the process and the outcome of each action. Learning and action go hand in hand. All actors and a variety of perspectives can be taken into account. People may use their own knowledge and experience as a basis for action, and add to that knowledge through action. New learning emerges through the process, and thus ongoing learning is fostered.

This framework has been used with Inuit in the Canadian Arctic, with a multicultural group of recent immigrants in Winnipeg, and with para-professionals, undergradutes, and graduate students at the University of Manitoba. In teaching this approach I have found that the greatest barrier comes from the existing mind-set of learners about the virtues of the scientific method. For that reason, those from other cultures or with little formal education often grasp it and use it more easily.

I do not profess to have a complete answer for how we can teach when we do not know where we are going, or for those complex or marginal situations which involve relationships or which require action before knowing. I hope, however, that the framework I have presented will help to advance our ongoing struggle in learning how to learn from doing and from experience.

References

Bateson, G. (1972). *Steps to an Ecology of Mind.* New York: Ballantine.
Bateson, G. (1979). *Mind and Nature.* New York: Dutton.
Schön, D. A. (1971). *Beyond the Stable State.* New York: Norton.
Schön, D. A. (1983). *The Reflective Practitioner: How Professionals Think in Action.* New York: Basic Books.

5

The Principal Meaning of Dialogue for the Construction and Transformation of Reality

Danny Wildemeersch

Wildemeersch cautions us against some of current orientations in experiential learning which take us down the route of individualized learning and self-direction at the expense of other concerns. By doing so we may lose that central dimension of learning – conversation or dialogue – by which we understand and transform the reality in which we live.

He sets the recent background to the theory and practice of experiential learning in radical critiques of traditional education in the 1960s. He finds that in the current climate in the West there has been a 'colonization' of the progressive ideas on experiential learning, often in naive forms, for narrow technological and consumerist purposes. Moreover, there is in much contemporary theory and practice an easy compatibility with the current vogue for self-direction and individualistic values. Taken down this route we risk legitimizing personal isolation and narrow instrumental learning. Drawing upon his phenomenological position and the work of other recent writers, Wildemeersch suggests that what is missing from many contemporary applications of experiential learning is that element crucial to our construction of reality: the centrality of 'conversation' or 'dialogue'. Indeed, without this we are less able to engage in the transformation of our reality and more likely to get caught up in the imperative of the status quo.

This chapter provides a reflective insight into other chapters which concentrate upon independent study and self-direction (Chapters 4, 7, 9 and 10) where student autonomy is a central concern. He also adds another dimension of analysis to Boud's discussion of social change traditions of adult learning (Chapter 3). Wildemeersch can also be related to those chapters where the issue of social change for community and societal transformation is the main focus (Chapters 18, 19 and 20). Keregero (Chapter 18), in particular, insists on dialogue as a crucial part of the transformational process where experiential learning is applied.

Introduction

Experiential learning as an approach to education has become quite a popular phenomenon over the last 20 years. In spite of its relative popularity, experiential learning remains a diffuse concept that encompasses many different view-points and theories referring to a wide variety of disciplines and practices, such as therapy, formal, non-formal and informal education, social and cultural work, community–organization, and organization–development. I want to explore some of the background of experiential learning with special reference to adult education. Furthermore, I want to present a phenomenological outlook that gives new meaning to experiential learning and education. In doing so, I also want to caution against orientations that over-estimate the value of individualized or self-directed learning. I shall stress the critical importance of 'conversation' or 'dialogue' as a basic element of human experience and learning.

Some considerations about 'romanticism'

From the 1960s onwards educational theory and practice have been strongly challenged by some radical approaches. Authors like Illich, Reimer, Goodman and Freire criticized the technological, alienating and even oppressive character of dominant educational practice. Many supporters of these critics were particularly susceptible to observations about the class-biased character of education, the limited practical relevance of bookish knowledge, the rigidity of curriculum planning, and authoritarian teaching methods, for example. Although the former radicalism has lost much of its popularity nowadays, some contemporary theorists like Aronowitz and Giroux (1985) and Shor (1980) continue to contest dominant educational traditions and keep on emphasizing the importance of these criticisms. However, the conservative era in which we live now, seems to bring little enthusiasm for their radical ideas, at least in most of the advanced industrialized countries or post-industrial societies.

These observations do not mean that the concern for alternative approaches in education has completely disappeared nowadays. On the contrary, some of the ideas of the above-mentioned authors have been integrated into mainstream considerations about education. The result of this process is a mixture of radical and liberal insights, which also characterize some approaches to experiential learning. In the field of adult and continuing education especially, the 'romantic curriculum' (Jarvis, 1983) has obtained a fairly important position. This type of curriculum, in opposition to the classical curriculum, emphasizes elements like student-centredness, creativity, experience, discovery, awareness, originality and freedom. The educational process should refer to real-life experiences and ought to imply a shared responsibility among learners and facilitators in the planning, execution and evaluation of the activities. Experiential learning has thus become a core element of this alternative type of curriculum development. One of the dominant representatives of this orientation is Malcolm Knowles (1980, 1984). His theory is grounded in basic assumptions about adult learners, e.g. their capacity for self-direction, the accumulation of experiences as a rich resource for learning, the readiness to learn as a function of the need to perform social roles, and their problem-centred orientation.

According to Brookfield (1985), these assumptions and especially the orientation towards self-direction, have explicitly or implicitly inspired a new kind of orthodoxy in adult education. Although the author is in favour of an experiential approach, he critically appraises some recent trends, which he ironically characterizes as follows:

> Adults are self-directed learners within whom lies a partly realized, innate potential for learning. Our tasks as adult educators are, therefore, to assess as accurately as we can those learning needs which learners perceive themselves to possess, and to engage in a warmly humanistic facilitation of learning in which these needs are met. This facilitation is one in which teacher and learner grow together in a satisfying, joyous and bountiful release of latent learning potential (Brookfield, 1985, p. 44).

This criticism also involves a warning that this new orthodoxy might turn adult education into an apolitical, acurricular, reactive and consumer-oriented enterprise which casts the educator in the role of marketing expert and technician of the teaching–learning machinery.

The above-mentioned naive assumptions about the nature of adult learning, which seem to inspire a mainstream orientation in adult education and, simultaneously, legitimize certain experiential learning approaches, have also been critically examined by other authors. They raise objections to a naive understanding of learning processes. In accordance with these objections, Tennant remarks that Knowles' assumptions are shrouded by some persistent myths, such as:

> the myth that our need for self-direction is rooted in our constitutional make-up; the myth that self-development is a process of change, towards higher levels of existence; and the myth that adult learning is fundamentally (and necessarily) different from child learning (Tennant, 1986, p. 121).

He identifies the origin of the notions of student-centredness and self-directedness in the 'ethic of individualism' which is characteristic for a middle-class biased type of adult and continuing education.

Day and Basket (1982, p. 150) formulate similar objections and consider Knowles' approach not as a theory of adult learning, 'but as an educational ideology rooted in an inquiry-based learning and teaching paradigm'. Referring to Day and Basket, Jarvis (1984) states that Knowles' basic assumptions, which underpin the so-called 'romantic curriculum', remain open to considerable debate. Furthermore, Jarvis makes clear that, however much the romantic approach to curriculum theory has become an important sign of the times, rooted in the progressive pedagogy of the 1960s:

> its significance should not obscure the fact that it attained the status of a theory in a time when the structures of a wider society were conducive to it rather than because it was valid theoretically or adequate as a description of the process of adult learning (Jarvis, 1984, pp. 37–8).

These observations suggest that we need to be careful about some of the taken-for-granted insights about adult learning. I consider these suggestions as an invitation to question the usefulness of some theories about experiential learning in relation to adult education. The debate about the 'romantic' orientation towards learning and education is challenging. There are some elements in it which require further attention. First, there is the observation that many experiential practices have a rather poor theoretical underpinning. Secondly, there is what I would call the 'paradox of self-direction'. Experiential learning is very much concerned with autonomy, which of course is an important objective in education in general. Yet, the concept of self-direction may simultaneously lead to isolation, individualism and poor learning. Thirdly, the assimilation of experiential approaches into technological frameworks is puzzling. Experiential learning is apparently becoming an easy victim of a consumer-oriented and technicist enterprise.

In the following I will elaborate the outlines of an approach, by which the above-mentioned distortion may be avoided. I will examine the usefulness of the phenomenological concept of the 'life-world' as a theoretical foundation for experiential learning and education. In addition to this theory, the centrality of 'conversation' as a means for reality-construction and -transformation will be emphasized. This argument may finally neutralize – at least theoretically – the paradox of self-direction and some technological distortions which are the result of a too naive understanding of experiential learning and education.

The construction and transformation of the life-world

According to Berger and Luckmann (1985), the reality in which we live is socially constructed. This means that to human beings reality cannot exist without the act of giving meaning to it. Consequently, all reality has a strong subjective dimension. In spite of this observation, a difference is made between 'subjective reality' and 'objective reality', just as human beings must distinguish between the 'inside world' and the 'world out there'.

Subjective reality has in continental European phenomenology traditionally been denoted as the 'life-world' of human beings. According to that tradition, the life-world is to be considered as a stock of taken-for-granted perspectives or as a reservoir of interpretation patterns which are culturally transmitted and organized in a communicative way. This stock of knowledge is composed of unproblematic basic assumptions which function as an implicit or tacit horizon in everyday processes of action and communication. It is the basis of inter-subjective sharing of familiar or new situation definitions and routinized everyday activities.

Objective reality, on the other hand, transcends the domain of subjective or private experience. Although it is basically a socially constructed reality, it has obtained an objective character, as it is not part of our routinized action and reflection patterns. To a certain extent, this reality becomes reified because we cannot conceive of it as a socially constructed reality. Most of the factual knowledge which is being transmitted in educational settings belongs to the domain of objective reality. The more the world grows complex and functionally differentiated, the more vast becomes this objective reality. In relation to the complicated world out there, our private world represents only a minor slice of total reality.

The following representation (Fig. 5.1), which is a somewhat simplified version of a figure developed by Schmitz (1983), may give a good insight into the nature of (experiential) learning. It has been conceived in close relationship to phenomenological theory concerning the life-world.

In relation to this representation, learning can be understood as a process of continuous exchange between the life-world of subjects and the objective reality which is present in society as a whole. The most important agents of these exchange processes are the groups that are part of the external objective world but, at the same time, are closely linked to the subjective reality of a person. It is especially the process of interaction between individuals and the groups they belong to, that enables the mediation between the subjective and the objective world. These groups are composed of 'significant' and 'generalized' others (Berger and Luckmann, 1985). Significant others are people whom subjects are closely related to, like friends and relatives, with whom they interact quite privately and intimately. Generalized others are the persons with whom subjects have a more distant, neutral relationship, like colleagues or classmates. Through face-to-face interaction within these groups we continually confirm or change our private and public roles and the way we understand reality. The groups to which one belongs, as they are composed of several subjective realities, represent segments of objective reality which are relevant to one's subjective understanding of life.

The exchange processes between objective and subjective reality are genuinely experiential because they necessarily refer to the stock of experiences which have been integrated into our life-world and to new experiences which spring from the interactions with the objective world. It is quite interesting to

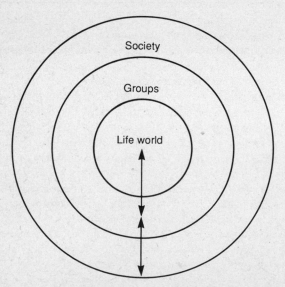

Figure 5.1   The nature of experiential learning (adapted from Schmitz, 1983, p. 115).

notice that Kolb (1984) also conceives of experiential learning in terms of a transaction between person and environment. The fascinating thing about it is that this distinction enables him to distinguish between two meanings of experience. There is the subjective personal meaning of experience, referring to the person's internal state, and the objective meaning referring to the environmental context. The disappointing thing about Kolb's theory, however, is that although he emphasizes the importance of the person–environment transaction, the transaction between people as a constitutive element to learning is not taken into consideration. Though this kind of reduction may be legitimate from a psychological point of view, it is rather unfruitful from an educational standpoint. For this reason I now want to draw attention to conversation as a constitutive element for experiential learning and education.

Conversation: the missing link in experiential education

According to Berger and Luckmann (1985), the conversation apparatus is a 'vehicle of reality maintenance' and, at the same time, a means for identity-building. In a very similar way, Freire (1972, p. 61) points at the necessity of conversation for the empowerment of human-kind:

> If it is in speaking their word that men transform the world by naming it, dialogue imposes itself as the way in which men achieve significance as men. Dialogue is thus an existential necessity.

In particular, the ongoing stream of conversation within the above-mentioned groups either confirms or changes our understanding of objective reality. This stream of conversation is to be considered as an important supportive element to learning processes of any kind. It helps the subjects involved to realize an interpretative integration of elements of the unknown objective reality into the patterns of familiar subjective reality. Simultaneously, objective reality can be redefined with the help of significant and generalized others.

As conversation is so crucial to everyday life, it is, *ipso facto*, decisive in relation to education and learning. For this reason, Schmitz (1983) also conceives of education in the first place as a specific type of conversation which is characterized by three functions. The first function is the interpretative function: adult education is to be conceived as a process of 'substitutive interpretation'. In the educational process the educator supports subjects in interpreting unresolved action problems. The act of interpretation includes the understanding both of the subject's life-world (subjective reality) and the objective reality. It also includes the capacity to facilitate the exchange process between subjective and objective reality. Brookfield perceives the centrality of this interpretative function in a very similar way.

> We may think of adult education also as a transactional dialogue between participants who bring to the encounter experiences, attitudinal sets, differing ways of looking at their personal, professional, political and

recreational worlds and a multitude of varying purposes, orientations and expectations (Brookfield, 1985, p. 41).

The second function is the expert function. In relation to this function the educator has to play an expert role in this exchange process. This is especially necessary when unknown items are removed at a considerable distance from the subjective patterns of understanding. In this case, the educator as an expert develops a multitude of means-to-end sequences in order to link objective to subjective reality.

The third function is related to the activities of context-organization. The specific role of the educator in this matter is to create a context in which participants to the learning process are temporarily liberated from the pressure of everyday routines. This context enables them to find new foundations to their understanding of reality.

A reduction of the three functions to two basic functions of adult education is relevant. The distinction which Habermas (1981) makes between communicative and strategic action as two forms of human rationality is highly interesting in this respect. Communicative rationality is the rationality by which people give meaning to their activities and their lives. It is basically interactive, because this meaning is grounded in the capacity of people to communicate or to question the validity of each other's arguments. Strategic rationality, on the other hand, is instrumental, technological or goal-directed. This rationality is governed by the capacity of people to develop and apply means-to-end schemes, in order to achieve predetermined goals. Relating the above-mentioned functions to both types of rationality, there is a clear parallelism between the interpretative function and communicative rationality on the one hand, and between the expert- and context-organizing functions and strategic rationality on the other.

Hence, the communicative function of education is to be understood in terms of substitutive interpretation or transactional dialogue. The process of identity-building, to which conversation or dialogue is constitutive, is a crucial aspect of the communicative function.

The dialogue about the learner's experiences in educational processes legitimizes these experiences and gives an active voice and presence to the ones who express them (Giroux, 1985).

Expert activities and context-organizing activities on the other hand, may be considered as basic elements of the strategic function of education. The character of these activities is essentially technological or instrumental. They are basically meant to organize the educational process in an efficient and effective way.

Social technology: The learner as an efficient data-processor

There is a growing conviction in continental European reflection on education that the only legitimate base of education is communicative rationality

(Gronemeyer, 1987; Masschelein, 1987). This conviction is supported by Habermas' argument that strategic rationality actually colonizes communicative rationality. In terms of the above-mentioned functions of education one could say that the expert- and context-organizing functions dominate the interpretative function.

The dominance of strategic action further implies that dialogue or conversation is consigned to some secondary position in relation to the educational process. Hence, dialogue is only appreciated as far as it is useful in terms of the goals to be reached. In this case, dialogue could even be replaced by a less democratic type of relationship on condition that the substitute is more effective. The comparison to democracy is indeed significant. Strategic rationality cannot recognize democracy as a value in itself, but only as a means to efficiently and effectively achieve goals which are situated outside the discourse of democracy.

This debate may seem of secondary importance in connection with reflections on experiential learning. The final argument in this paper is that this is not the case and that experiential learning, which is being uncritically fitted into the above-mentioned strategic schemes, is subjected to unfruitful technological reductionism. There is evidence that social technology is nowadays infiltrating some experiential approaches which stem from the humanistic tradition. This evolution coincides with a growing consumer orientation, especially in adult education.

> The humanistic concept of the adult learner . . . is being replaced with the objectified notion of the adult learner as a consumer. According to this way of thinking, the goal of programme-development is to establish the conditions whereby the consumer, a collection of traits and preferences, rather than a person, is willing to exchange valued resources for the adult educator's 'product'. What learners learn and whether learning has any value is relatively unimportant as long as 'consumption' remains high (Beder, 1987, p. 112).

A reduction of the communicative dimension of education is very striking in the field of self-directed learning or independent study, which is considered to be an important orientation of experiential learning. As already mentioned, Brookfield is extremely critical about this evolution and especially deplores the growing lack of conversation or dialogue among learners and facilitators.

> Assistants are frequently relegated to a position of subordinate importance . . . as the individual learner is conceived as a master chef, choosing ingredients (resources) and blending these into a highly distinctive, individual dish (Brookfield, 1984, p. 67).

This remarkable negligence towards the communicative dimension of education goes hand in hand with a strong influence of the 'ethic of individualism' both in theory and practice. This ethic of individualism is characterized by Tennant (1986) as follows. In the first place there is a moral axiom which places the individual at the centre of a value system which relegates the 'group' to second place. Secondly, there is the notion of autonomy, or self-direction, according to which an individual's thoughts and action are his own, and not determined by agencies or causes outside his control. And, finally, there is the notion of self-development which is steeped in the romantic tradition.

A remarkable illustration of this ethic of individualism is to be found in Evans (1985). In his reflections about the future of our society Evans pictures a shift from education to learning. The way he conceives this transformation symbolizes to me a farewell to dialogue and a welcome to individualized technicism. Traditional types of education are criticized, while the future learner is presented as an autonomous person who is no longer dependent on interaction and communication with other people.

> The family, the community and the church contribute relatively little to people's learning. Schools and colleges contribute relatively less than they did. Learning at work either through the nature of employment, or through in-house courses, has increased markedly. Even more significant is the rise of the media as a source of learning. And there is all the compelling evidence of the learning individuals accomplish for themselves. The balance has changed again, with formal educational institutions becoming relatively less important, and informal learning systems becoming relatively more important (Evans, 1985, p. 93).

Although this picture of autonomous learners seems attractive, it should be clear that a radical application of the concepts behind it tends to reduce the learner to an efficient data-processor rather than recognizing the process of learning and education as a fundamentally communicative act.

Conclusion

In this paper different issues have been taken into consideration. Certain technological tendencies are criticized. I have argued that some romantic or naive assumptions about the nature of learning and education may enhance the colonization of dialogue or conversation in learning and education. In opposition to this evolution, communication is presented as a basic dimension of the way humans understand and transform the reality in which they live. Consequently, I have emphasized the predominant role of communication in order to make sense of experiential learning and education.

References

Aronowitz, S. and Giroux, H. (1985). *Education under Siege*. Massachusetts: Bergin and Garvey.

Beder, H. (1987). Dominant paradigms, adult education, and social justice. *Adult Education Quarterly*, **2**, 105–13.

Berger, P. and Luckmann, T. (1985). *The Social Construction of Reality*. Harmondsworth: Penguin.

Brookfield, S. (1984). Self-directed adult learning: A critical paradigm. *Adult Education Quarterly*, **2**, 59–71.

Brookfield, S. (1985). A critical definition of adult education. *Adult Education Quarterly*, **1**, 44–9.

Day, C. and Basket, H. K. (1982). Discrepancies between intentions and practice: Re-examining some basic assumptions about adult and continuing professional education. *International Journal of Lifelong Education*, **2**, 143–55.

Evans, N. (1985). *Post-education Society. Recognizing Adults as Learners*. London: Croom Helm.

Freire, P. (1972). *Pedagogy of the Oppressed*. Harmondsworth: Penguin.

Giroux, H. (1985). Introduction. In Freire, P., *The Politics of Education*. London: Macmillan.

Gronemeyer, M. (1987). Ecological education a failing practice? In Leirman, W. and Kulich, J. (Eds), *Adult Education and the Challenges of the 1990's*. London: Croom Helm.

Habermas, J. (1981). *Theorie des kommunikativen Handelns*, 2 vols. Frankfurt: Suhrkamp.

Jarvis, P. (1983). *Adult and Continuing Education*. London: Croom Helm.

Jarvis, P. (1984). Andragogy – a sign of the times. *Studies in Adult Education*, **16**, 32–8.

Knowles, M. (1980). *The Modern Practice of Adult Education*. Chicago: Association Press.

Knowles, M. (1984). *The Adult Learner: A Neglected Species*. Houston: Gulf Publishing.

Kolb, D. A. (1984). *Experiential Learning*. Englewood Cliffs, NJ: Prentice-Hall.

Masschelein, J. (1987). *Pedagogisch handelen als communicatief handelen*. K. U. Leuven, Fac. Psychology and Educational Sciences.

Schmitz, E. (1983). Erwachsenenbildung als lebensweltbezogener Erkenntnisprozess. In Schmitz, E. and Tietgens, H. (Eds), *Enzyklopädie der Erziehungswissenschaften (Band 11)*, pp. 95–123. Stuttgart: Klett Cotta.

Shor, I. (1980). *Critical Teaching and Everyday Life*. Montréal: Black Rose.

Tennant, M. (1986). An evaluation of Knowles' Theory of Adult Learning. *International Journal of Lifelong Education*, **2**, 113–22.

6

Experiential Learning:
A New Orthodoxy?

Avtar Brah and Jane Hoy

Brah and Hoy provide a critical analysis of some current accounts of experiential learning and reflect on what it might mean to change the agendas of educational institutions. They distinguish 'learning from experience', as used within education movements focused on social transformation (such as through workers' education or the women's movement), and 'experiential learning', as it is currently constituted within the economic climate of Britain in the 1980s. Their work is concerned with critically examining how dominant ideologies mediate the ways in which we interpret experience. Reflection on experience may make social reality clearer; it may also 'obscure and distort'. They consider the interpretation of personal experience needs to be related to the wider social structure. They implicitly pose the question: how can social transformation objectives be reconciled with individual and economic objectives? (a point also addressed by Wildemeersch in Chapter 5).

Brah and Hoy challenge the extent to which the assessment and accreditation of experiential learning may only refine and extend the skills of those whose social positioning in society already ensures them greater access to opportunity and choice. Further, to what extent does the current tendency to equate experiential learning with self-acquired skills ensure vast areas of experience remain unamenable to certification, given the limited experience reflected in dominant frameworks of meaning? (see, e.g. Chapters 11, 14 and 20).

Overall they raise the question: how might certain assumptions underpinning the use of experiential learning approaches in education (in the curriculum or at entry) result in outcomes that are contrary to those originally intended?

This chapter arises out of our work as tutors and organizers on award-beating courses in Community Studies. We work in a Department of Adult Education in a University.

Traditionally, urban community studies in Britain tend to emphasize either community issues focusing on the experience of white working-class neighbourhoods or on planning, economic and urban changes. What we have tried to do is find ways in which urban communities are seen as heterogeneous groupings whose experiences are shaped by their social position within society as a whole.

We have also tried to avoid the tendency to analyse, say, economic change as if it were an abstract process outside of human control. In other words, we work from a perspective which emphasizes human agents as subjects rather than the objects of political, economic and social policies. Such a project demands an approach which bridges the dichotomy between human agency and structure, through a systematic integration of questions of, for example, racism, class, gender and sexuality. Our approach contains a historical perspective which is used to illuminate the continuities and discontinuities between past and present. Our aim is to develop an educational practice which maintains questions of social justice and equality at the heart of its approach.

Questions of student experience have always been central to adult education. However, we feel that we need to look critically at the concept of experience and not take it as an unproblematic 'pregiven'. In this paper we want to address some of the issues we think are often ignored. These are issues we ourselves have had to deal with in the process of working out course content, teaching methods and in struggling for recognition of this work within our department. It is important to note that the majority of students are working-class women, a substantial proportion of whom are black, having origins in Africa, Asia and the Caribbean. In this article we use the term 'black' to refer to all those groups who are subjected to a specific form of racism constructed on the basis of skin colour. In this sense 'black' is a political colour. In Britain, black is normally used to refer to people of African, Caribbean and Asian origins. Parts of the programme are also taught by part-time tutors but this article is based on our experience as full-time staff of the department.

Politics of experience

Our starting point is that although experience is important we would argue that the concept of experience is an ideological construct. Rather than accepting experience as a given, there is a need to deconstruct and unpack it. What is 'experience'? Can experience ever be constituted outside of social relations? We do not think so. Each of us, though unique as individuals, are positioned within society alongside hierarchies of power constructed around such factors as class, caste, racism, gender, age and sexuality. Social encounters, as for instance in a classroom, are therefore mediated within the parameters set by this broader social context. So, for example, the colour of a person's skin is not a neutral category. It is imbued with different meanings in different social contexts. The experience of being black in present-day Tanzania is quite different from the experience of being black in Britain, where there is a history of Empire and racism. In other words, *all experience is shaped by concrete social conditions*.

There is, however, a complex and sometimes contradictory relationship between personal biography and social history, between the nature of experience and social structure. Individual experience cannot simply be read off from the 'social' because of the unique elements of individual histories. Yet the converse is also true, as the group history is not simply the sum total of individual biographies. In any group of women, for example, each woman has a unique story to tell. But the way that experience is shaped will depend upon the particular form sexism takes in her society and her position in terms of, for example, class or caste. So although her own account of her life remains important it may not necessarily aid us in fully understanding the position of women in a society. This is particularly likely to be the case if the woman does not interpret or present her experiences in terms of the opposition which she faces. We suggest, therefore, that stories of experience are mediated through a *lens of ideology* which may obscure or distort as much as it illuminates social reality.

To take another example, white and black residents of inner-city areas may have much in common in terms of their economic and environmental conditions, their structural location within the class structure, and their positioning in relation to particular state policies. Yet, this may not always be recognized as such by white residents because racism constructs black people as 'outsiders taking away white jobs and housing'. So we may find that white residents perceive black people as a threat and as a cause of the economic and social decline in the inner-cities, rather than as people with whom they share a similar experience of poverty and oppression. Similarly, a white working-class student may speak of her experience in terms of her street being 'taken over' by 'immigrants'. The answer lies not in dismissing her as having 'false consciousness' or in simply condemning her for being 'racist'. Nor indeed is it a matter of 'validating the students' experience'. Instead, our responsibility as tutors is to enable all students to develop analytical frameworks within which to examine and interrogate experience. In other words, the aim is to *critique* rather than *criticize* 'commonsense' understanding of experience. Depending on the context certain experiences may need to be valued while others may need to be challenged.

The value of any experience will depend not so much on the experience of the subject, important though this is, but on the struggles around the way that experience is interpreted and defined and by whom. These struggles are constructed around relations of power between different social groups around cleavages such as racism, class, gender, and sexuality. We see these social relations as interlocking, enmeshing realities rather than discrete and separate experiences, although they may be so perceived. This approach finds particular expression in the work of Hall *et al*. For example, they have argued that blacks live their class through 'race' (Hall *et al.*, 1982). We would, however, like to extend the application of this important insight to white groups, for they too live their class through 'race': only the racialization of white subjectivity is often not visible to white people by virtue of the fact that white colour is a signifier of 'dominance' in Britain. Similarly, both black and white groups experience their gender and sexuality through 'race'. We therefore need to develop an understanding of the processes which construct us as 'white female', 'black female', 'white male', 'black male', etc.

Learning from experience or 'experiential learning'?

In this section we want to make a distinction between experiential learning as an educational ideology from the practice of starting from personal experience as a vehicle for learning. For us, the two are not synonymous. In fact, the practice of starting from personal experience has a long history which includes a number of different traditions. Learning from experience has been actively used by workers' movements as part of the process of developing strategies to challenge oppressive structures (Simon, 1965). The anti-colonial movements also used the shared experiences of the colonized as a springboard for the mobilization of people against the colonial system. Similarly, in the post-war period the Civil Rights Movement, the Black Power Movement, the Women's Movement and the anti-racist struggles in different parts of the world have sought to address the links between personal experience and 'the social'. Approaches to learning from experience have also been very influential in adult education, particularly through the work of Freire, who developed the idea of 'conscientization'. This refers to the development in the learners of a critical understanding of social processes and an awareness of their capacity to change society (Freire, 1972).

Despite some contradictions within these traditions, the central point is that they do not separate individual experience as independent of the power relations in society. Instead, individuals are enabled to make sense of their personal stories by making links between autobiography, group history and social and political processes.

A somewhat different approach which also utilizes notions of experience derives from humanistic psychology. It has become dominant in post-war Britain and found expression in the education of both young children and adults. In primary education, a child-centred approach has been used as a means of encouraging wider spontaneity and creativy in learning. As such it has long been associated with many possible outcomes, but a major problem with this approach has been that it tends to assume that there is an inherently natural and spontaneous development of children which can be measured through play. As recent critiques have shown, this approach has been shown to reinforce stereotypical views of 'normal' growth and development in young children (Henriques *et al.*, 1984; Walkerdine, 1983). Another problem is that it tends to separate out the young child as the object of study from the social context in which she lives. Keddie (1980) has argued that there is a 'remarkable similarity between the ways in which adult educators and primary school teachers construct their student-centred ideologies respectively. This means that adult education is bedevilled with some of the same problems as primary education. We recognize that teachers in both sectors may be very committed to enabling children and students to express themselves. But we need to bear in mind the ways in which classroom practice is still influenced by popular and professional ideologies, and assumptions about normative behaviour. The degree to which students will feel free to voice experiences will be mediated by power relationships in the classroom. Moreover, the slippage which may occur in using experience as a means of eliciting teaching material is, for us, dangerously close to a counselling mode whereby the structural dimensions of experience come to be located primarily within the individual psyche. The experiential method-ology can thus perpetuate the individual–social divide, rather than treat human subjectivity as both constituted by and constitutive of social relations (Henriques *et al.*, 1984).

One example of the way this can happen in the UK is that when black students are present in a class, they are encouraged to talk about experience of being 'black' as if this were merely an expression of difference. This individual reflection on experience may fail to acknowledge the reality of racism. Tutors who operate in this way may avoid taking responsibility for either their own racism or that of white students and of the institution in which they work. This approach also implies that black students have nothing to learn about the social determinants of different racisms and that they do not need to explore with others what this means to them. Similarly, where questions of sexuality are concerned, both tutors and students may be reluctant to challenge the domin-ance of heterosexist norms. Unless such issues concerning heterosexist norms are structured into the curriculum, we reproduce the invisibility of process through which we acquire our sexual identity. In particular, it excludes an understanding of lesbian and gay oppression. In other words, even if 'every-body has their say', the ideology of pluralism in effect masks relations of power and domination.

To reiterate, while we accept some of the positive features of a student-centred pedagogy, there is no guarantee that it automatically exposes or challenges power dynamics inside and outside of the classroom. For instance, we know that sharing individual experiences can be an important way of learning to value ourselves and develop empathy with others. As we have already pointed out, using experience to relive and reinterpret the past has always been part of reclaiming the histories of oppressed groups. But there is a difficulty in assuming that people have the same understanding of the structural determinants of their experience, so that the method by itself does not automati-cally lead to a liberatory practice.

More recently in Britain there has been an increase in the provision of courses for adult students who wish to return to study or employment. Most of these take the form of 'access' programmes which are closely linked to courses in higher education or specific training courses for employment. Some of the initial impetus for these courses came from outside the formal education sector, e.g. from within the black communities and the Women's Movement. However, these demands for positive programmes were paralleled by a rather separate development involving the Manpower Services Commission[1] whose primary

1. The Manpower Services Commission, or the Training Agency as it is now known, was set up in 1974 by the Conservative Party as a small public agency. It has since become a large national enterprise with a budget of over £2500 million and a brief to advise the Government on national manpower policies and to execute them under ministerial authority. It runs the state employ-ment services, carries out government training and temporary work programmes, supports training in industry and more recently vocational courses in schools and colleges. It also monitors the labour markets and conducts research on manpower matters. For an extended critique of the MSC, see Benn and Fairley (1986).

aim has been to 'develop and maintain a more versatile and productive workforce' through retraining and updating (MSC, 1983). It is clear that these two strands represent quite different and often diametrically opposed political perspectives on the question of experience. It is in this context that the discourses on 'experiential learning' have emerged. Perhaps one of the more influential forms for this tendency is that provided by some of the publications of the Further Education Unit (it was established in 1977 as part of the Department of Education and Science to advise further education, primarily the 16–19 age group) and the Learning from Experience Trust (FEU, 1987).

What is significant about 'experiential learning' is not that it uses experience as a vehicle for learning, because as we have noted above there are other approaches that can lay claim to the validity of this, but that the emergence of the concept of 'experiential learning' represents an ideological shift. There is a movement away from the language of 'adult *education*' towards the terminology of 'adult *learning*'. We see this as a matter of the educational process being reduced to questions of 'learning techniques'. The experiences of students then become valid mostly in terms of the extent to which they are translatable into skills and attitudes that lend themselves to accreditation. In addition to reproducing the problems already discussed, this new tendency reinforces the ideology of individualism and the free market which is characteristic of the political and economic climate of the 1980s. In this era of high levels of unemployment and increasing centralization of state control in Britain, we see this new ideology of experiential learning as tying in with the shift from education to training under the umbrella of organizations such as the Manpower Services Commission.

It will be apparent that, throughout the 1970s and 1980s, there has been much talk about student-centred pedagogy and 'experiential learning' without a parallel emphasis on 'what is to be learnt'. According to Yarnit (1980), for example, this 'obsession with form at the expense of content' reveals a superficial 'radicalism'. In our view, the content and process embedded within an adult educational encounter are both equally important. We believe that the use of learning from experience in education can be fruitful, provided there is no dichotomy between content and form. Our aim is to enable students to interrogate the world of appearance, and to expose the underlying relationships of inequality as part of the struggles for social change. One implication is that we must develop non-hierarchical modes of teaching and learning, but this does not mean that the tutor becomes simply a 'facilitator' of student experience. The tutor must play an active role in constructing and presenting well-integrated and coherent frameworks within which to locate and understand individual as well as group experience.

We will try to illustrate this point with reference to one of our courses entitled 'Race, Community and Society'. We have consciously avoided an approach which starts with asking students to share their experiences. Instead, we begin by underlining the notion of the historical specificity of racism, as this allows one to avoid sterile arguments as to the relative importance of different racism (e.g. anti-semitism *vs* anti-black racism). Each racism has a particular history: it arose from a particular set of economic and social circumstances, has been perpetuated via specific mechanisms, and has found different expressions in different societies. Hence, in Britain today, we are faced with several racisms – anti-Jewish, anti-Arab, anti-Irish, anti-black, and so on. But the one that is currently most dominant is the one directed at people whose skin colour is not white. In other words, colour is a crucial element in contemporary British racism, although by no means the only one. Therefore, our primary focus in the course was on anti-black racism, though we did make comparisons with anti-Irish racism and anti-semitism. In order to understand anti-black racism, we examined, among other aspects, the history of colonialism and imperialism; looked at ways in which neo-colonialism operates on an international scale; analysed the processes of class formation since the period of slavery; and studied the role of black labour within these historical processes. We compared the experience of black, Jewish and Irish migrations. We studied the changing conceptions of 'race' over different historical periods, establishing that 'race' has no scientific validity as a biological concept but that it remains a potent analytic and political construct in illuminating various phenomena. We also explored the role of academic and political discourses on 'race' in organizing 'commonsense' racism, and analysed specific state policies and their effects on different sections of communities. Finally, we addressed questions of gendered subjectivities formed with racialized contexts (Brah and Hoy, 1987; Brah and Deem 1986).

It will be evident from what we have said that although questions of experience permeate the whole course they are not treated in isolation from social context. This means that there is no pressure on the students to 'bare their souls', yet they are enabled to examine the personal within the social and political and vice versa. In fact, as the course is participatory there are often lively and heated discussions and debates about each others' views of the world, how they relate to students as individuals, and as members of particular groups: for example, to working class, black people, or women, and to the course concepts and materials to which they are exposed. As tutors we do not stand apart and are therefore an integral part of the process. We have come to recognize that our power, both inside and outside the classroom, is mediated through our gender, sexuality, class and whether we are black or white.

Conclusion

In this article we have attempted to raise some questions about the social construction of experience. We have argued for the continuation of traditions which utilize experience as a means of transforming oppressive social structures. We have contrasted these liberatory traditions with the ideology of 'experiential learning' which we suggest is fast becoming a new orthodoxy. As Fanon (1985) reminds us, everyone is subject to ideological forces but the range of relations of domination and oppression means that as subjects we experience them differently. We may or may not accept or challenge dominant ideologies. Whether we do is mediated by the specificity of historical and social conditions, including what goes on in the classroom and what is included in the curriculum.

Empowerment means identifying and acknowledging where power lies and the structures which uphold it and challenging those structures in struggles towards a more equal society.

References

Benn, C. and Fairley, J. (1986). *Challenging the MSC.* London: Pluto Press.

Brah, A. and Deem, R. (1986). Towards anti-sexist and anti-racist schooling. *Critical Social Policy*, **16**, 66–79.

Brah, A. and Hoy, J. (1987). Politics of urban experience: Teaching extra-mural courses. *Multi-Cultural Teaching*, **6**(1), 22–6.

Fanon, F. (1985). *Black Skin and White Masks.* London: Pluto Press.

Freire, P. (1972). *Pedagogy of the Oppressed.* New York: Herder and Herder.

Further Education Unit (1987). *Assessing Experiential Learning.* Project Report. London/York: Longman/FEU.

Hall, S., Critcher, C., Jefferson, T., Clarke, J. and Roberts, B. (1982). *Policing the Crisis.* London: Macmillan.

Henriques, J., Holloway, W., Urwin, C., Venn, C. and Walkerdine, V. (1984). *Changing the Subject.* London: Methuen.

Keddie, N. (1980). Adult education: An ideology of individualism. In Thompson, J. (Ed.), *Adult Education for a Change.* London: Hutchinson.

Learning from Experience Trust (1987). *Resources Materials for Assessment/Experiential Planning.* London: LET.

Manpower Services Commission (1983). *New Training Initiative.* Task Group Report. Sheffield: MSC.

Simon, B. (1965). *Education and the Labour Movement 1870–1920.* London: Lawrence and Wishart.

Walkerdine, V. (1983). It's only natural: Rethinking child centred pedagogy. In Wolpe, A. and Donald, J. (Eds), *Is There Anybody Here from Education?* London: Pluto Press.

Yarnit, M. (1980). Second chance to learn. In Thompson, J. (Ed.), *Adult Education for a Change.* London: Hutchinson.

Part 2

Coming to Know

2. Perspectives

One of the things that happens whenever you get yourself into a significant educational experience, almost by definition, is that you start to see things differently. You start to see yourself differently, you start to see the world differently. I think that a very important missing ingredient is the continued opportunity for reflection and reappraisal. Not so much of competence but of interests and values and orientations and so forth.

What happens in this society is that people tend to get deskilled. So experiential learning is about giving some of those skills back. It is very much at the practical level. Even if you look at those skills from a theoretical framework it's still about whether you can put it into practice or not, that matters.

At school, we were given quite a lot of information about the poor little children overseas – which was reinforced in my Sunday School as well – and I was thinking about how we still have this tendency to say, well, let's learn about a Sikh. Let's learn about the Asian family. We ask someone who is black to talk about their experience, as if it were the same experience for black women and men, for working class and middle class. But culture is created and recreated every day. And I have also been thinking, why should we keep doing this – getting them to tell us *their* stories. Because their story is also my story. Part of my history is involved in their history. I have a relationship to this country's past. I am a white person whose history is bound to that past, to their past. So I start then to reflect on my *own* history and my *own* knowledge and where that comes from rather than say, I need to know these other peoples' stories. We need to ask questions about that. What is this knowledge for? What are we going to use it for? What is the purpose of this knowledge and this experience? Who decides what experience is valid and what it means?

Wisdom needs to come back into the picture and we need to say, not only what I *know*, but what I *am* is a very important part of my contribution to society. It is not enough simply to churn up marketable commodities that have to be useful in a business or an academic context.

7

Learner Autonomy: A Case Study

Lucy Horwitz

What happens when a learner has little choice but to satisfy a requirement in a course that a certain subject, in this case, algebra, has to be studied and a standard attained for achievement over the whole course? This, we may say, must be incompatible with experiential learning aims. Horwitz shows how for the 'traditional' discipline of mathematics and for adult learners (most of whom have been alienated from mathematics in their formal education), algebra can come alive. She also discusses how through her approach she tries to promote their autonomy. For Horwitz, promoting learner autonomy is the primary goal. The secondary goal, enabling the students to attain a given standard, is achieved through the first. Struggle is involved but the learner is 'engaged' in that struggle. Horwitz examines some of the assumptions from which students tend to approach their learning as well as giving us examples of how she promotes autonomy and teaches algebra. This chapter will be useful to those who work in areas they believe do not obviously lend themselves to experiential learning methods and who have a hard time thinking through ways to 'reach' the learner. Because Horwitz works with adults who have traditionally been under-represented in higher education, by virtue of their race, gender, socioeconomic and prior educational background, her discussion is relevant to access issues.

This chapter could have been placed in Part 3, 'Creating New Possibilities for Learning', for Horwitz writes about using experiential learning in an institutional context as well as about learners coming to 'know what they know', as she puts it. The chapter provides a useful accompaniment to Salmon (Ch. 21) who explains the notion of 'personal stance' in relation to the teacher and learner. This chapter may also be read with Boud's analysis of different ways of approaching autonomy (Ch. 3).

The role of autonomy in both formal and experiential learning, and the relationships between these abstract terms in a very concrete learning environment is the concern of this chapter.

I had better explain how I use the term 'experiential learning'. In a trivial sense, all learning is experiential. Even sitting through the most boring traditional class is an experience. But, in my vocabulary, experiential learning is the process of acquiring knowledge and skills outside of the formal or traditional methods commonly encountered in the academic classroom. It implies active participation of the learner in a real or simulated context where what is to be learned is embedded in a larger setting, one which is encountered in real life or which simulates real life. For instance, the usual college French course, as an example of formal learning, can be contrasted with the experiential learning alternative of picking up French by living in Paris for a year.

The current interest in experiential learning is nothing new. The history of education is the path of a pendulum, constantly swinging from one extreme to the other, rarely stopping in the middle, where the truth so often lies. From Dewey and Montessori, to 'Why Johnny Can't Read', from 'the new math' to 'back to basics', experiential and formal learning have been ends of that pendulum. Too much time has been spent arguing over the relative merits of each. It is clear to me that experiential and formal learning must be integrated to produce whole human beings capable of realizing their full potential. It is learner autonomy which best mediates between the two, and it is only the autonomous learner who is capable of that much desired integration.

Just as there are two poles in educational practice, there are two extremes in writings on education: speculations from the ivory tower and reports from the front; or, if you like, theory and practice. My preference has always been for reports from the front. I have tended to attribute this preference to the general weakness of educational theory, but in the context of thinking about experiential learning, it occurs to me that it is not only the weakness of theory, but the strength of direct experience that dictates this preference. The best reports from the front plunge us into the experience that the writer has had and allows us to share, and to learn from that experience, e.g. Ashton-Warner's (1963) work with Maori children, Herndon's (1965) report from the ghetto, Holt's (1964) account of suburban despair, and Postman's (1969) account of revolution in the classroom.

Much as we may need sound educational theory (and we could use a good deal more than we have), there is always a terrible gap between theory and practice. The raw data of the learning experience gets translated into theory and then the theory has to be retranslated into practice. A lot gets lost in translation. The advantage of reports from the front is that we can see them more immediately as applicable (or not) to our own difficult situations. What follows then is my dispatch from the trenches.

In my case, the battleground is the College of Public and Community Service (CPCS), a part of the University of Massachusetts, which serves adult learners who wish to either begin or continue their university education in the area of human service work. The student body is non-traditional in that it is older (average age 35); it has a larger proportion of minority students than any other 4-year college in the state; and that the vast majority of students work, take care of families, or both, while enrolled in the college. The programme is competency-based. The central idea of competency-based education, as practised at CPCS, is the separation of learning from evaluation, with credit given only for the outcome of evaluation, however the learning took place. Students are evaluated at entrance, given credit for relevant knowledge and skills, and told what further learning must take place before a degree can be granted. That further learning may take place in the courses offered by the college, or may be independent, work-related, or acquired in any other way.

Learning methods are, at least theoretically, quite flexible. The curriculum is much less so. And in the area of basic skills, it is particularly rigid. Some mathematics, including elementary algebra, is a non-negotiable requirement for graduation. As anyone familiar with American education might guess, it is often the mathematics requirement that prevented these very students from pursuing higher education at an earlier stage.

So it is hard to imagine a situation less amenable to experiential learning or more likely to destroy students' feelings of autonomy. My choice of the battle ground metaphor was not arbitrary. Yet it seems to me that examining the relationship between experiential learning and learner autonomy in a context that in many ways militates against both, provides a unique opportunity to look at possibilities without ignoring the difficulties. If, by learner autonomy, we mean the exercise of free choice as to what is learned, how it is learned, and how it is used, then clearly my students' autonomy is limited in a number of ways. It is these limitations I would like to consider now, in the light of what is, could, or should be done about them.

The first limitation is in the choice of what is learned. Algebra, for my students, is a requirement, and there is no way around it. This situation causes a good deal of lamentation, not only on the part of the students, but also a few of us on the staff. Some of us would like the learner to have more free choice in what to learn, but few of us would opt for no requirements at all. It is just not that simple. Students clearly cannot make autonomous choices to study fields that they do not know exist. Nor are they likely to choose fields which are totally foreign to their interests or experience. Students with no mathematical knowledge are very unlikely to choose to study algebra, or to be in a position to gauge accurately its usefulness to them. They are often angry and frustrated. They feel that they are being treated like children, yet they often lack the experience to be able to sort out cause and effect. They cannot distinguish the institution's or teacher's shortcomings from their own. Frequently, they blame themselves for being 'stupid' when they are merely the victims of inadequate education. At the same time, they will blame the institution for setting up 'unnecessary pre-requisites', by which they might mean the insistence that basic mathematics be mastered before algebra is begun.

True, there is no easy answer to this problem, but we, as educators, have a responsibility to allow students greater participation in the decision making, and an opportunity for the kinds of experiences that will make their input meaningful. There must be a balance between autonomy and guidance. In the case of my college, the guidance in what is to be learned takes the form of coercion. For questions of how to learn, it is almost non-existent.

When it comes to the issue of how to learn, our students are severely handicapped by their past educational experiences. Learning which has taken place informally, on their own, or in work settings 'does not count'. Formal learning has been almost entirely of the most traditional, teacher-directed sort. Especially in mathematics, there has been very little attempt to make the subject attractive, available or useful to the average student. Their exposure to alternative forms of learning has been almost nil. Who has read Knowles (1970), Kidd (1973), or Kolb (1984)? Not the traditional teachers my students have been exposed to, and certainly not my students themselves.

So here we are, students who have on the whole been coerced into an algebra course they would much rather avoid, and further handicapped by a lack of experience in approaching the kind of learning that is now required of them; and me, their teacher, not at all convinced of the reasonableness of this particular requirement, but determined to salvage something from the situation. What has evolved for me is the realization that teaching algebra is my secondary goal. My primary goal is to help my students become more autonomous learners.

It has become a commonplace of cognitive psychology that intelligence is to a certain extent domain-specific. It is my contention that the same is true of learner autonomy. I know any number of students who are capable of demonstrating their autonomy at home, at work and in the classroom, as long as the classroom is one that deals with words rather than numbers. I have had students who held extremely responsible jobs, made decisions involving millions of dollars of public money, but who would ultimately insist that I tell them whether the solution to an equation they had just solved and checked was correct or not.

It therefore seems essential to me that we address the issues of learner autonomy in every classroom and every learning situation. So I begin my classes every year with a discussion of what a pain it is to have to take algebra. Here they are, adults who want to work with alcoholics or be lawyers' aides or organize housing, and they are being asked to do this crazy stuff with x's and y's that they maybe saw once in high school and hoped never to see again. But now that they are here, they actually have a lot of choices. They can make a commitment to learn the stuff well, or they can squeak by. They can work independently, or they can work together. They can attend class faithfully and take notes or they can simply collect the materials and work on their own. We talk about it: what the benefits are, and what the costs are. Some say: 'Never mind all that, let's just get on with it.' Others want to talk forever about how to find the tutoring room so they will not have to actually get to the algebra. We talk about that.

Then, as we begin to get into the material, we talk about expectations. The number of false expectations that students have is truly mind-boggling. For example, there is a surprisingly common belief among adult learners who are new to academic pursuits that if they have to think about it, work at it, study it, then they are stupid. There are unrealistic expectations about how long it should take to learn something and what the process is. Perry (1981) talks about students learning more effective reading methods: 'Students who read word by word often told us that our recommendation to "look ahead" was commending to them a form of "cheating" in which they refused to participate.' My students frequently expect that they should be able to read a chapter of algebra and then do all the exercises at the end without looking back. Looking back is cheating, or it proves that they are stupid.

We talk about expectations in detail. How long should it take to do the homework? Anywhere from 5 minutes to 5 hours. It depends on a lot of things, and we talk about those. What do you do when you get stuck? If you cannot get a problem right away, how long should you keep at it? Or should you just go on to the next one? These questions do not have right or wrong answers, but they are important because they allow students to share their experiences, to feel 'normal' and thereby gain the confidence they need to feel autonomous.

There are certain things that come up in every class that I teach. The central theme is 'KNOW WHAT YOU KNOW'. By writing it on the blackboard in big capital letters, it is my way of making it overt, i.e. this is the issue. You have to sort out what you have learned from what you have not, to know absolutely the extent of your own knowledge and your own ignorance. You cannot swim around in a sea of uncertainty, feeling 'I think I've got it', 'I did this one right, but I'm not sure I can do it again', and 'I know how to do it, but I can't write it down.' Until you 'KNOW WHAT YOU KNOW', you do not own your knowledge, and so you do not know anything.

The autonomy training gets acted out in more subtle ways all semester. For example, there is a running battle between me and the students about answers. I will not give them the answers to the homework. Instead, I give them the opportunity to ask questions. 'If you're not sure of the answer, ask. We'll work it out together,' I'll say. And we do. 'But why can't you just tell us?' they'll ask, 'It would be so much faster.' 'Because,' I say, 'life does not provide the answer in the back of the book.' Sometimes they laugh. Probably because they have no intention of ever using any of this stuff in real life. But some of them get it. They begin to think about what that means, not only for learning algebra, but for learning other things.

Or I will give a quiz. 'Not fair!' they'll scream the first time, 'You didn't warn us.' 'What kind of warning are you likely to get if you're driving through the desert and you have to figure out if you have enough gas to get to the next town.' So some of them accept the surprise quiz. But then I tell them not to put their names on the quiz. 'Why not?' someone will complain. 'I got it right. I want credit.' 'There is no credit. Getting it right is all the reward you need. Who are you doing this for anyway? Yourself or me?' But then I make them hand in those quizzes. The ones with no names on them. Why? That's my surprise quiz. Are they learning anything? I need to know. Not individually, but collectively. If they all did badly, then surely I must take the blame. And then, when they have handed in the quizzes, we go over the problems immediately, while they still remember. This is their time to check themselves, to see how they are doing. It is their responsibility to check what they have learned. KNOW WHAT YOU KNOW.

And then comes the hardest part – developing autonomy in making use of their learning. There is no point in putting these adults through the hoop of algebra, which for many of them is real torture, if there is no payoff, no benefit. So I want the people in my class to take responsibility not only for learning, but also for using algebra to solve real-life problems.

This brings us back to the role of experiential learning. One cannot teach something in the complete isolation of the classroom and then hope that a transition will automatically be made to real life. If they are to take their new knowledge out of the classroom, the connections must be made in the classroom.

So I encourage students to bring in their own problems, from work, from other classes, from the newspapers, from any conceivable source that is *real*. I have them make up problems. Problems that they really want to know the answers to. And so we bring the real world into the classroom, with discussions ranging from their personal budgets to the national debt.

This may sound like a completely backward approach to the problem of autonomy, and in a way it is. First we force them to learn algebra, and then I bribe and cajole and harass them into using it. It is my original definition of experiential learning stood on its head. Instead of specific learning embedded in a real situation, I try to bring reality into the artificiality of the classroom. If this manoeuvre succeeds, then haven't they been coerced into something I have no right to call autonomy?

I would like to answer that question with an example of how this method can work. As I have mentioned before, an ever-recurring argument in my class is about my refusal to give them answers unless they ask the questions. In my last algebra class, the students were so insistent on being given answer sheets, that I finally said, 'Okay, I'll make some up, and I'll leave them on the desk, and those of you who absolutely can't live without them can pick them up after class.' Well, I made up the answer sheets, but the next week it snowed and class was cancelled, and the week after that I forgot, and no one said a word. So I waited to see what would happen. On the last day of class, I mentioned the fact that our plan to have me provide answer sheets had never materialized, and I wondered why no one had complained. They all agreed that they really had not needed them after all. They compared answers with each other, they asked questions in class, and when they really got into trouble they came to my office. But they all felt good about not having needed answer sheets. They felt in charge.

Learner autonomy is not, as I keep insisting, something one is born with, or something that drops out of the sky, or even something that comes automatically with experience. It is learned, just like everything is learned. Some people will have a head start because of their predisposition or their experience. But autonomy is learned, not in any straightforward way, but in bits and pieces. There is no autonomy without competence. There is no autonomy without confidence. We do the best we can.

References

Ashton-Warner, S. (1963). *Teacher*. New York: Simon and Schuster.

Herndon, J. (1965). *The Way it Spozed To Be*. New York: Simon and Schuster.

Holt, J. (1964). *How Children Fail*. New York: Pitman.

Kidd, J. R. (1973). *How Adults Learn*. New York: Association Press.

Knowles, M. S. (1970). *The Modern Practice of Adult Education*. New York: Association Press.

Kolb, D. (1984). *Experiential Learning*. Englewood Cliffs, N.J.: Prentice-Hall.

Perry, W. G. (1981). *Cognitive and Ethical Growth: The Making of Meaning in the Modern American College*. San Francisco: Jossey-Bass.

Postman, N. (1969). *Teaching as a Subversive Activity*. New York: Dell.

8

The Autobiography as a
Motivational Factor for Students

Marie Redwine

Redwine is included in this section, 'Coming to Know' for how she evokes the experience of adults in a residential orientation programme at the commencement of a degree programme based on distance learning. She discusses how the preparation and sharing of autobiographies boost their self-esteem and their self-confidence for returning to study. The process also enables continuing links with other students and a keen appreciation of the relevance of prior learning. Redwine asks us to understand the personal feelings of the students and staff on the programme. She then shows us how the autobiography is endorsed more formally through their studies when the students return to their home base. The chapter provides a useful contrast with O'Reilly (Chapter 9) in that he too is concerned with mainly adult students returning after a 'break' from formal education. Redwine concentrates upon the support and cohesiveness of the initial programme, O'Reilly on the discontinuity between the intended 'rationality' of the educational world students enter and the richness of their 'incoherent' experience.

Redwine shows how portfolio work can produce a basis for APEL (see Chapters 1 and 22), but in ways that emphasize process as much as product. Readers may wish to make contrasts with Criticos (Chapter 19) on institutional–community relationships, Wildemeersch (Chapter 5) on the incorporation of experiential learning into traditional educational programmes, and Brah and Hoy (Chapter 6) on the social construction of experience.

Southwestern Adventist College in Texas has been conducting a non-traditional programme for older adults since 1978. The Adult Degree Program (ADP) is an independent study plan based on traditional college courses. The purpose of independent study is to provide an educational option for adults who, for a variety of reasons, cannot pursue an education in the traditional sense of attending classes on campus. In the SAC Adult Degree Program, following a 10-day orientation seminar on campus, students study at home. They come from all over the country. The distance travelled to get to a seminar is often hundreds and even thousands of miles.

The purpose of this chapter is to discuss what goes on at an orientation seminar and to deal with what students and staff experience during this time. Particular attention is given to the requirement that each student write a lengthy autobiography and share it.

The traditional student chooses a school and changes her life to fit the social demands of the school. The non-traditional student instead seeks to fit the school into an already busy life, where school is an 'and also' rather than an 'either/or' proposition (Garrison, 1984, p. 27). The question arises, 'What characteristics in a programme will lead to success?' Non-traditional programmes, relieved of conventional schedules and requirements, are not for everybody, regardless of how innovative or flexible it may be. Adults who are returning for higher education via non-traditional methods find that independent learning requires a degree of self-discipline and self-motivation often unknown to them.

At our college we believe that coming to the orientation seminar and being on campus, visiting classes and meeting other students with similar goals will strengthen the possibility of success in the programme. Without exception those who take the time to come to the orientation seminar, are glad they did. This is why the requirement continues, although I am sure there are some potential students that are unable to come because of this requirement. Our seminars are kept small, usually 12–16 in number. Onderkirk *et al.* (1986) see the small group experience as a 'buffering' effect for their students that motivates them to take responsibility for their own learning while at the same time providing a social support group with which to feel a shared obligation and help in time of need.

In the next few pages I would like to share with you some staff and student experiences of orientation seminars.

On the day of the commencement of the seminar I, as director, am anxious. I wonder if the students will all come and if we told them everything they needed to know to find the place. Then the participants arrive and I meet them at the appointed place and hour. Five from California, two from Colorado, three from Oregon, one from Virginia, two from Michigan, one from Canada, and yes, the one from Bangkok did make it. A very cosmopolitan group! They have come far from their families, homes and friends. In most cases they are strangers to one another. They have taken a big step and it is somewhat frightening. I eagerly greet them. All I need is a face to put with the name and other data I have stored in my mind about each one. It does not take long. I feel comfortable with the group immediately. This will be another good seminar!

The orientation seminar proceeds with introductions and a sharing of where they come from, the subject they hoped to major in, and a bit of personal data about themselves. To motivate them, the teacher tells them that 'It will be hard, but you can make it.'

After a brief overview of the seminar schedule they go right into the first project, writing their life story. It is important to get into the writing because, in just 3 days, they will be asked to share their rough draft with the group.

The writing and sharing of the autobiography is one of the unique features of our ADP. Most of the students are older adults who have gone through or are going through transitions. This sharing of autobiographies does at least three things:

1. It acts as a catharsis and helps the students deal with many areas in their lives that they have not dealt with. Because of the very nature of the students, there are many commonalities. They dropped out of school and got married and/or started working. They had problems with parents as teenagers; they often have low self-esteem. Many of them are women who have gone through one or more divorces, and a disproportionate number in our programme are single parents. Adults enter or re-enter the educational cycle with needs and characteristics that are very different from those of 18- to 22-year-olds.
2. It binds the group together and forms a support group for the next year when they are studying independently. A call or a letter to or from a fellow seminar participant is always encouraging.
3. It serves as a basis for asking for credit for particular aspects of their experiential learning. As the participants relive their lives, they recall learning experiences they might not otherwise have thought of.

The students are given guidelines, and suggestions on how to get started; perhaps for one a chronological outline will work best; or maybe a list of transitions will get another going. They are also allowed to read autobiographies of students who are already in the programme. By reading other autobiographies they are able to get into their own histories easier. The work on their life stories is interspersed with lectures and films, for example, and they are given time to review portfolios, and to simply reflect. Some like to go to their rooms to write alone, whereas others choose to be with the group where they can 'try out' parts of their story on anyone who will listen.

On sharing day there is tension in the air. Usually they have talked it over among themselves and one person has agreed to be the first to speak. There is one who 'wants to get it over with'. With the sharing of the story come laughter, tears, anger, and other kinds of emotions. Each person in turn gives his/her reaction, constructive criticism, and support to the presenter. It might just be a 'Wow!' The presenter is very vulnerable now and needs affirmation. After just a few autobiographies have been shared there is a different atmosphere in the group. They are more supportive and caring for each other; a bond is forming. Someone who may have been thought to be snobbish is now seen as shy or hurting. One who was thought to be aggressive is now seen as a person who wears a mask, perhaps to cover up inner turmoil. The camaraderie is very good and the cohesiveness of the group increases throughout the rest of the seminar. Those fortunate enough to have had a fairly stable childhood and adult life experience compassion at a new level, and perhaps for the first time have an understanding that life is not always easy or the way it 'should' be.

As students evaluate where they have come from, they gain a new appreciation of where they are going. Their commitment to higher education during this re-evaluation is thus strengthened. The process of generating an autobiography and reflection on their past invokes insights that have been dormant and unarticulated (Boud *et al.* 1985).

In addition to the autobiography, students write competency statements and develop goals and projections. 'Competency statements' are written statements about things the students feel they are competent at or can do well. They are meant to affirm what they are good at and thus are meant to raise their self-esteem. They are given help to explore the past, present and future in an effort to raise a sagging self-esteem and to become sufficiently motivated to succeed at college classes on an independent basis. One student wrote of her experiences in the seminar:

> Our personalities were different but blended together so as to make an enjoyable group. We had fun together and shared pain together [the autobiographies]. I have been touched by each one and as a result will grow to be a better person. The group has made me look at me, 'Rebecca', sometimes being disappointed in what I saw but at the same time being made aware that there is room for wholesome change in my life. I will never be the same as a result of the seminar, hopefully I will be better.

Another says:

> I have been introduced to not only people but to friends that will vicariously go with me from now on. I have a goal and heart's desire is to see the goal accomplished.

And still another student reveals:

> Group support and acceptance is very important. Though we'll never meet this way again, I feel that the experience will stay with and encourage us.

For many, the autobiography takes away prejudice, class rank, status or anything that would get in the way of learning. As one student put it:

> This discussion was one of my favorites because I have learned that if anyone could read anyone else's autobiography, we have no reason to feel either inferior or superior to one another. We all have a story behind the visible appearance of us all.

And, finally, a student testified that:

> A tremendously rich, and fulfilling experience after the moaning and groaning of the assignment, a mountain top experience, to share auto-biographies with strangers who become dearer than blood relatives. Amazing!

Boud *et al.* (1985) found that as students reflect on their feelings, they restimulate the pride they have experienced in accomplishments as well as identify and remove obstructing feelings. He states that this occurs because the process identifies even 'failure' as a learning experience. As students write their autobiographies, they are forced to look at their background and to their own accomplishments.

Warren and Breen (1981) conducted a study on the perceptions of pro-gramme administrators as to the educative values of portfolio assessment programmes and contracts. From this study three kinds of learning were judged most important. All involved changes in the student's attitudes toward them-selves: an improved self-concept, a more realistic view of abilities, and a greater sense of 'ownership' of achievements. Working through the autobiography serves this purpose and therefore helps the student to get on to important things like being successful in their classes.

Students frequently mention that the autobiography provided bonding for the group as they heard each other's life stories, and that it gave a sense of community with the fellow students. This provides a motivation for them after they leave the campus as they follow each other's progress via our *Newsletter* and through personal correspondence. Throughout the seminar, the students listen to lectures, see films, visit professors, obtain syllabi, and purchase books they will need to complete the work outlined. Late in the week an 'outing' to the nearby city is planned to provide a break from work on campus. We visit museums, the theatre, and 'eat out'. By now all are 'old friends' and feel that they have known each other for years.

The final days of the seminar are packed with activities that include preparing or up dating resumés, listening to professors lecture on topics that range from how to study and how to do a research paper, to a review of basic English rules, and learning styles, temperaments, etc. Time is spent on degree plans, advice and the last stage of the portfolio: experiential credit. This section of the portfolio ranks high in value. Students may receive up to 33 hours of college credit if they can document their knowledge. Our faculty recognizes that a lot of learning occurs outside the classroom: experiences in the work place; interaction with colleagues and family; and seminars attended. Through the portfolio process this knowledge can be turned into college credits.

When the seminar is over and students are ready to go their different ways it is common to see tears, hugs, and hear promises to call, write, and to meet back at the 3-day interim seminar a year later. As director of the progamme, I have been very involved with this group; on call, as it were, 24 hours a day. I have listened to their stories, I have laughed with them, I have cried with them, helped them set goals, and, with the college staff, have helped them towards finishing a degree in spite of the obstacles they may experience. I am somewhat drained but know that this will pass. I am refuelled by the thoughts of the success of past groups, with individual successes, and with each graduation that includes a good percentage of ADP students.

Independent study is not for everyone. I know that some will fail again, and this is sad. The motivation and discipline required is tremendous. Even though all students desire a degree very badly, I know that some will not be able to cope with demands of the workplace, the family, their old habits of failure and their lack of confidence. We at the college will do what we can to keep them interested. Each one will be contacted frequently with progress reports, newsletters, personal letters, and telephone calls.

The student returns home registered for 12 credits of classes; one of them is 'Portfolio Development'. They are expected to finish at least 12 credits during the next year. There is no maximum, however, to what they can complete. During the orientation seminar they go through each section of the portfolio in rough draft form. They now edit and refine what they did at the seminar. They have up to 4 months to complete this work. Each page is placed in a durable plastic page protector and then in a loose-leaf notebook. Often pictures of themselves and their family gives the reader a better perspective of the writer.

When completed, the portfolio is then shipped to the ADP office. It is received with excitement and eager anticipation by the director and staff. It will be checked to see if the student asked to be evaluated for experiential credit. A faculty member who has expertise in that area will be assigned to evaluate the material, using guidelines developed for their on-campus class as a criterion. The student needs to present documentation that reflects learning at the level of a traditional student, who has completed their work on campus. If this has been done the student is given unconditional credit. If it is good but not quite good enough the instructor will require additional work in this area. They will mark the evaluation with conditional credit and will state the condition. The professor also has the option of denying credit.

When the portfolio has been evaluated in each of the areas for which the student is seeking credit, it is taken to a review committee for final approval. When approved, an elective credit is given for the completed portfolio. The student will now know the number of hours they have been credited with and which classes they have been given credit for. It can be as many as 33 hours.

The following are a few excerpts from the conclusion of portfolios telling what the writing of the portfolio has meant to the author:

Then came the assignment of this portfolio for the ADP. It has been worthwhile, not easy or exactly what would be described as fun, but definitely worthwhile. It seemed that at each step I found another contradiction to be re-evaluated, a painful experience to be put into proper perspective for the first time, an attitude or belief to be considered and consciously rejected or accepted.

In many cases it was extremely painful. But mixed with the pain was a kind of exulting – a feeling that it *is* possible to make sense out of life, to determine what and why you believe what you do and to do something about it. That is a feeling that had been missing from my life for several years.

The process is not yet complete but time passes and this portfolio is long past due. I've still been unable to formulate long term goals in a concrete format, although I've finally understood the root of the problem . . .

This project has started an awful lot of good things in my life, and for this I will be eternally grateful to the staff of the college for requiring it. While the path to take is still not entirely visible, the way to proceed upon it has been greatly clarified by the inspection and introspection involved in displaying my life in this manner.

The autobiography was my gift to myself. Does every person feel that his life is a unique study? I finished this effort with a deeper understanding of my individuality and with that realization came a giant serving of self-worth.

I'm at peace with my past, I'm satisfied with the present, I'm confident of my future.

I learned a lot about myself. I reaffirmed that I do have a lot of strengths, that I am knowledgeable, and that my many years of experience have taught me things that others have learned in the classroom. I also found as I attended classes that my love for academics has not diminished over the years, that I still love learning, and I can still stay in the top percent of the class.

I know that many long hours of work are still ahead of me before I reach my goal. Completing this portfolio is just the first of many steps yet to be taken. But right now, as I type this last page, I feel a real sense of accomplishment.

In conclusion, I want to say that a commitment to return to college is a major emotional trauma for the non-traditional student. In my experience, evaluating one's life through the process of writing an autobiography is an appropriate way to validate that commitment and it serves as a catalyst, recognizing new directions in one's life.

References

Boud, D., Keogh, R. and Walker, D. (Eds) (1985). *Reflection: Turning Experience into Learning*. New York: Kogan Page.

Garrison, D. R. (1984). Predicting dropout in adult basic education using interaction effects among school and nonschool variables. *Adult Education Quarterly*, Fall, 25–38.

Onderkirk, W., Spanard, J.-M. and Leavitt, D. (1986). The best of both: A program designed to offer the benefits of independent study and group interaction. *The Sixth National Conference on Adult and External Degree Programs*, October 1–4, p. 89. Chicago, Illinois.

Warren, J. R. and Breen, P. W. (1981). Preface. In *The Educational Value of Portfolio and Learning Contract Development*. Columbia, Md.: The Council for Advancement of Experiential Learning (CAEL).

9

On Being an Educational Fantasy Engineer: Incoherence, 'The Individual' and Independent Study

Dave O'Reilly

O'Reilly challenges the extent to which educational institutions devalue the richness of incoherent experience. Placing greater educational value on conceptual clarity and skills as the outcomes of experiential learning may distort the unique fabric of an individual's lived reality. He suggests that this issue needs to be seen in the context of industrialized societies where male-related assumptions about 'autonomy' and objectivity prevail. In contrast, he draws on the work of the neurologist, Oliver Sachs, who balances scientific objectivity with his active engagement with subjective phenomena and respect for his patients as individuals, rather than cases, and for us operates in the 'new paradigm', as discussed in Chapter 22.

O'Reilly relates these issues to his own political and personal concerns and struggles as a tutor in a non-traditional higher education setting. He raises wider issues that are echoed by Salmon (Chapter 21), Wildemeersch (Chapter 5) and Brah and Hoy (Chapter 6). For example, how and with what consequences might such assumptions permeate the process related to the assessment and accreditation of prior learning? When, in educational programmes, we seek to introduce experiential learning into the curricula, are we unduly obsessed with 'wrapping it up' at analytical and rational levels, or proving that there has indeed been a comprehensive 'transfer of learning' to 'real life'? To what extent do we impede our understanding of complex individual and social realities through our failure to value experiential learning that may still be tacit and intuitive, not yet coherent, but no less rich in its possibilities?

Recently, a colleague at the School for Independent Study asked me how I respond to the question 'What do you do?' from someone I have just met. He was relieved to hear that, like him, I have great difficulty offering a coherent response. A similar difficulty faces me now, as I work on this paper so that it will make sense to you, an unknown reader. It is not easy. Yet the first thing each of our students is expected to do in devising an individual programme of study is to write a statement of personal experience. What I intend to explore here are the risks involved in moving from experience that is incoherent and private to making a public statement about one's self.

Let me start by saying that I treasure my own incoherence and that I value incoherence in my students. That may sound a risky statement for me as an educator. Most of the education courses I have encountered place a high value on logical analysis and coherent argument, in keeping with the high value placed on rationality in Western culture (I have discussed these issues more fully elsewhere: O'Reilly, 1986). Even non-traditional models of education, such as experiential learning cycles, which recognize incoherence as a stage in the learning process, may still place higher educational value on the ultimate achievement of greater conceptual clarity and comprehension. I value coherence too, but I wonder why our incoherence is so undervalued.

Perhaps part of the reason is that coherence is closely related to another key-stone of Western culture: our notion of 'the individual'. This is again relevant to my educational work, since individual autonomy in learning is given a high value in the practice of independent study (see, e.g. Stephenson, 1988). Indeed, I put a high value on my own autonomy as a tutor in the school, yet I have a few reservations about the notion. One is the suspicion that autonomy is more of a male-orientated value in our society: for example, representations of 'the individual' purveyed by Hollywood movies loom large in Western culture – usually male, often violent, e.g. Clint Eastwood as the lone cowboy, Charles Bronson as the lone vigilante, Humphrey Bogart as the lone investigator or (in *Casablanca*) the lone lover – 'a man's gotta do what a man's gotta do'. In contrast, women may be offered role models that emphasize collective values, e.g. the mother, the nurse, the nun, even the teacher. Yet nearly all of us brought up in a traditional Western mode are subjected to processes of learning that reward individual academic achievement, measured in competitive examinations.

These are commonplace observations of a complex dynamic (cf. the analysis in Apple, 1982), but enough to sound a warning bell. As Susan Buck-Morss (1987, p. 203) writes:

> It has been argued by more than one social theorist that individual autonomy is valued by industrial society, not as an end in itself, not with the goal of freedom, but as a means of social control. The internalisation of social constraints, maintained by anxiety and insecurity, produces cultural traits of obsessive cleanliness, submission to regimentation, asceticism and the felt need for 'rational' domination of both inner and outer nature – traits that have in fact become synonymous with Western 'civilisation' and historical 'progress'. They are rationalised as necessary for industrial efficiency, but they are inherently authoritarian and their political implications need to be made explicit.

The latter point is crucial. What is the form of social relations that gives specific meaning to individual autonomy in any context? How do the educational processes of independent study (as we practise it at North East London Polytechnic) define, shape and delimit the boundaries of 'the individual'?

Hard questions. Rather than engage with the positions of social theorists, edifying though that might be (Buck-Morss has in mind Adorno, Foucault, Horkheimer and Reich), or attempt a coherent (and therefore idealized) account of debates on such questions within the School for Independent Study, I would like to offer you something perhaps a little less coherent (a little less industrialized?). Perhaps Oliver Sacks' book *The Man Who Mistook His Wife for a Hat* (1985) might help to reveal a connection between the politics of incoherence and the politics of the individual.

I read the book a while back. It is about people who cannot think 'normally', who are missing some vital capacity to maintain a coherent front. Though written by a neurologist, it spoke powerfully to me about educational matters – about the very narrow band of mental functioning that gets endorsed by higher education; about the importance of recollected experience in establishing personal identity; about Sacks' own capacity to conduct an enquiry that is scientifically objective while remaining engaged with the subjective meaning of phenomena; and about Sacks' ability to reflect on his encounters and turn them into such a wonderful book.

Sacks reflects on a series of 'cases' from his neurological practice. From an obsessively objective scientific viewpoint these would be patients with pathologies; for Sacks, they are also unique individuals, with whom he engages in a quest for their identity, for the meaning of their human condition – an endeavour that calls forth, as Sacks' mentor, the Soviet neurologist Luria, would have it, a 'romantic science' (Sacks, 1985, pp. ix–xii and p. 224). Already this is an exciting revelation for me, having for 15 years been lecturing in social aspects of science and technology, teasing and cajoling science and engineering students into confronting the consequences of a reductionist approach to experience – experience stripped down to experiment – when the results of that approach are reapplied to the world as technology. Of course, there are valuable attempts to expose the values implicit in an apparently value-free science and to identify better values, but at the level of ideas, intellectual discourse tinges even the strongest commitments with impersonality (cf. Albury and Schwartz, 1982; Capra, 1982; Raskin and Bernstein, 1987). Now Sacks is 'doing science' in a way both deeply personal and intellectually challenging – going even beyond Primo Levi's (1975) reflections on being an industrial chemist, so beautifully conveyed in *The Periodic Table*.

Both Sacks and Levi are reflecting deeply on their experience, as we would encourage our students to do in independent study. Levi deals with his Jewish origins, his time in Auschwitz, the interplay of cultural and personal in his life; Sacks too is Jewish, and in some ways his 'stories' are reminiscent of Freud's (1901) *Psychopathology of Everyday Life*. While Freud deals with the significance of relatively minor aberrations of remembering and forgetting, the very identities of Sacks' patients are put at issue by their condition. Ironically, some of the most striking accounts concern people who have no grip at all on their experience, who have no capacity to recollect, nothing on which to reflect.

One such is 'The Lost Mariner' (Sacks, 1985, Ch. 2), Jimmie, who has no memory beyond 1945, and who in the 1970s is fixed in a world gone by. Nothing sticks, nothing new connects. Jimmie functions in a way that is tolerable in an enclosed mental institution, though Sacks observes that he maintains his identity only by constant effort. Bewildered by contemporary events for which he has no frame of reference, Jimmie finds repose in contemplating simple things (perhaps 'eternal' things, perhaps, for Jimmie, unproblematized things) – in watching children play, in nature, above all in worship, where 'Clearly Jimmie found himself, found continuity and reality' (p. 105). Less fortunate in Sacks' view is Mr Thompson, who must also 'literally make himself and his world up at every moment' (p. 105), but with no discernible place of repose. Mr Thompson has slid from a state of human being to a state of Humean being, where each event is unconnected to what goes before and what comes after, a continuous amnesia (q.v. Hume, 1739: Book 1, esp. pp. 251–62, 'Of personal identity'). Sacks recalls a passage from the autobiography of that great observer of bourgeois absurdity, the film-maker Luis Bunuel: 'I can only wait for the final amnesia, the one that can erase an entire life' (Sacks, 1985, p. 32).

Or erase an entire culture. In a chapter in *New Ways of Knowing* (Raskin and Bernstein, 1987), Buck-Morss chronicles phases in the cultural colonization of a Cretan village by the two-way traffic of incoming tourists and outgoing 'guest-workers'. In connection with the villagers' pending loss of cultural identity, she writes:

> But a mere sense of history is not enough to safeguard against illusion. Granted the construction of intelligibility in the present involves a recon-struction of the past, the reading one gives to the past is a highly political act (Buck-Morss, 1987, p. 210).

For the people in Sacks' book, the political consequences of their failures to construe a presentable imitation of 'normal reality' are severe – segregation in institutions, useless lives, 'treatment'. Few will find physicians as sympathetic as Sacks.

On the streets of New York, Sacks observes a bag lady mimicking every passer-by. This 'grey-haired woman in her sixties . . . was caricaturing everyone she passed . . . within a split second she had them all'. Then she desperately turns into an alleyway and 'with all the appearances of a woman violently sick, she expelled, tremendously accelerated and abbreviated, all the gestures, the postures, the expressions, the demeanours, the entire behavioural repertoires, of the past forty or fifty people she had passed'. This is Tourette's syndrome. Overwhelmed by her experience, 'the super-Touretter' is 'driven to incoher-ence, an identity delirium' (Sacks, 1985, pp. 116–18).

I look at the piles of books on my desk as I write, the splurges of quotation in the text, and I laugh.

Are Sacks' observations slightly alarming? Do the various syndromes de-scribed echo transient segments of my own experience? Maybe they are always there for all of us, routinely filtered out of our normal stream of consciousness or dismissed as temporary aberrations. Significantly, they raise issues of the individual's sense of being, of being individual and coherent. This surely lies central to the Western grasp of reality, where coherence resides – in *me* – the cogito of Descartes, 'I think, therefore I am'.

'I think, therefore I am' or 'I laugh, therefore I am?'   ·

As much as anything, our conceptions of being and knowing are fundamental to our educational philosophies. In people devoid of 'normal' conceptualizing abilities, we can discern with Sacks the importance of concrete apprehension. A world that lacks unifying abstractions may still be experienced in extraordinary depth and richness and unified by the narrative, symbolic force of music or art. One of Sacks' most moving portraits is that of Rebecca (Sacks, 1985, Ch. 21), 'a wholly "unremarkable" young woman, a simpleton, with whom I worked twelve years ago. I remember her warmly' (p. 167).

> Rather suddenly, after her grandmother's death, she became clear and decisive. 'I want no more classes, no more workshops,' she said. 'They do nothing for me. They do nothing to bring me together . . . I'm a sort of living carpet. I need a pattern, a design like you have on that carpet. I come apart, I unravel, unless there's a design.' I looked down at the carpet, as Rebecca said this, and found myself thinking of Sherrington's famous image, comparing the brain/mind to an 'enchanted loom', weaving patterns ever-dissolving, but always with meaning (Sacks, 1985, p. 175).

Despite her backwardness in conceptual thinking, Rebecca finds her meaning, becomes a complete person 'poised, fluent, with style', in performing drama. The converse seems less likely, that an education system which offers only cognitive development will help people find any meaning in what they learn.

In tutoring independent study, I am preoccupied above all with the tension between personal meaning and objective knowledge. I see each student arrive with a dream of what her learning might be, what his future might be. The dream pattern carries the individual's life story interwoven with all the facets of experience that inform her story. That experience being what it is, often painful and confusing, the dream is not necessarily cosy, the pattern not necessarily beautiful in a conventional sense. But in any case, the first task for the student is to translate the personal dream into a coherent programme of study that can be publically validated as a basis for an accredited award. This is where I might be able to help the learner.

I might be able to help as a translator. After all, I am reasonably articulate, though once I was not: as a child, like everybody in the world, and as a working-class person, like many of our students, at school. Though it is a long time ago now, I can still feel something of the loss in becoming articulate, in losing touch with my childhood non-verbal experience of the world and in losing touch, especially at the aptly-named Grammar School, with my sense of belonging in a rooted culture. Curiously enough, I was raised in the docklands of Liverpool, where my father laboured, and I work now near the Docklands of East London. As I help a local person who has become a mature student to write a programme of study, I can remain aware of the alien cultural norms implicit for that person in writing a document which sets out in coherent, logical, grammatical prose, the pattern of the person's life to date and the plan of it for the next 2 years.

For the unwary, the educational dream might become entrapped in the bureaucratic requirements of validation boards, degenerating into a form-filling exercise; or it might be pinned down too soon to a rigid plan of work, rather than keeping open possibilities and living with creative uncertainty; most insidiously of all, it might get dissected on a timetable, which looks such a reasonable requirement but carries the full force of objective linear time, the common matrix of Newtonian science, of commercial and industrial organization, and of political planning and control. As Parjanen (1986) has written in his discussion of myths of time in educational practice:

> In the professional training which follows upon basic schooling the conditions of work life exert such a powerful influence that for both teacher and pupil time-bound efficiency becomes a self-evident requirement . . . Bowles and Gintis, in their well-known *correspondence theory in the sociology of education* (1976), claim that it is precisely the function of education to accustom young people while still at school to the social laws and practical requirements of work life. In addition to stress on discipline, mutual competition, submission to authority and individualism, this correspondence also involves an attitude to time (pp. 7–8).

> . . . Both the generally educational and the professionally orientated school observe a practise in which the predetermined division of available time, with the fragmentation it inevitably involves, presents an obstacle to holistic and deep learning and promotes *a surface or serialistic style of learning* (p. 9).

Though contemporary science is moving beyond 'single vision and Newton's sleep', and though we move en masse into the fragmented culture of postmodernism, the shadow of totalitarianism hangs over too many of the world's education systems. Indeed, some of the elements of a totalitarian framework of knowledge, such as the presumption of a single objective dimension of time, may be so integral to our ways of thinking that we expect them to be reproduced in the stories that pass for our collective history and even in the autobiography of the individual. This means for me, as I grope my way towards a more liberatory pattern of education (let's call it O'Reilly's Dream), that I need to be patient with the inevitable frustrations and contradictions, and to be gently, but relentlessly, subversive of my own practise.

In this pursuit, I am sustained in many ways. I owe much to the gifts my students bring me in their learning. I am carried forward in an endeavour shared with my colleagues in the School for Independent Study and with the global community of educators I am coming to know through events such as the First International Conference on Experiential Learning. And, of course, for all I have said about language and loss, through writings, reading remains for me an important realm of experience. To detail all these influences would be no less than an autobiography.

The writer Samuel Beckett has said that the experience of the individual is an incoherent experience and must be conveyed incoherently. In these few words I have done my best to convey something of my experience of independent study, especially of the tensions between the objective and the subjective, the private and the public, the personal and the political. So it is that I sometimes respond to the question 'What do you do?' by claiming to be an educational fantasy engineer.

'And what do you do?'

References

Albury, D. and Schwartz, J. (1982). *Partial Progress: The Politics of Science and Technology.* London: Pluto Press.

Apple, M. W. (1982). *Education and Power.* Boston: Routledge and Kegan Paul.

Bowles, S. and Gintis, H. (1976). *Schooling in Capitalist America.* New York: Basic Books.

Buck-Morss, S. (1987). Semiotic boundaries and the politics of meaning: Modernity on tour – a village in transition. In Raskin, M. G. and Bernstein, H. J. (Eds), *New Ways of Knowing: The Sciences, Society and Reconstructive Knowledge*, pp. 200–36. New Jersey: Rowman and Littlefield.

Capra, F. (1982). *The Turning Point: Science, Society and the Rising Culture.* New York: Simon and Schuster.

Freud, S. (1901). *Psychopathology and Everyday Life*, Vol. 6 of *Standard Works*, Strechey, J. (Ed.), 1960. London: Hogarth Press.

Hume, D. (1739). *A Treatise of Human Nature: Being an Attempt to Introduce the Experimental Method of Reasoning into Moral Subjects.* Reprinted and edited by Selby-Bigge, L.A., 1888. Oxford: Oxford University Press.

Levi, P. (1975). *The Periodic Table.* Translated into English, 1985. London: Michael Joseph.

O'Reilly, D. (1986). Personal learning and objective assessment. *The New Era* (London), **67**(3), 68–71.

Parjanen, M. (1986). Professional continuing education – Higher education for sale? Paper presented at the Gottlieb Duttweiler Institut, Ruschlikon, Switzerland (available from the author at the Institute for Extension Studies, University of Tampere, Box 607, SF-33101 Tampere, Finland).

Raskin, M. G. and Bernstein, H. J. (1987). *New Ways of Knowing: The Sciences, Society and Reconstructive Knowledge.* New Jersey: Rowman and Littlefied.

Sacks, O. (1985). *The Man Who Mistook His Wife for a Hat.* London: Gerald Duckworth. (References here are to the paperback edition published in 1986 by Pan.)

Stephenson, J. (1988). The experience of independent study at North East London Polytechnic. In Boud, D. (Ed.), *Developing Student Autonomy in Learning*, 2nd edition, pp. 211–26. London: Kogan Page.

Though I have not referred to them specifically in the text, I have been influenced and encouraged in writing this piece by several of the chapters in:

Boud, D. and Griffin, V. (Eds) (1987). *Appreciating Adult Learning: From the Learners' Perspective.* London, Kogan Page. Of especial interest were Margaret Denis and Ingrid Richter on 'Learning about intuitive learning: Moose-hunting techniques' (pp. 25–36), Stephen Brookfield on 'Significant personal learning' (pp. 64–75), and Peter Reason and Judi Marshall on 'Research as a personal process' (pp. 112–26).

10

Generating Integration and Involvement in Learning

Mary K. St. John Nelson

Working in a traditional academic setting in the USA, Nelson and Peterson (Chapter 16) devised a Learning Model of Experiential Education (LMEE) in order to enhance personal motivation and the relevance of courses for the student. Here experiential learning is used in the sense of non-classroom-based learning, such as field trips and internships. Nelson believes that too often students feel driven by their courses, rather than in control of the process. The key to this model is to use experiential learning as a basis for helping students integrate three potentially separate domains: personal aspirations, career goals and educational plans. Students clarify these through planning for and becoming involved in an action phase (the experience), followed successively by reflection, analysis and synthesis phases which yield further degrees of integration between the three domains. Examples of the application of the model are given with a discussion on outcomes showing how the process can facilitate integration as well as greater coherence and relevance in learning. Readers may wish to compare this approach with that of Stanton and Giles (Chapter 17).

This chapter could equally have been placed in Part 3 but we have included it here since its emphasis is on the personal and the individual. Readers working in the milieu of traditional academia will be able to consider how Nelson found compatibility between a traditional course and an experiential learning component to enhance student involvement. In this context, the 'learning to learn' capacities that Nelson suggests result from the application of her experiential learning model, are more likely to be applied to personal, rather than social, needs and goals. We have here a useful contrast with the approaches discussed by Keregero in Tanzania (Chapter 18), Serrao and Jensen in India (Chapter 20), Packham et al. across an entire college in Australia (Chapter 13), and the approaches advocated by Wildemeersch (Chapter 5), Brah and Hoy (Chapter 6) and Salmon (Chapter 21).

Introduction

A student does not come to college primarily to learn things, to store an intellectual garret with an assortment of odds and ends. He [as originally written] comes to college to learn how to learn, what to learn, where to learn, and why to learn (Wriston, 1987).

I believe that the meaning of this quotation has significance for educators, particularly those in the experiential camp. I interpret this quotation to mean that facts and figures will soon be forgotten, but that the real purpose of education is to imbue students with newly developed skills that will transfer to new learning – for their lifetimes.

Wriston's statement provides a standard by which we might judge the impact that our own teaching methods have on students and on the process of teaching and learning. As an educator in a college dedicated to general education within a broader university setting, I have developed a personal educational philosophy. That philosophy embraces the need for students to be involved in their own education. Thus it was from a concern for making education relevant to the lives of students, for seeing a need to increase the motivation of learners, for believing that knowledge and theory should apply to individual conduct and that the educational process should accommodate, for the learner, a system of values, that the idea and the development of a model that would help to facilitate these things began to take shape.

This chapter will explain how and why the model, which I have developed with a colleague, came about (Peterson and Nelson, 1986). It will describe our experiences in using the model as an integral part of a course at the University of Minnesota, discuss the outcomes of this experiment, and conclude with how the process of teaching and learning was affected.

Development of the model

Our model emerged out of a realization that students could benefit by understanding how to learn, what to learn, where to learn and why to learn. Theory related to experiential learning provided the basis for developing a decision-making model to enable both the faculty and the students to better understand the outcomes of their decisions. The key was student involvement.

Student involvement has been identified as the first of three critical conditions of excellence in America's colleges and universities:

> The first of these three conditions – and perhaps the most important for purposes of improving undergraduate education – is student involvement . . . The amount of student learning and personal development associated with any educational program is directly proportional to the quality and quantity of student involvement in that program (National Institute of Education, 1984).

Experience plays a central role in descriptions of learning processes within both behavioural and traditional experiential theories (Dewey, 1938; Lewin, 1951; Piaget, 1970). It is the concrete experience, which is followed by the collection of data and observations about the experience, that ties those theories together (Kolb, 1984, p. 21). In all cases, experience leads to some action by the learner: continuing the same behaviour, modifying that behaviour, or choosing a new experience.

Keeton and Tate (1976) also emphasize experience followed by action in their definition of experience learning as:

... learning *in which the learner is directly in touch with the realities being studied* ... [It typically] involves not merely *observing* the phenomenon but also *doing* something with it.

These conceptions of learning helped to shape the development of the model.

Another motivating factor in our quest to make the educational experience more meaningful for students came from my observations of what was going on around me. Students were often rushed through the curriculum, taking a full load of credits, often having to work to pay their tuition, and often dealing with a myriad of conflicting demands. For them, too much happened too fast. From what I observed and heard, I concluded that students were more concerned with survival skills than with educational pursuits. They worried about how they would make it through a class or a term. They felt that they had little control over becoming truly educated. I felt that this must reduce their commitment to the learning process. It seemed that they did not understand the 'how–what–where–why' of their educational pursuits. Their purpose, all too often, was merely to survive.

It was in response to these concerns that we developed a model which would centre on the *process* of learning – one which would foster reflection, evaluation and further action, and would actively involve students in making decisions about their education and their lives. My colleague and I debated and discussed the issues related to such a learning model. We shared our ideas with a few valued colleagues and after many drafts produced *The Learning Model of Experiential Education* (Peterson and Nelson, 1986).

The Learning Model of Experiential Education (LMEE) was developed with an emphasis on learning as a dialectic process in which the learner progresses through stages of experience, analysis, and action, not unlike other similar models. However, in the LMEE the process takes into account the need for the learning experience to interrelate all parts of the student's life: personal aspirations, career goals and educational plans. The LMEE emphasizes the need for students to bring these three areas of their lives into harmony with each other – that is, to understand what education is needed for becoming successful in a particular career and what kind of lifestyle is associated with that career. How can that harmony be accomplished? With a deeper understanding of the interrelatedness of decisions and how they might affect not only a student's education but other areas of their lives, students come to discover for themselves the 'how, what, where and why' to learn. In the LMEE (Fig. 10.1) that process of recognizing the interrelatedness is described.

In describing this decision-making process, we begin at the base of the diagram, recognizing that individuals come to a learning experience with certain personal aspirations, career goals and educational plans. These may be very conscious, somewhat vague, or quite unconscious. In any case, students may be making decisions within each of these domains without considering or realizing the impact a decision in one area may have on another. The domains – personal aspirations, career goals, and educational plans – are set apart in the

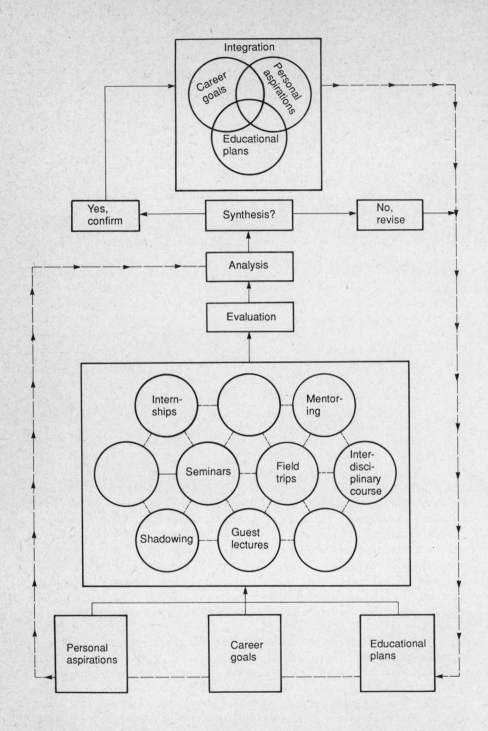

Figure 10.1 Learning Model of Experiential Education.

model. Even though the students may perceive them to be integrated, the domains often exist in a state of separateness. The important decisions that students make in each of these areas may not lead them in the same direction. In order to discuss these three domains further, it will be helpful to clarify our terms.

1. *Personal aspirations* represent desires or ambitions concerning one's personal life. Individuals have ideas about what sorts of things they want out of life, e.g. status and respect, freedom to pursue leisure time activities, opportunity for travel, satisfying personal relationships, recognition, spiritual growth, social and community awareness, and material rewards.
2. *Career goals* are projected career plans that will enable a person to pursue an occupation which will fulfil the personal needs and values considered to be the most important (Tennyson *et al.*, 1980). Career goals should flow from, as well as contribute to, one's personal aspirations. These are often defined in terms of the positions one desires, e.g. personnel manager, owner/manager of a small business, sales person, or advertising executive.

   Traditionally, the assumption is made that students have career goals well in mind and only have to be educated in order to realize these goals. Emry and Page (1985), however, claim that some students have not identified a career direction, many are confused, and still others have made career decisions based on inadequate information.
3. With *educational plans*, students make use of learning experiences to accomplish goals. Most recognize that some education or training is usually necessary in order to achieve career goals, e.g. courses, seminars, workshops, educational programmes, degrees, or conferences. When students ask, 'What is this course going to do for me?', educators need to be able to provide answers; but without knowledge of the students' personal aspirations and career goals, they cannot advise students well as regards their educational plans.

The action phase of the LMEE begins when the individual has an experience. A variety of choices have been identified in this model. Some of the experiences available in our institution include field trips, internships, guest speakers, or independent studies. The experiences are not limited to these examples. The important thing is that the action, whatever it is, is purposefully chosen by the student for the purposes of testing a theory or gathering information.

Having had the experience, the student proceeds to the reflection phase, which in the LMEE has been fleshed out to include three stages: evaluation, analysis, and synthesis.

Evaluation, in this model, is defined as the initial appraisal of the relevant experiential activity. Individuals automatically have a reaction to any activity but, in this context, the initial evaluation is more than a reaction and cannot occur in just one step. The experience can best be appraised through, for example, group discussions, written questionnaires, journal writing, or comparing post-tests with pre-tests. Whatever the method of appraisal, it often includes reflections on feelings, both positive and negative, about the recent experience (Boud *et al.*, 1985).

Analysis occurs when an entity is separated into its component parts to determine their relationships to one another. As individuals evaluate the experience, they begin to determine what influence one domain might have on another. In this phase, students begin to be aware of how personal aspirations influence, and are influenced by, career goals and educational plans and how all three have a symbiotic relationship to one another.

This leads students into questioning whether or not the three domains reinforce and support each other. *Synthesis* occurs when the students' personal aspirations, career goals and educational plans are brought from a state of separateness to a state of integration. Most important for the students at this point is the realization that any decision they make will have an effect on the symbiotic relationship of the three domains.

One of two conclusions is possible: 'Yes, there is harmony and agreement among the three components; efforts in all three domains are moving the individual in the same direction.' If this is the case, then synthesis exists. However, the more likely answer is, 'No, there is not harmony among the three domains.' Rarely are decisions made by consciously examining the impact of that decision on all domains of one's life. If harmony does *not* exist, a change in one or more domain is necessary.

At this point, given that students desire to achieve harmony in all three domains, students can perceive more effectively what further experiences will contribute to integration. The LMEE recognizes that 'looping back' (to the right of Fig. 10.1) again and again, until students are satisfied that the three domains are merging, is a natural and desirable part of the process. This 'looping back' will encourage students to select an alternative experience and go through the process again in order to re-evaluate their directions in the light of that new experience.

The final phase of the LMEE illustrates a state of integration, whereby previously separate elements are now experienced as a harmonious, interrelated whole. This model can help individuals recognize that the three domains of their lives can fit together and enhance one another, leading towards accomplishment of the individual's overall objective, which is defined as *harmony* among a person's aspirations, career goals and educational plans.

It is important to recognize that the state of integration, even having been achieved to one's satisfaction, is not permanent, because change in life is inevitable. The process will continue to repeat itself for many reasons, as individuals:

- observe others in situations they desire for themselves;
- get new information;
- participate in new experiences; or
- outgrow their circumstances and seek change.

Any of these processes may lead to dissatisfaction with their present state.

The LMEE thus suggests the *processes* whereby individuals can better understand the necessity for making decisions that require them to look at each issue separately, so that they can see how these parts can be integrated. It is the experiential component that makes possible the new insights that aid students in their decision making.

The experiment: Applying the model

We used the LMEE in an experimental course in 1985 and again in 1987 at the General College, University of Minnesota, to examine the usefulness of our theoretical model. A field trip from Minneapolis to New York was an integral part of the course and served as the experiential activity. Twelve students enrolled in the course in 1985 and 15 in 1987. Both groups of students were asked to identify their personal aspirations, career goals and educational plans in a pre-test, as well as to indicate how sure they were of their responses. Data were also collected regarding knowledge and attitudes of the various business fields in which the students had identified an interest. In the course, students attended six seminars prior to taking the field trip. The preparation included studying the businesses they would be visiting, preparing to interview people in New York in selected career positions, and attending lectures on areas such as finance. They also learned how to keep a journal and participated in planning their itinerary for the trip.

The 1-week field experience in New York set up an intensive schedule of tours through various businesses in areas where there was an expressed interest, such as finance, advertising, public relations, marketing, design and manufacturing, as well as in government. Students were also required to attend an artistic performance and visit a museum of their choice as well as spend time with at least one of the ethnic communities of New York. Students kept journals on all their activities in preparation for the final paper they would be writing.

Upon returning to the University of Minnesota campus, three post-trip seminars were held so that students could reflect upon and discuss their experiences on the trip, their new insights, and their feelings about the experiences. This sharing of information helped them to organize the data they had collected in order to prepare a final paper. The final paper required the students to reassess the pre-trip statements describing their personal aspirations, career goals and educational plans, and to determine the degree to which they now viewed the three domains to be integrated in light of their new insights. The students also took a post-test which provided data that would be compared with the pre-test data in order to determine whether or not significant changes had occurred.

Outcome of the model's application

I will report some of the findings and share some of the students' comments before discussing the outcomes of the course and the value of the model as a guide to students' reflections and planning. Data analysis of the 1985 pre-/ post-tests indicated the following:

1. All but one student indicated at least one change in career goals, and the number of students having a specific job in mind increased from 50 to 83 per cent.
2. The number of students who were sure about a specific job increased from 33 to 83 per cent.
3. Students' perceptions of how well they understood the workings of six different types of businesses increased.
4. Students indicated unexpected gains in defining their educational goals and they became more aware of the importance of better-defined career goals. For example, before the field trip, most students believed that their most important expectation of the course was to gain a better perception of the business world. After the trip, most students specifically identified a better understanding of different businesses and better-defined career goals as the most important contributions of the course.

(The analysis of the pre-/post-test data from the 1987 trip was not completed at the time of writing.)

The following selected comments written by the students in trip journals, final papers, and open-ended questions in the pre- and post-tests illustrate some of the insights that students gained from this experience:

The 1985 group:

In my personal life, the field trip has given me something to base decisions on what kind of lifestyle I would like to lead in the future and what type of lifestyles go along with various careers.

I thought this course was one of the most educational . . . I have ever attended. It has given me a better understanding as to what I want for my career goals and has opened the door for internship and job opportunities. I received an excellent educational and cultural experience that has enhanced my education.

Since I have made my career decision I now know where I am going! I have a destiny and it feels good. It feels so good that I am confident in my future and in myself.

This course has reinforced the idea of constantly setting new goals for myself and to achieve them as best as possible.

My career goal changed from being very vague to being very specific and the field trip to New York helped me to make that decision.

The 1987 group:

My career goals are more narrowly defined as a result of this course. I am more determined to have the life style I'm striving for.

I would say I became more open to various career choices.

It helped to clarify my career goals and to assure me that I had made the right choice . . .

This course has had a large impact on my career, education, and personal goals. I will not know the extent, though, for a long time.

I have more enthusiasm and confidence to follow through on my goals and dreams. I was impressed with what was accomplished by people in New York and it challenges me to do the same.

It [the course] reinforced many of my ideas.

The field trip had an impact on my career goals and that is that I will try to achieve the highest level of success I feel is possible for me.

This course opened my mind to new alterantives. It has made me think about myself and has given me a better understanding of who I am and what I want to accomplish.

My desired life style has changed dramatically after this trip.

This experience helped to show me that something was lacking.

The quotations above were very typical of the comments heard during and after the field experience. They do not, however, tell the whole story. The students experienced and absorbed so much in 1 week that many pieces had to be fitted together through the processes of evaluation, analysis, and then synthesis before they could reach those conclusions. The conclusions that students expressed suggested to me three categories.

1. In the first group, students who had some idea of what their future plans would be, whether they were certain or vague about them, had those plans reinforced. These students expressed greater confidence and a clearer picture of where they were going and what they had to do to achieve their goals.
2. Students in the second group found that they had made choices in one or more of the domains that now seemed inappropriate for them. This group expressed an interest in exploring other options. There was some surprise that a choice they had made was not based on reality as they now perceived it. They were relieved that they had discovered it while they could still make changes.
3. Still others, who fell into the third group, came to realize that although one or more of the decisions they had made were not appropriate for them in the light of their new insights, they were not able to make changes because they were so near graduation. For this group, the frustration was the greatest because the experience came too late. They now realized that they had made some decisions without fully considering how those decisions would affect the other domains of their lives.

Some conclusions can be drawn about the groups as a whole. Nearly all the students recognized the value of setting goals for themselves and then analysing the impact that those goals might have on other areas of their lives. In the post-trip discussions, all of the students indicated that they would continue to seek other experiences that would further test whether or not their personal aspirations, career goals and educational plans were in harmony with each other and leading them in the same direction. Whether they do this or not, or whether they were verbalizing what they thought I wanted to hear, is not really important. What is important is that the students learned to view the integration of different domains in their lives as a desirable state, not easily achieved and not static.

The data collected and the students' comments indicate that there was some progress made in moving from a state of separateness to one of integration. That was illustrated by those in group 2, who recognized the need for changes and became open to new options. Using a model such as the LMEE seems to have served this group well in learning how to conceptualize the process, as they seek other experiences and reflect on those experiences when making further decisions. This resulted in a broader view of their educational options and a sense of having more control over their futures.

Those in group 1 who found that they were satisfied with the degree of integration in their lives had no need for immediate change in the paths they had chosen. For them, reinforcement of their decisions felt good, and this was a motivating factor. As we have already recognized, however, the process is not static, and future changes might place any of the members of this group into one of the other categories.

At first glance, for the students in group 3 who experienced the most frustration, it might seem that the whole course was nothing more than an unnerving experience and also that the model was of no real value to them. What had they learned – that they were 'off the track'? Even though they were near graduation, these students may come to realize that this does not mark the end of one's education. They might begin to look at educational opportunities for their lifetimes. It may be that for this group, the LMEE will be a most useful conceptual tool that they can take with them after graduation and use as they work through the important decisions in their lives.

Reflections

As an educator, I felt that never had one experience yielded so much 'food for thought'. This experiment has been reinforcing, but it also has raised many questions. The feedback from the students has suggested that some changes had occurred for them and that those changes could be attributed to the field experience and the guidance and learning processes that supported it.

Many faculty members and administrators are not sure how an institution can provide experiential learning opportunities and traditional curricula at the same time. We have shown how traditional content in a discipline (business) can be enhanced with an experiential component (field trip) in ways that are complementary rather than competitive. How successful might this be for teaching curricula in other liberal arts disciplines? What documentation exists (or could exist) that would support such experiential learning?

We might apply Marland's (1974, p. 229) definition of career education to experiential learning and view it as:

> . . . a process, not a different curriculum. It enhances the learner's purposefulness in learning and, accordingly, the instructor's effectiveness and personal satisfaction.

In this process, the educator's role is changed from that of a lecturer to that of a teacher/adviser whose task it is to help students to make sense out of their educational experiences. The teacher/adviser no longer has sole responsibility for enlightening, educating and motivating students through a lecture. That responsibility can be shared with students as they become more actively involved in their learning. The teacher/adviser now has the responsibility of co-ordinating experiential activities that will contribute to an understanding of the course content. The teacher/adviser now serves as a catalyst, questioning and interacting with students. Through this interaction students can help to determine *what* activities will best help them to learn.

As a teacher, I had to deal with the fact that I would have less control than I would have had in a lecture–review–quiz method of teaching. I experienced some concern as to whether or not the students would be effective in taking control of some aspects of the course. Although their level of motivation was high enough, so that they all accomplished the pre-trip planning and require-ments satisfactorily, many did not realize the importance of these things until the end of the course. One student commented: 'There is no way you could have fully prepared us for that experience in New York! If I had to do it over again, I would have worked harder at preparing for it myself.' I might suggest that the risk of having less control is worth it if students come to this realization. Those students who shared this attitude have learned something about *how* to learn.

In order to facilitate a shift in the focus of the educator's role from lecturer to teacher/adviser more easily, a model that will help educators to see ways students can be involved in their learning may be useful. It has long been recognized that

> learning usually proceeds best when both students and teacher are clear about the relationships between objectives and activities designed to serve them (Chickering, 1977).

The LMEE has served effectively as a tool which helped students better understand the separate domains for which they made decisions and to help them visualize the process by which those domains – personal aspirations, career goals and educational plans – can become integrated. The result is a better understanding of *why* and *how* to learn in ways that are satisfying and effective in relation to their goals.

Experiential learning breaks down the classroom walls and encourages students to seek knowledge and test classroom theory in whatever environment may serve them best. As this example has shown, students travelled several thousand miles to test their decisions. For others, that trip may be only across campus to the library or to a local firm. In any case, students are being involved in decisions about *where* to learn. They soon discover that there is no limit to the resources that students and educators have at their disposal.

The post-trip statements made by students indicated a fairly high degree of satisfaction with not only the learning but also the personal development that had occurred as a result of this course.

In addition, students in both groups began to develop into a cohesive unit, perhaps due to activities that required them to work on assignments in small groups and to select room-mates for the week in New York. This 'bonding' served them well later when meeting a rigorous schedule in New York, as I observed students taking care of each other in a new and strange environment. In addition to accomplishing their own goals, the students demonstrated their concern for each other, and a greater sense of responsibility for their 'community'. There is all-too-often a different attitude in the competitive environment of a classroom.

Conclusions and recommendations

This chapter has described the process that students went through and how a model can be used to help them evaluate, analyse and synthesize their field trip experience. In the main I have discussed the outcomes of these processes, but much more needs to be explored concerning what was done in the course to *engage* students in the process of analysing, evaluating and synthesizing their experience. For example, what are the processes that can help students move from one phase of the model to the next? What are the activities that help to bring learning experiences out into the open so that students can reflect upon and evaluate the extent to which their learning fosters interaction in their personal aspirations, career goals, and educational plans? What are the experiential activities that make feedback more salient, so that it will bring about a state of synthesis? What is effective and what is not in moving students towards integration?

This experience raises certain other issues. How useful would this methodology be in other circumstances? We used the LMEE in a class situation, but would it be as useful for students to take away with them to use individually as learners. In a class situation there is a certain amount of structure and influence imposed on the student by the instructor. Is the LMEE a model which can be relevant to promoting autonomy and greater commitment to self-directed and life-long learning? Can it be used in secondary as well as post-secondary educational systems?

We need more information about how students can be helped to develop skills that will transfer to new learning throughout their lifetimes:

> Good teaching is hard . . . it demands not only a balancing act, but a willingness to dissolve classroom walls and engage with our students and colleagues in different ways. But we also have an advantage. As scholars, we know the vulnerability of exploration as well as the excitement of discovery (Cafarelli, 1988, p. 1).

I believe we, as educators, will experience the excitement of discovery along with our students if we are willing to risk vulnerability by helping students to become more involved in their own learning.

References

Boud, D., Keogh, R. and Walker, D. (Eds) (1985). *Reflection: Turning Experience into Learning*. London: Kogan Page.

Cafarelli, K. (1988). Editor's comments. *Focus*, **3**(2), 1.

Chickering, A. W. (1977). *Experience and Learning: An Introduction to Experiential Learning*. New Rochelle, N.Y.: Change Magazine Press.

Dewey, J. (1938). *Experience and Education*. New York: Kappa Delta Pi.

Emery, A. and Page, N. R. (1985). Cooperative education and student career identity. *Journal of Cooperative Education*, **21**(3), 20–8.

Keeton, M. T. and Tate, P. (Eds) (1976). *Learning by Experience – What, Why, How?* New Directions for Continuing Education, No. 1. San Francisco: Jossey Bass and CAEL.

Kolb, D. (1984). *Experiential Learning*. Englewood Cliffs, N.J.: Prentice-Hall.

Lewin, K. (1951). *Field Theory in Social Sciences*. New York: Harper and Row.

Marland, S. P., Jr. (1974). *Career Education: A Proposal for Reform*. New York: McGraw-Hill.

National Institute of Education (1984). *Involvement in Learning: Realizing the Potential of American Higher Education*. Study Group on the Conditions of Excellence in American Higher Education. Washington, D.C.: NIE.

Peterson, S. L. and Nelson, M. K. (1986). Learning Model of Experiential Education: A guide for decision making. *Journal of Cooperative Education*, **22**(3), 16–28.

Piaget, J. (1970). *Genetic Epistemology*. New York: Columbia University Press.

Tennyson, W., Klaurens, M. K. and Hansen, L. S. (1980). *Education and Work Competencies Needed by Experiential Education Personnel: A Program for Teachers and Counselors*. Falls Church, Virginia: National Vocational Guidance Association.

Wriston, H. M. (1987). As quoted in *The Teaching Professor*, **1**(7), 4.

11

Coming To Know: A Personal Experience

Julie Wylde

Originally a letter to us, Wylde conveys for us the essence of the title of the section: 'Coming to Know'. The letter reveals how she has come to recognize the significance of learning that derives directly from her life experience as opposed to that derived from externally received learning. The letter encapsulates Belenky et al. (1986), to which we refer in Chapter 22, at two critical levels. First, beyond received knowledge on their spiral of ways of knowing, is the emergence of 'subjective knowledge': that is, a perspective from which truth and knowledge are conceived as personal, private, subjectively known or intuited. Secondly, the leap to 'constructed knowledge', in which women view knowledge as contextual; experience them-selves as creators of knowledge; 'and value both subjective and objective strategies for knowing' (ibid.) Wylde conveys a deep sense of the meaning of her personal knowledge. As the reader you are invited to compare Wylde's experience with your own. The question may also be raised as to how such learning would be accredited for higher education outcomes? If it were deemed invalid, on whose criteria and on what criteria? (see also O'Reilly, Chapter 9). Wylde provides a living example of how personal stance (Salmon, Chapter 21) influences our experience of any formal curriculum.

The journey I took through my research into experiential learning was a hard, long and bitter one.

As a child I was told to swallow nasty things because they were good for you, but the savour of old stomach-wrenching potions lives on, and now my stomach heaves at the sight of a doctor's prescription. And so it was with experiential learning. The reason I cannot write lucidly about the process of carrying out my research into this area is that I feel nauseous re-experiencing the bitter emotions that snared me throughout – the anguish, anger, confusion, self-doubt, sadness and hopelessness.

Because my own road was so hard, mine is a small but, to me, precious harvest. It could get lost in a scholarly, and orderly arrangement of words.

Mine are very simple things which no doubt have been said before, but I was blind to their meaning until they became part of me.

Now ripe and juicy fruits of learning tumble into my consciousness as I go about working in the world – with myself and with other people. They taste good and I am sure that there are still some peaches waiting to fall.

For example, I have learnt that it is only possible to use something I have read or heard, if that 'something' connects with my own experiencing. A fact is something that connects with my gut, regardless of whether it is supported by theories and research. Whether or not it is a fact worthy of further exploration and refinement I will trust myself to work out. I have the equipment and I am able to use it.

I have learnt to make a practical working distinction between role-plays and simulations, so often confused in the literature on training. I classify role-plays as 're-enactments of past experiences', and I use them to re-live experiences and gain more insight into past events. I classify simulations as the enactment of fantasies – 'what will happen ifs'. I use them to develop insight into the future.

Finally, I have learnt that I cannot learn when I am tired, confused, angry, or nervous. I cannot experience something new, outside of myself as interesting and challenging, if the interest and challenge is already being channelled towards a quite separate, prior and more powerful internal experience.

It sounds so amazingly obvious doesn't it? It is hardly worth saying. The final thing I have learnt is that life does become more clear and more purposeful when I take responsibility for making up my rules for myself and give up looking over my shoulder, waiting for someone to come up and clap me on the back and say 'That's Right! Here is a prize!' That's all I really want to say.

12

Action Learning: A Vehicle for Personal and Group Experiential Learning

Ian McGill, Susan Segal-Horn, Tom Bourner and Paul Frost

In this chapter, McGill et al. *discuss their own experience of a particular form of experiential learning – 'action learning' – originally developed by Revans (1980). The authors examine how this methodology can provide a focus for people working together to explore their personal development needs and objectives. The essence of this group's application of action learning is that no one person functioned as the facilitator. For instance, the structure, time management, and the balance between achieving goals ('task') and maintaining effective group relationships ('process') was managed cooperatively by the group itself. The authors give the background to the group's forming. The setting is an academic department where considerable innovation, based on an experiential learning philosophy and methodology, is taking place. The initial motivation for establishing the action learning set came from an awareness that students were being asked to work more experientially; some staff felt that they too could use this form of experiential learning as a means of extending their own understanding about such learning, for team building, and for problem solving. The set thus meets not just personal development, but also staff development, needs and interests. The authors discuss the procedures traditionally involved in action learning, and ways in which they adapted these for their own purposes. They also describe the learning and group processes, and the values and norms, which characterized their 'experiment'. They conclude by identifying key outcomes that came out of the action learning process over the 6 months of their first round of meetings.*

Readers may wish to read this chapter alongside Wildemeersch (Chapter 5), in terms of dialogue, Boud (Chapter 3), in terms of autonomy, Hutton (Chapter 4), in terms of learning from action, and Packham (Chapter 13), with regard to staff development strategies to support organizational change. They might also like to consider the processes described in relation to the perspectives offered by Brah and Hoy (Chapter 6) and Salmon (Chapter 21).

Introduction

Action learning has its origins in the pioneering work of Reg Revans (1980), and its primary use has been for organizations as a means of promoting management and project development. Our interest is in developing action learning in much wider contexts as we consider this approach to learning is a very effective one. At a personal level it can promote learner autonomy. In group and community contexts the action learning approach provides its users with an accessible form of effective group working. Accessible is meant in the sense that it does not require expertise that is difficult to attain. In higher education course programmes it can be the core basis for personal and group learning. The approach can enable learning to be experienced as an enhancing, shared and cooperative process where issues of difference arising from gender, race, sexuality and disability can be acknowledged and struggled with. Thus action learning can also create a supportive framework for change and innovation.

To appreciate how this can be achieved it is helpful to define action learning as we use it – a means by which people learn with and from each other by attempting to identify, and then implement, solutions to their problems/issues/ opportunities. This definition lays emphasis on progressing tasks that are problematic but may embrace a much wider set of learning needs, retaining the emphasis on implementation and cooperative endeavour.

Traditional action learning also utilizes an external facilitator or adviser who may reduce her or his role as the group develops. We are interested in the practice of non-facilitated (or self-managed) action learning groups or 'sets' as they are sometimes called, within or outside institutional contexts.

The background

The potential of action learning was first considered at the Brighton Polytechnic, England, as a result of the development of a part-time postgraduate Masters research programme. Research into alternative learning methods suggested that action learning provided a promising vehicle for research degrees in management aimed at part-time students. However, it rapidly became clear that action learning could be used much more widely than this. It offered staff, as well as students, a means of addressing and learning from their own concerns and problems. Consequently, as part of the process of building up an experienced team for the Masters course and in the spirit of learning from doing, an interested group of staff began meeting as an action learning set.

At its formation the set comprised five persons: four with academic and one with administrative responsibilities; three men and two women; ages ranged from 32 to 47; white and able-bodied. The only common denominator deliberately built in at the beginning was that each person had a specific responsibility which placed additional work demands on them and their relationship to the institution and their colleagues. It was from these 'additional demands' that the set members drew their initial problem statements for the tasks they wished to work on with the set.

Procedures

From the outset there were three important ways in which this set differed from the traditional notion of an action learning set as developed by Revans. First, action learning sets in organizations tend to have a 'client' outside the set to whom the set members are responsible for the progress of the task or problem. Although we were each working on real problems directly pertinent to our job responsibilities, we did not have a client. Secondly, and in our view most importantly, we decided to work without a set adviser – we would do that task ourselves. Thirdly, we set up our particular group voluntarily. While all working in the same organization the set was not formally recognized by the organization.

We all knew each other as colleagues in the Polytechnic but not very closely. One of our set wanted to get experience of the process of operating a set before he implemented the Masters course. He felt strongly that as the process was an integral part of the course and distinct from traditional approaches to teaching and learning in higher education, that by doing it himself he could best learn how it worked! He approached colleagues whom he thought would have some empathy with him and the idea, and five agreed to start the set. This followed some initial reading on action learning (Pedler, 1983; Revans, 1980). From our first meeting onwards, however, it was apparent the set had no wish for 'expert' input and that much of the interest of set members was in constructing a model that suited our needs. All of those who agreed to start the set were interested in how a set would work as well as wanting to resolve a 'knotty' issue. Thus set members had a concern for their task and a concern for the process by which the set worked.

At the first meeting, procedures and ground rules were established regarding the life expectancy of the set, frequency and duration of meetings, time allocation at meetings, the issue of confidentiality, note-taking and time-keeping. Time was high on the agenda: we all had very full working and home lives and time was the major constraint on our willingness to commit to this new activity. It constituted the clearest 'cost' in agreeing to participate in the set.

For the inaugural meeting, members had agreed to provide a one-page summary of the problem or issue they wished to work on, including objectives, perceived barriers and possible solutions. Eight meetings were agreed over a period of 6 months. All of the dates and times of the meetings were fixed by mutual agreement at the first meeting and then adhered to rigidly. One of the most influential conventions to emerge was that meetings once fixed would not be set aside for any other demand which arose subsequently. It was also a convention that should anyone cause a meeting to be rescheduled, they must accept responsibility for organizing its replacement.

Meetings were to last 2 hours. At each meeting time was allocated in the ratio 2:1:1:1:1, with the double allocation rotating among members in turn. Note-taking by one member at each meeting was confined to amendments or additions to ground rules and recording the 'contract' of each member for the next meeting. A rota for note-taking and time-keeping was established. Time-keeping was strictly adhered to: set meetings started and finished on time. Information exchanged at set meetings was to be treated as totally confidential. The confidentiality rule was elaborated further at later meetings to permit information (possibly of a very personal nature) acquired outside the set, to be used openly inside. This was a particularly delicate issue, since the set comprised individuals who were colleagues, and whose personal and professional relationships would continue outside the set and after the set was disbanded. The decision to allow such information to be used was an important step in the development of the set. It reinforced the growing climate of trust and openness.

Two special full-day meetings were included for a half-way review and final evaluation. Each of these day sessions proved to be significant events leading to both qualitative and directional changes. The half-way review session was begun by giving positive feedback to each other. This took the form of each member identifying three qualities that they appreciated about each of the other members of the set. It was hoped that this would help to sustain morale during a gruelling day; but it provided an additional longer-term benefit in fixing the set as a place of positive reinforcement. The second full day was the final evaluation meeting of the set, for which each member had agreed to provide their own assessment of the costs and benefits of the action learning experience. The substance of that day led directly to the analysis on which this paper is based.

Processes

In a group with no set adviser, all facilitating of set activity and learning is in the hands of the members themselves. For this reason, the process skills which were used within the group were of extreme importance in the fulfilment of tasks and survival of the set. Some of the more important group processes are outlined, as these are critical to the success of a set. Success is defined here in terms of achieving outcomes satisfactory to individual members and to the effective maintenance and coherence of the set over its life.

For each person, personal commitment to the set and the way it worked was a priority. Being at the set was very important compared to other activities associated with our work. This generated a feeling of protectiveness towards the time of the set. Something that required so much effort to protect and sustain could not fail to attain significance. It was simultaneously both a discipline and a space to breathe, and consider ourselves and how we lived in our busy lives. The fact that one member came to view the set meetings as of decreasing personal and professional relevance, by contrast highlighted what the meetings represented to the other set participants. The position of this member will be returned to.

We gained support from each other. There was a sense of effort and fair exchange in the time, advice, and attention of others each received. While it was generally felt that the members of the set uncritically supported each other, one member did not feel that the set was supportive in its questioning. This member gradually withdrew from the set giving lack of time as the reason, having attended five of the eight meetings. No specific statement of resignation was received. Yet the other set members felt that the three successive apologies for absence were a resignation, and were perhaps more clearly aware of this than the absent member. On a couple of occasions the rest of the group discussed how it had 'failed' its colleague, until talking this through gave rise to the perception that 'succeeding' or 'failing' was not something in the gift of the set; it was something individuals could only do for themselves. The others in the group did take responsibility for endeavouring to maintain this member in the group. The lasting question is whether the remaining members could have done more to ascertain the differences in outlook between them and the departing member.

We confronted each other in a supportive way. This was not an encounter group. Nobody was to be *made* to face up to anything about themselves. The questions posed would enable an individual to reflect constructively on their situation. For example, one question posed to the first author was what would be the impact of a particularly taxing work programme upon his personal relationship with his partner, something he had unwittingly not considered. He had made assumptions as a man about the work overriding the partnership and the needs of and impact upon his partner. At about the same time he had been addressing his sexism and his relations with women, yet had not thought through that in relation to those closest to him. The set brought the issue to him in the closest way. That simple question certainly enabled a subjective confrontation to take place as well as reflecting upon and acting on sexism in the wider sense.

The questions could just be listened to and then thought about privately afterwards. The set always explored 'Why? What for? Is that really the best way? Is that really what you want?' The emphasis was on constructive discussion of alternative ways forward. Set members had different backgrounds and lives and the problems brought to the group were different. However, there were so many threads in common, that the situation of the other was very real. A frequent comment referred to the realization, 'that I am not alone in this organization in terms of my concerns and ideas'.

Listening was one of the most important things we all did for each other. People became increasingly generous of their time and attention to others, realizing that listening and learning are linked. It became clear that we were learning about ourselves and our tasks while listening to the others. It may be that this is what is at the heart of all support groups, and this action learning set was definitely a support group in Reg Revans' sense of 'comrades in adversity'. One of the set described this process as 'relieving oppressions'.

The climate of developing trust was the groundwork on which everything was laid. Set members who had been working colleagues and strangers, often for some years, evolved a genuine intimacy once the set had established itself as open, non-competitive and non-threatening.

Caring as a form of positive reinforcement to each other was a key feature. The concern of others let us be kinder to ourselves. Often when exploring and analysing the self, we are only able to be critical. Being positive about ourselves seemed to require the participation of others: 'Caring for each other: this emerged slowly and was unexpected in its depth', as one of our set put it.

The set worked. It was effective. Tasks that seemed daunting initially progressed; objectives were achieved or reviewed. It cannot be emphasized too strongly that success at the task itself was part of the process that welded the set together and gave it purpose. The set was not just a talking shop. Working contracts were made and we all felt the obligation to meet them, meeting by meeting. They gave a clear sense of purpose. At the same time, meeting or failing to meet the contract was not the responsibility of the set, but of the individual. The contract was to help the person not the set. However, the growing sense of loyalty to the group and its expectations often led the individual to do better for the set than they would for themselves.

Values and norms

From the preceding account, certain formal, explicit values emerged:

- confidentiality (within the set);
- priority (of the set);
- openness;
- commitment;
- self-discipline;
- equality: leadership without leaders means that task and maintenance functions are the responsibility of every member.

A corresponding set of implicit norms grew more slowly to underpin the distinctive culture of the set:

- trust;
- caring for each other;
- protective yet challenging towards each other;
- encouraging risk-taking;
- non-prescription, that is not saying what a person 'ought' to do;
- loyalty to the set and each other;
- effort: 'by contrast, think of how you behave in other meetings of whatever kind';
- an imperative to action after each meeting;
- recognition and use of each other's skills: 'I was surprised at my intuition in respect of others in the group';
- clarity and tenacity towards the explicit values;
- an intellectual interest in the process;
- the bringing of gifts (e.g. bottles of wine, fruit, etc.);
- success: 'tasks have been accomplished'; 'enjoyment'; 'more control over my life'; 'learning more about me'; 'learning more about the others';
- acknowledgement of difference: we did not necessarily have the same values and attitudes to our lives outside the set.

In attempting to distil a more general value framework from this experience, three features, which although possibly relevant in facilitated sets, were identified as essential for the success of a non-facilitated set. First, egalitarianism as an approach to relations and commitment within the set are especially necessary for non-facilitated sets where there is no formal or informal leader. Secondly, responsibility for the total activity rests with all the participants. Non-facilitated sets have an advantage in this respect beyond the voluntary participation and mutual agreement on procedures common to all action learning sets. This shared responsibility may be a factor in the fairly rapid growth of strong personal ties within the set, which in turn contribute towards integration and task achievement. Thirdly, an empathy toward the process is essential by all who participate in it. This is not to deny differences between set members.

Outcomes

The considerations below were the result of explicit reflection about the way in which the set operated towards the end of its first round of meetings. We wanted to draw upon the experience, learn and record what it was about our process that would be useful in the future of this and other sets.

Initially, members of the set had three types of misgivings about the activity. First, and dominating everything else, were time costs. Secondly, there was a concern about the ability to manage our continuing relationships as colleagues in the future. Thirdly, was some straightforward scepticism about the point of it all. Instead, as one of the set recalled, 'a turnaround of anticipated perceptions occurred'.

The first great discovery was that although each member of the set period-ically suffered severe stress over pressure of time, the anticipated time costs of participation in the set disappeared. Instead, set meetings were energizing and motivating. A theme which emerged more and more strongly for us was the notion that energy can be substituted for time. The set generated its own list of things that generated energy, and top of the list was set meetings. Others included finishing something; feeling good about yourself; having spoken to friends that you trust. As one of us said: 'The group released energy and it felt good afterwards for individuals.'

Secondly, as far as working relationships were concerned in and outside the set, membership of the set certainly influenced the behaviour of its members. One way of grouping the types of influences and the learning that arose from them is to use the three types of outcome proposed by Hackman (1976): informational, affective, behavioural:

1. *Informational outcomes* involved input to member's beliefs and knowledge:

- facts about each others' lives;
- similarities in the problems we faced;
- things other people knew about and could either tell us or help us with.

2. *Affective outcomes* involved impact on members' attitudes, values and emotions:

- its okay to talk about yourself;
- its okay to get things wrong;
- its safe to trust other people.

3. *Behavioural outcomes* concerned impact on the individual and social behaviour in the group:

- bringing and sharing gifts;
- expressing affection feels good;
- pleasure in company and small rituals.

By all these means the experience of the set qualitatively changed and deepened our working relationships. One visible outcome has been a series of initiatives in short-course, workshops and new course developments pioneered by set members in cooperation with each other, building directly on the shared knowledge and understanding gained in the set.

It is important to convey that while the set worked for us it did so often because it was uncomfortable. A participant could well have been in the midst of a silence in the set when s/he was struggling with an 'unpalatable' reality about themselves (like the example above of the impact of a work programme on the set member's relationship with his partner and his sexism), or an uncertainty about their sense of purpose or why they had been avoiding something. Here is learning at its most critical, where disjuncture in the person's way of seeing reality is at issue. In these situations it was important that the others in the set did not collude in order to keep the individual 'safe'. It was often messy and exposing but not embarrassing because of the overall parameters of confidentiality and trust.

Scepticism at the start of the set's life was in a very short time replaced by commitment, and is best expressed directly:

> The real thing for me is that I could not imagine my original agenda now; the hidden agenda has been isolation in the working environment – feeling alone and not being able to talk about it. The group gave support to me for the real concerns, and I had a sense of this function for all of us.

> Significant impact and push in the early sessions turned round my attitudes, followed by a change away from the task to an outlet for the major disruptions in my life.

The effectiveness of the set consisted in revealing the connections between tasks and the person doing them, often most importantly to the person themselves. When asked to evaluate costs and benefits of membership of the set, costs were largely unspecified while benefits were many and clearly perceived. They can be grouped under the following four headings: group support; self-discovery; learning about others; task development and completion. The benefits were effective because they were linked:

> I gained support for my task but also for reflection on the essentials: relationships, work, the rest of life and the need for balance.

It is necessary to note the problem of causality: Were these causal or correlative relationships? What difference did it make having the set?:

> It's been useful but I would have done the life changes anyway. However it is difficult to dissociate the life changes from the workings of the group.

> Task completed. It would have been anyway but not as well and with more pain. The set provided useful traction.

> More control over my life – cannot say how much was due to the set.

Simple recurrence of the theme tends to the view that it cannot all be coincidental.

To the genuine surprise of members of the set, the early task orientation very soon gave way to a concern with process and person:

> The manifest function was quickly replaced by the latent function, that is, a framework for exploring the self and others.

> We got beyond the initial issues to the real matters.

What this meant was that issues which started off as task issues, like getting a new course developed and implemented, tended to reveal themselves as personal development issues as discussion progressed.

The shift to more reflective and personal development themes that emerged 'behind' the initial task may have been a result of the stage most of us were in in our working careers. We had a good deal of work experience in and out of higher education and were at an integrative stage in our lives. The significance of the stage in the life-cycle has been noted elsewhere in the literature of experiential learning. Kolb (1984) has expressed the relationship with sensitivity:

> The developmental model of experiential learning theory holds that specialization of learning style typifies early adulthood and that the role demands of career and family are likely to reinforce specialization. However the pattern changes in mid-career . . . Perhaps it is inevitable that specialization precede integration in development, inevitable that youth be spent in a search for identity in the service of society, until in a last reach for wholeness we grasp that unified consciousness that has eluded us.

Conclusions

It is difficult to suggest prescriptive generalizations for all non-facilitated sets, from a specific experience. We started two further rounds of meetings and simultaneously each started new sets with other colleagues in the Polytechnic. It is only appropriate to state what worked for us. One factor emerged as critical: a common value framework and empathy about the process (whatever the content). Without these it is unlikely that sufficient bonding and trust would have been generated to enable the set to achieve for its members. Moreover, we did not detect resentment from colleagues who were not members of the sets. This was partly because our meetings were not a formal part of the Polytechnic structure. Secondly, that those who did think the sets a good idea were able to join the new sets.

A limitation which we have since learnt is that we took perhaps too much for granted about what was common among us (and in the process made assumptions about our backgrounds and experience). It is critical to encompass differences of personal experience among set members such as gender and race, as well as the impact of these differences in wider contexts of prevailing oppressions. Commitment to self-growth, development and change is enhanced in this process.

Two other factors which have already been mentioned in the discussion are of sufficient importance to return to here. The set was successful; it worked. It was not just a talking-shop or a support group. Action as well as learning was taking place, although of a more complex sort than originally envisaged. Tasks were progressed or completed, but as part of a larger agenda of developing needs. Lastly, the absence of a set adviser was experienced as an advantage. It made the set totally responsible for its own learning from the outset and hastened the growth of intimacy which made the shared learning possible. The non-facilitated style seems particularly appropriate for a reflective action learning set.

In a wider context, some of us are now organizing courses with action learning sets as the core vehicle for learning by students engaged on the courses. These are led by staff acting in the role of set advisers, though it is recognized as a role in which the aim is to become expendable as the set members acquire the facilitating skills. The action learning process is part of the wider task of shifting towards student-centred learning and is an excellent example of how learners can take ownership of their own learning. Action learning sets also lend themselves to project-based learning and can be used for individual and group projects. The approach has contributed to our personal development but also to our development as practitioners of experiential learning in higher education. Finally, the approach lends itself to community-based learning as a focus for effective group working.

References

Hackman, J. R. (1976). Group influences on individuals. In Dunnette, M. D. (Ed.), *Handbook of Industrial and Organisational Psychology*. Chicago: Rand McNally.
Kolb, D. A. (1984). *Experiential Learning*. Englewood Cliffs, N.J.: Prentice-Hall.
Pedler, M. (Ed.) (1983). *Action Learning in Practice*. London: Gower.
Revans, R. (1980). *Action Learning*. London: Blond and Briggs.

Part 3

Creating New Possibilities
for Learning

3. Perspectives

In academic worlds, there is this hierarchy of theory over practice and I see experiential learning as a way of breaking that down. It sets up something that is more equal and develops people in new ways. I think many of us come to experiential learning through our own experience, and struggles with wider problems.

Issues of assessment and accreditation of experiential learning enable academics to see how naked their own understanding of assessment is and it raises very fundamental questions. For example, what is a programme? What is coherence? What is progression? These questions have to be addressed and answered, and the process and the understanding within institutions will change – but it won't happen dramatically or overnight.

I think it is critically important to create institutional diversity and, by accrediting experiential learning, get new kinds of students coming into your institution with new kinds of experience. Some of the empowerment that comes from validating how much they know can make them something of a force for change. Their presence provides you with a continuing infectious mechanism to keep working with academics and departments.

Experiential learning is about empowering the student to challenge the educational system, and how knowledge is prepackaged. They force us to recognize that the ways we see the world are not *their* ways. They start to teach us. The thing is, can *we learn* from the experience?

One of the things that most of us have glibly accepted is that any learning that takes place experientially in some way has to be formally approved, accredited or given some sort of seal of approval. This is almost a contradiction to where true experiential learning should lead. We mustn't create a myth around experiential learning.

Experiential learning can empower. Empowerment means being able to take on an educational system or speak to power and shaking it to your own motives and own purposes.

13

Our Faculty Goes Experiential

Roger Packham, Roger Roberts and Richard Bawden

Institutionally in higher and continuing education, the introduction of experiential learning approaches and methods tends to be incremental, with its advocates initiating new ideas on the margin of mainstream and traditional approaches. Packham and colleagues take us through the process by which an institution, its staff and students, planned and implemented change with experiential learning as the core mode and philosophy on all course programmes. The authors confront the political issues arising from this degree of change and how support is won; how effective orientation is critical for students in the early stages of the programme; how experiential learning in one area of the course impacts on others; and how the changes implemented were integral to a systems relationship with the wider community (in this case, the agricultural community). They reflect upon their own experience of this profound change and the need for continuing staff development. They cite the importance of staff learning what it means to be effective facilitators of learning and of student involvement in assessment. They also discuss the structural changes required to make the organization of the college empathetic with the experiential approach. They provide a 'new paradigm' perspective (see Chapters 4 and 22) in relation to action-based project learning embracing Kolb (1984) and systems theory in particular. The institution and the 'model' continues to develop! Their approach may be contrasted with Stanton and Giles (Chapter 17), Nelson (Chapter 10) and Peterson (Chapter 16), where forms of experiential learning are being introduced in more traditional contexts. This chapter might also be considered in the context of issues raised by Brah and Hoy (Chapter 6) and Salmon (Chapter 21). Finally, McGill et al.'s (Chapter 12) discussion of action learning as a vehicle for self-managed staff development is relevant here.

For 10 years the Faculty of Agriculture at Hawkesbury Agricultural College, Australia, has been developing experiential programmes, experientially. We have been creating changes based on conceptual explorations of what we experience. This perforce is a process of continual evolution: we experience, we observe, we conceptualize, we act and we reflect; we also change as the environment about us changes. We are thus strong supporters of the model developed by Kolb (1984), embracing the concepts of Dewey (1910), Lewin (1951), Piaget (1952) and Bruner (1966) – although this is *not* where we started. The start was a strong desire to change, to improve our situation both as a Faculty of Agriculture and in respect of the opportunities and competencies of our graduates. However, we had no clear idea of how to achieve this, given the myriad of often conflicting ideas of faculty members and the complex, messy issues of power and politics that have to be researched when introducing innovation and radical change.

Origins of the change

People and organizations can be looked at as continually interacting with their environment. Feelings of curiosity or discomfort with aspects of this environment will lead to change in the person or organization experiencing such feelings. Up until the late 1960s, Hawkesbury Agricultural College had a long period of relative stability. Throughout the 1970s and 1980s, the College as a whole, and the Faculty of Agriculture in particular, has been changing and learning in response to a turbulent environment (Emery, 1977) – in education, agriculture and the region. In the early 1970s, the College moved from offering its own awards independently (Hawkesbury Diploma in Agriculture) to offering centrally accredited awards as part of the College of Advanced Education Sector. An upgrading of the agricultural course was necessary as a result of this, and took the form of more 'in-depth' teaching of technology, on the assumption that graduates would be better able to use this knowledge to 'solve' the problems of agriculture. Bawden *et al.* (1985) have described the problems agriculture was facing during this period. The upgraded programme brought our graduates into direct competition with University graduates, and pressure mounted to upgrade the new diploma to a degree. Considerable disquiet was apparent in the Faculty at this, based on concerns as to what the role of the Faculty and its graduates should be. A review process was started, but this focused on the curriculum, and the collective bargaining that occurred between departments was not providing a way forward, and was proving unsatisfactory for the parties involved.

Richard Bawden was appointed Faculty Head in 1977, and was able to catalyse discussion and debate around a number of issues, but particularly:

1. The State of Australian agriculture from a social as well as a production viewpoint.
2. The nature of learning and how people learn.
3. The systems approach to understanding complexity and managing change.

These debates changed people's appreciative system (Vickers, 1983; Checkland, 1986). Previously, staff were only able to offer technological solutions through a didactic educational paradigm. These new ways of viewing the issues, using a different epistemology, provided a way forward. A vision was established of a new type of graduate, who would take a holistic approach to social and economic aspects of agriculture, as well as to the production aspects. They would be educated using the knowledge gained from research into how people learn, in a learning environment designed to optimize such learning (see Burgess, 1977; Knowles, 1978; Brundage and Mackeracher, 1980; Kolb, 1984). In addition, the epistemology would be based on a systems approach (see Spedding, 1975, 1979; Emery, 1981; Vickers, 1981; and Checkland, 1982).

Having established the vision, the task was now to turn this into functional programmes.

Implementing experiential learning

There was no recognized model for implementing experiential learning about agriculture at institutional level. The programme devised to actively pursue these ideas could not be rigorously planned and implemented since guidelines did not exist to allow such an optimizing solution.

Initially, a set of activities and structures was established to put the change in motion. A group of staff representing a range of disciplines and factional interests pioneered this task, basing the course design and curriculum on what they considered to be appropriate theoretical concepts. They did not all share the same views about what should be achieved or how to do it. It was more a case of strong leadership by a 'few' with a vision which enabled the changes to take place.

This group did not contain the Faculty Head, whose input was only a model of how he thought his vision could be implemented. The group was relieved of teaching duties for only 1 day a week to plan the development, since they were required for the rest of the time to keep existing programmes running. It was originally hoped to plan and start the new course over a year – in fact, it took two. The development was complicated by the fact that not only was the proposed learning process different, but the adopted perception of the competencies of the resultant agriculturalist was also radical. Such changes posed a serious threat to the established values held by a great many individuals and groups who were involved during and after these developments. These included the current students and recent graduates, who saw the new developments as undermining their qualification; staff who saw their traditional roles being removed and no clear guidelines being provided to enable new roles to be developed; the administration of the College, which was being asked to support a new development very much on trust, and which would involve different models of resourcing and administering in as yet unknown ways; and the agricultural community at large, which was being asked to support the development in direct ways by opening up their farms and organizations to students, and indirect ways by helping to get the new programme accredited. The fact that the Faculty goes from strength to strength 10 years later is a testament to the enthusiasm and commitment of a significant proportion of the Faculty in coping with the change themselves, and persuading these other groups to support us, or at least to give us enough rope to hang ourselves!

After initial enthusiasm, the development group reached an impasse, principally created by its attempts to use the Faculty Head's model. The group had examined this model closely, found it unworkable, but did not feel it could reject it. Eventually, this issue was confronted, a new acceptable model developed, and the old one rejected. The group now worked interdependently with the Faculty Head, and a creative and productive process led to the accreditation and introduction of the new course in 1981. However, while an operational plan had been devised, we were still sailing uncharted waters, and much remained to be done. The course has continually changed since it started, based on a particular model of experiential learning and action research (Kemmis and McTaggart, 1988). From that beginning, a range of courses has evolved. While change has been a feature, the underlying concepts, goals and values have remained to provide stability in the Faculty.

Many incoming students, most of whom come straight from secondary school, experience considerable difficulty coping with the change to experiential learning, despite our efforts to forewarn and prepare them. As we gain in experience, however, so this orientation process improves. Empowering them to effectively and efficiently learn experientially and to substantially develop their learning autonomy causes considerable anxiety in the early stages of our programmes. Their development by completion of their programmes, however, is very rewarding to them and to us. It is our view that students with post-school experience develop autonomy faster, and we continue to explore ways of assisting the school leavers to develop as quickly.

The original programme and activities have changed considerably. They have been described in part by Bawden *et al.* (1984) and Bawden and Valentine (1984). Let us now document the current structures and activities of the Faculty, using the degree programme – Batchelor of Applied Sciences (Systems Agriculture) – as the programme example.

Programme structure and activities

It is essential that planned tactical activities have matching structures. Structurally, the programme is based around three phases (periods of two or three semesters of learning between summative assessments), each having a particular thrust but directed to common competency themes of Learning Autonomy, Systems Agriculture and Effective Communication.

The focus is always on real life as the source of the experience for learning. The phases are therefore structured to enable this to occur but with increasing degrees of complexity in the real-life situation, concurrent with increasing student competency – a confluent approach. Students are expected to 'find out about' these situations as a prelude to 'taking action to improve' them.

The initial phase (two semesters, each of 16 weeks) first uses the College farms as the experiential base, but soon extends to add access to the world of agriculture outside. Students (and staff) are constantly encouraged to expand their experience outside the institutional boundary. Assistance to do this is provided by the Faculty through an 'outreach' structure (Lundie-Jenkins *et al.*, 1985) and the individual contacts of staff.

Learning activities for all Phase 1 students for 1988 are summarized in Fig. 13.1. Students will work on these tasks in groups of about 15, together with three staff consultants. Group activity is traditionally resourced through a great variety of inputs from both within and outside the Faculty and the College.

The Personal Action Plan allows students to initiate and incorporate learning activities for themselves. Students in Phase 1 also exercise autonomy in managing the Rural Development Task.

The second phase (three semesters) focuses on the concept of situation-improving for others in a co-learning relationship. To do this successfully is regarded as a competency, critical to becoming a 'Hawkesbury Agriculturalist'. This notion does not need to be confined to agriculture – it could equally apply to a wide range of professions/careers in other institutions or programmes.

In the second phase, the activities of the first stage (one semester) are used to prepare for working and learning in an off-campus situation the following semester (stage 2): this provides a very real experience in which to learn about change to improve agricultural situations. The thrust of this experience is to learn how to explore situations and identify relevant issues with the student's host(s). Students are periodically visited on-site by staff, and they also participate in regional workshops related to expected learning outcomes. The role of off-campus experience has been more fully described by Lundie-Jenkins *et al.* (1985).

In the final stage (one semester) the student is based back on campus, with a brief to pursue agreed situation-improving strategies on behalf of their client/farmer. There is an emphasis here on change and action which is assessed summatively before the student progresses to Phase 3.

Phase 2, as with other phases, is under continuous monitoring and change as we learn to make it more effective and efficient. Among the problems encountered in implementing Phase 2 is that three (mostly discrete) sets of needs and expectations have to be managed primarily by the student. Figure 13.2 attempts

---

1. *Orientation to the Faculty*: emphasis is on the support resources available to the learners.
2. *Personal Action Plan*: development and implementation of a validated individual learning experience.
3. *Farming Task*: learning experientially how to deal with technological issues in agriculture.
4. *Farming Activity Task*: developing a map of the territory of agriculture.
5. *Rural Development Task*: an off-campus group exercise.
6. *Off-campus Agricultural Situation Improving Task*: based on a cooperating farm.

Figure 13.1 A summary of the staff-initiated experiential tasks for degree students.

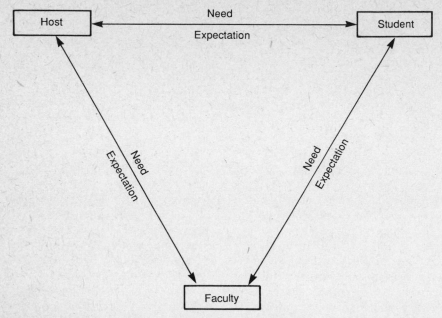

Figure 13.2   The relationship occurring during Phase 2.

to portray this complex relationship. Additionally, a process of 'client' transfer (from Faculty to another) has to take place. In most cases, the student identifies the host as the client for whom the student is intervening.

Greater clarity about situation-improving in this context is developing as we learn from our experiences. One of the authors, R. Roberts, is action-researching this aspect.

Phase 3 (two semesters) requires that learners undertake projects which continue to develop the prescribed competencies. There is freedom of choice on the content of the project and the methodology used. The projects may be undertaken by individual students or by small groups of two or three. A staff member is often one of the learning group. In every case learners are expected to interact regularly with the Faculty. The projects are of a consultancy type, in that there is a 'client' who links the content of the project situation with the student learner(s) who take the role of 'helper' or situation improver(s). We prefer to use the term situation improver rather than problem solver. This is based on the notion that in the type of problematical situations in which our senior students participate, there is no finite solution, because the nature of the problem changes as the environment in which it exists changes. They can only take action to make it better than what it was perceived to be. Because each situation is unique, making changes to improve it has to be largely experientially learned. Figure 13.3 has been developed to assist in the identification of the nature of the situation (problem).

A methodology appropriate to deal with particular types of situations has been incorporated with the spiral as a guide (Fig. 13.4). At each level, the

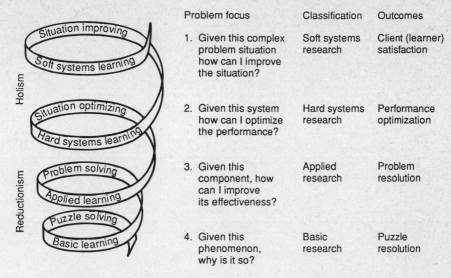

	Problem focus	Classification	Outcomes
	1. Given this complex problem situation how can I improve the situation?	Soft systems research	Client (learner) satisfaction
	2. Given this system how can I optimize the performance?	Hard systems research	Performance optimization
	3. Given this component, how can I improve its effectiveness?	Applied research	Problem resolution
	4. Given this phenomenon, why is it so?	Basic research	Puzzle resolution

Figure 13.3   The Hawkesbury hierarchy of approaches to problem solving and situation improving (after Bawden *et al.*, 1985).

process of learning follows the same experiential cycle. It is the methodologies, techniques and skills used to follow the cycle that differ.

While the activities a student is involved in are initially staff-managed, they become increasingly student-managed. The former are referred to as *tasks*, and the latter as *projects*. By Phase 3, all activities except assessment are student-managed around projects. *Learning projects* have been described by Tough (1971). The anatomy of such a learning project operating in the Faculty is shown in Fig. 13.5 and is based on the learning cycle of Kolb (1984).

At the start, learners try to develop as 'rich' a picture as possible of the situation regarded as problematic. *Diverging* techniques are required here. At some point, analysis of this picture will begin, drawing on methods of *assimilation* to create patterns and themes which begin to provide insights into the problem. Out of the more useful insights will arise a need to *converge* and look for concepts, generalizations and 'answers'. This created knowledge will provide a way forward to improve the situation, which then needs to be tried out in some way in the environment within which the issue was embedded, using processes of *accommodation*. This cycle of learning is not unidirectional, and iterations between the stages will continually occur.

Learners are introduced to a range of techniques to help them with each stage of Kolb's learning cycle, and are encouraged to seek out others of their own. These suggest the range of methodologies a learner might use. Some of these techniques are shown in Fig. 13.6.

Learners are also encouraged to explore their own learning styles – the way they habitually change experiences into meanings, values and strategies. This helps them to identify the strengths and weaknesses of their personal style, as illustrated in Fig. 13.7.

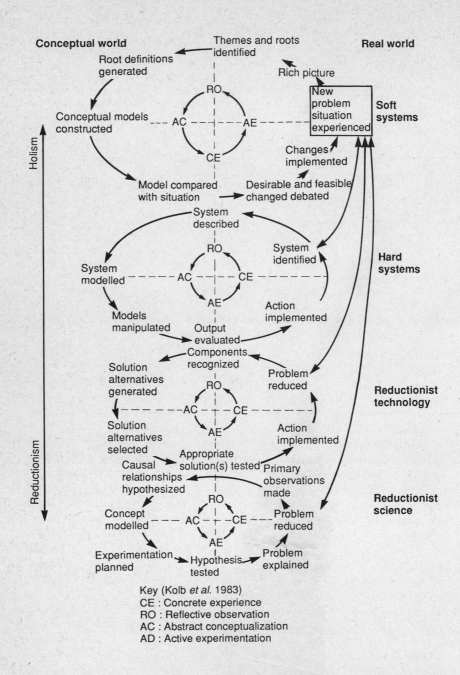

Conceptual world   **Real world**

Themes and roots identified

Root definitions generated   Rich picture

                                               New problem situation experienced   **Soft systems**

Conceptual models constructed   AC — — — AE

                                 RO

                                 CE

Model compared with situation → Desirable and feasible changed debated   Changes implemented

                        System described

                        System identified   **Hard systems**

                        RO

System modelled AC — — — CE

                        AE

Models manipulated   Output evaluated   Action implemented

            Components recognized

Solution alternatives generated   Problem reduced   **Reductionist technology**

                        RO

            AC — — CE

                        AE

Solution alternatives selected   Action implemented

            Appropriate solution(s) tested

Causal relationships hypothesized   Primary observations made

                        RO

Concept modelled AC — CE   Problem reduced   **Reductionist science**

                        AE

Experimentation planned   Hypothesis tested   Problem explained

Key (Kolb *et al.* 1983)
CE : Concrete experience
RO : Reflective observation
AC : Abstract conceptualization
AD : Active experimentation

Figure 13.4 The Hawkesbury spiral of problem-tackling methodologies (after Bawden, 1985).

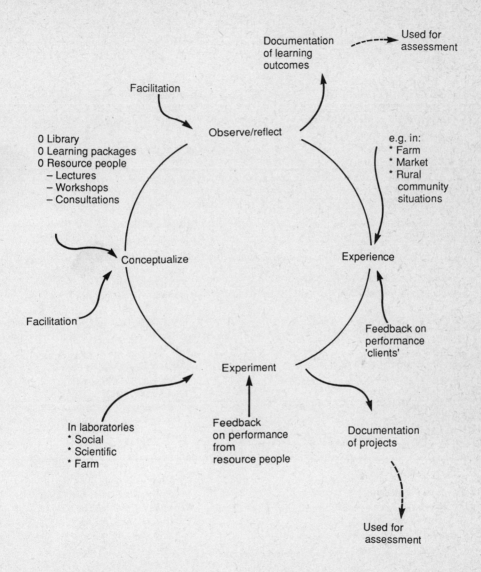

Figure 13.5   The anatomy of an action learning project.

Assimilation
  Force-field analysis
  Mind-mapping
  Root definitions
  Conceptual models
  Game theory
  Hypothesis forming

Divergence
  Brainstorming
  Active listening
  Role-play simulations
  Consciousness-raising
  Synectics
  Browsing literature

Convergence
  Decision trees
  Linear programming
  Validating conceptual models
  Crystal-ball imagery
  Experimenting
  Lateral thinking

Accommodation
  Goal setting
  Consensus seeking
  Implementing change
  Debating
  Critical-path scheduling

Figure 13.6   Some techniques of learning appropriate to activities of the learning cycle.

REFLECTIVE
OBSERVATION

Assimilation
Strength: planning,
  formulating theory
Excess: castles in the air,
  no practical
  application
Deficiency: no theoretical
  basis for work,
  unable to learn
  from mistakes

Divergence
Strength: generation of
  alternatives
Excess: paralysed by
  alternatives

Deficiency: inability to
  recognize problems/
  opportunities,
  ideas poor

ABSTRACT
CONCEPTUALIZATION

CONCRETE
EXPERIENCE

Convergence
Strength: Design,
  decision making
Excess: Premature closure,
  solving the wrong
  problem
Deficiency: No focus to
  work, theories
  not tested,
  poor experimental
  design

Accommodation
Strength: Accomplishment,
  goal-oriented action
Excess: trivial improvements,
  tremendous accomplishment
  of the wrong thing
Deficiency: Work not
  completed on
  time, not
  directed to goals

ACTIVE
EXPERIMENTATION

Figure 13.7   Strengths and weaknesses of different learning sytles (after Carlsson *et al.*, 1979).

Kolb *et al.* (1983) have prepared a learning style inventory to assist people in identifying and learning about their own learning style. However, it should be emphasized that the process is not seen simply as one of acquiring a set of techniques appropriate to each of the four stages of the learning cycle. Different techniques rely on the acquisition of skills, and thus different people will be more or less successful in using them. The techniques themselves need to be combined in a variety of ways to form a number of methodologies, or ways of approaching different problem situations. Four broad classifications of methodologies are presented in Fig. 13.3.

How a person views a particular situation, and the contingent methodology therefore selected, will depend to a large extent on that person's values, beliefs and attitudes; what has been called their world view or *Weltanschauung* by Checkland (1982). It is a key aspect of our programmes that learners are encouraged to look at situations from a variety of perspectives and viewpoints. This concept is presented in Fig. 13.8.

A simple example is 'the problem' of acid soils which has been discussed by Duff *et al.* (1985). This can be looked at as a chemical, ecological, social, economic or political issue, depending on the reason for examining the problem. Thus a number of analyses from different perspectives are often needed. The explorations of science can provide the insights for the action solutions of

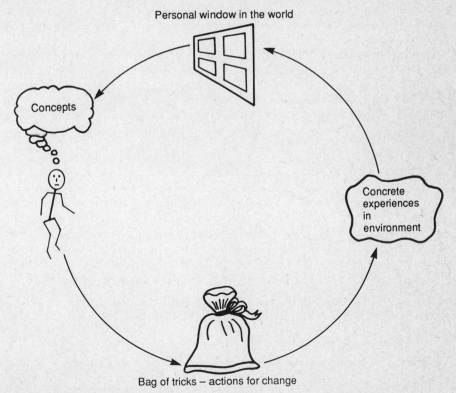

Figure 13.8 The relationship of the situation improved to the problem situation.

technology; these in turn can provide optimal solutions for purposive systems – those with clearly agreed goals; a range of possible solutions provided from such a 'hard' systems analysis can provide opportunities for ways of improving 'soft' socio-technical systems that have no clearly agreed goals. All levels of this spiral of approaches are complementary, and learners are therefore encouraged to use different methodologies on different aspects of the same issue. A similar approach to this has been advocated by Miller (1985). He discusses these issues in the context of environmental problem solving, and uses the terms 'tame' and 'wicked' when describing problem types.

Besides structuring the course into Phases, other structures have been developed to support the learning process. These include the formation of various types of *interest groups*, and the development of a range of learning resources known as *learning packages*.

Interest groups

These can be both formal and informal and are formed for specific purposes. They are a medium whereby students and staff can share ideas, information and experiences by working together on learning projects in a climate of interdependent learning. They may be based on the aim of gaining specialist knowledge, such as animal nutrition, soil science, sheep production, etc.; or around career aspirations such as inter-national rural development, farm management, extension, teaching, etc.

Membership of a learning group is voluntary and selected by the learner. Informal groups often do not have staff as members, although staff may be called on to provide particular resource expertise. Groups may also form to provide a support mechanism for students with similar learning projects. These groups are increasingly using human and physical resources outside the Faculty that they have located.

Learning packages

These are resources and activities that support the experiential learning process. They are designed to make the learning process as efficient as possible. They are usually discrete, of relatively short duration, and available at short notice. Two major categories of learning packages have been defined: those concerned with the *process* of learning; and those concerned with *content* related to agricultural situations. Key elements of learning package provision are:

- Resource material is presented in a form that can be accessed by individuals.
- Material is presented in a variety of formats where feasible.
- Group workshop activities are used where concepts can be highlighted and skills developed.
- Packages often contain laboratory and field-skills training exercises.

These packages provide both for in-depth learning activities, and for activities which contribute to a widening of horizons and a stimulating learning environment, such as seminars, tours, debates, farm walks and visiting lecturers. A particular type of learning package is the printed pamphlet, which focuses on the concept of a particular agricultural area, such as aspects of animal production, farm business management, etc. These are organized by a functional management grouping of the Faculty, known as AGPACK. This group of staff have the responsibility of organizing and requesting the production of an appropriate range of this material to service the needs of learners. Available learning packages are listed on a computer databank available openly, and learning activities and staff movements are listed on a computer information program, know as AGBULL. This lists events as far ahead as possible, and is updated weekly.

While initially timetabling was left open, it has proved necessary to introduce a broad weekly timetable structure to allow efficient use of laboratories, other teaching spaces, support staff and academic staff. The timetable remains as flexible and as open as possible, while attempting to avoid major clashes of interests for students and staff.

Assessment of experiential learning

Both summative and formative assessment is used in the programmes. Summative assessment is conducted at the completion of each phase. This assessment determines whether the learner progresses to the next phase, or in the case of the final phase, whether the student graduates. There is provision for students to repeat phases or to progress conditionally. A learner is considered as being either satisfactory or unsatisfactory in each of the three prescribed competencies. No grades are assigned, but at graduation a 'Merit' award can be made.

Validation of learning is a vital element in the process of learning. Students are expected to take responsibility for this aspect, and not rely on staff to 'examine' them. Validations need to be obtained at various stages in the learning project, as shown in Fig. 13.7. They are provided by the appropriate people, and they refer to different competencies and skills gained by the student. Validations may include:

1. Feedback from the situation explored as to the client's reaction to the learner's approach and any outcomes of the project from their perspective.
2. Reflections by the learner about the methodology used, techniques and skills developed, the process of learning itself, and what the project has meant to the learner in terms of personal growth.
3. Feedback from staff or other resource consultants on their use of particular concepts, methodologies, techniques and skills.
4. Feedback from peers on their role as a group member, or other aspects the peer is qualified to comment on.

Taken together, such validations build up into a package that answers the questions:

- What did I plan to do, and why?

- What happened?
- How did it happen?
- How did I learn?
- What did I learn?
- Where does this lead me?

Periodically, the validations from all learning projects are brought together by the student, and integrated into an application to progress/graduate. It is this document that is presented for summative assessment. The focus is always on competency development, and a competency matrix was developed to provide a guideline for both staff and students in assessment. This matrix (Fig. 13.9) is currently under active review to improve its usefulness.

The progression document is only part of the total summative assessment process. Two staff (three at graduation) will read the document, and then listen to an oral presentation by the student in support of their document. Considerable freedom is allowed in the nature of this presentation, the major constraints being time and space. The panel then makes a recommendation based on the total process (submissions, validations, interview). The whole of the exercise is considered different from the sum of the parts, and the outcome is judged accordingly. At graduation the team of three staff are joined by a relevant external person to ensure community acceptance of the standard of graduate.

At each summative assessment period, small staff teams are established to focus on each programme group of students, or year groups within a programme. These core teams ensure equitability, and make recommendations on outcomes of assessment to the Faculty Board of Examiners.

Formative assessment through validations (feedback and confirmation of desired outcomes) is an ongoing process. It occurs during most learning activities whether they be group or individually pursued, and student-, staff-, or co-managed.

In addition to ongoing validation, a few time slots are put aside for students to present themselves in staff-organized formative assessment sessions. Often students use these opportunities as 'trial summatives'.

Students are particularly expected to respond to formalized feedback received from tasks and projects.

Staff roles in experiential learning

Staff are no longer seen as the sole controllers of learning; neither are they the sole sources of knowledge. Thus the roles staff play have changed, as discussed by Burgess (1977). They can be summarized as follows:

- To provide support to the learner.
- To provide access to resources for learning.
- To provide critical feedback to learners.
- To assist in the management of the Faculty, including student assessment.

Increasingly, staff are meeting these roles by joining with students in action research projects.

To graduate a student must demonstrate evidence of:

	Autonomous learner	Systems agriculturalist	Effective communicator
Affective Attitudinal and value-related elements **Feelings**	1. Desire to learn 2. Commitment to personal development 3. Self-motivation	4. Professional commitment to agriculture 5. Empathy with rural values 6. Social awareness and responsibility to environment 7. Appreciation of and confidence as a systems agriculturalist	8. Sensitivity to and respect for others 9. Appreciation of concepts of leadership 10. Desire to communicate effectively 11. Desire to help
Conative Actualized behaviours and behavioural intentions **Doings**	12. Situation improving/problem solving 13. Experiential learning 14. Information accessing 15. Effective learning 16. Critical evaluation	17. Situation improving in agricultural systems 18. Accessing appropriate agricultural information 19. Operating, allocating and innovating in agricultural systems	20. Effectively communicating 21. Translating and communicating relevant information 22. Helping others to learn 23. Providing effective leadership
Cognitive Intellectual elements **Thinkings**	24. Effective processes of learning 25. Self-concept development 26. Conceptualization skills 27. Information field development 28. Creativity 29. Critical thinking abilities	30. Development of information base 31. Conceptual development of relevant 'maps' of agricultural systems 32. Systems perspectives and contingency views 33. Perceptions of the Hawkesbury intellectual map	34. Models of the process of communication 35. Interpersonal relationships 36. Helping relationships 37. Leadership models

Figure 13.9 The competency matrix for the degree programme (from Bawden and Valentine, 1984).

Staff also act as facilitators of learning to a nominated number of students. Staff will meet with these students both individually and in groups. As facilitators, staff try to foster interdependent learning activities between members of all groups in which they operate, encouraging the expression of the different competencies of group members. In this way staff aim to help groups to achieve the goals set out in Fig. 13.10.

The change to facilitating, rather than directing learning, has not been easy for staff. From the outset, emphasis has been placed on staff development activities to support this area. Staff have had the opportunity to attend workshops and discussions with many 'experts' or resource people in this area. Models of facilitation have been examined, including those of Rogers (1969), Heron (1975), Burgess (1977) and Knowles (1978). The six-category intervention analysis model of Heron (1975) has proved particularly useful, but staff are encouraged to develop their own personal styles.

In providing access to resources, staff will raise the awareness of students as to what resources are available within their own area of expertise, or where to go for other resource needs. They play a role in initiating interest groups, as described above. Staff have a major role in the design and conduct of learning packages, as also described above. One of the outcomes of the development of these has been the need for staff to reflect on, and distil out, the concepts of their various discipline areas. This is generally accomplished by a team of staff drawn from a particular discipline area interacting with academic communities outside the College (see, e.g. Turnbull and Gamble, 1986). Finally, as resource people, staff will act as consultants to individuals and groups on learning projects within their scope of expertise.

Staff provide written validations to learners whenever appropriate. All staff participate in the periodic assessment of students' progress: this is organized at Faculty level to ensure equitability of staff loads. Other aspects of critical feedback are given during facilitation.

The last role staff play is in the management of the Faculty. All staff are involved to some degree, either as a member of a programme management team, or in the management of one of the functions supporting the programmes. These are discussed below, but include such aspects as laboratory organization, learning package development, and staff development. Task force groups frequently develop to deal with unease about structure and/or process. Leader-

---

1. To identify the learning goals and learning strengths and weaknesses of group members.
2. To improve the effectiveness of members as autonomous learners in achieving these goals.
3. To improve members' abilities to communicate effectively.
4. To improve the way by which they help others to learn.
5. To improve the effectiveness of their group as an interdependent learning system.
6. To provide opportunities for the validation of competencies, and feedback on performance.

Figure 13.10   Goals of learning facilitation.

ship of these functions is provided by staff, either elected by the Faculty, or appointed by these elected leaders: leadership is not only dependent on academic rank.

In all their activities, staff are encouraged to act as role models for students in the processes of experiential learning and action research. They work with students in such projects that are of interest to them, that traditionally would not have involved students. An example is outlined below, which concerns the organizational restructuring of the Faculty (Macadam *et al.*, 1985). Often out of such projects new management functions and roles emerge and staff may voluntarily pursue these as managers for undefined periods.

Organizational structure

As learning activities require matching enabling structures, an organization needs to have an effective management structure to perform its activities.

The introduction of the changes outlined above led to a sense of unease among staff and students regarding the way the Faculty was meeting the needs of the new programmes. Relatively minor adjustments were made to the Faculty structure when a clear mismatch between needs and resources emerged, but the basic hierarchical, discipline-based, traditional academic organizational structure remained. There was an awareness of a need for radical change to occur, but the complexity of the issues meant that a way forward was not obvious. An action research process was launched by the Faculty, led by two senior Faculty staff members and a small group of interested senior students. The soft-systems methodology of Checkland (1982) was used, and the outcome was a total restructuring of the Faculty. This has been described by Macadam *et al.* (1985). Repercussions from this subsequently led to a more general reorganization of academic management throughout the College as a whole. The key feature of the reorganization was that it was along functional, rather than departmental (discipline-of-knowledge) lines. A conceptual model of the Faculty as an education system was developed in order to help identify the key functional areas. These were then organized along two dimensions:

1. The programmes of the Faculty, both formal and informal.
2. The organization of functions and resources to support these programmes.

Organizational management theory was used in the development of these models and practices, including ideas proposed or described by Emery (1977), Kast and Rosenzweig (1978), Beer (1981) and Kolb *et al.* (1983). Some of the concepts used included:

- An organic, rather than bureaucratic structure.
- A flat rather than steep pyramid of control.
- Operational management units to be small, with high unit autonomy.
- Much opportunity to be provided for communication among, and contributions from each, staff member.
- Sharing of values and objectives.

- Continuous learning about, and resultant rearrangement of functions (as opposed to prescription through 'standing orders', and only rearrangement of parts).

It is felt that these organizational structural changes have allowed the Faculty to stabilize at a higher (or meta-) level, and have been a critical component of overall Faculty development. Without them, the new programmes could not have been sustained. Three of the most important functional areas to emerge were those of learning package development, staff development and outreach. It is difficult to envisage how these activities could have evolved and been managed under a departmental structure.

Reflections

As reflective practitioners (Schön, 1983) we continually reflect on our programmes in an attempt to improve them. In writing this paper, we have drawn together some of these reflections relating to the overall developments of the last 10 years. A key outcome for us was a recent quote from one of our cooperating farmers, who had recently hosted a student during Phase 2 of the programme. The student had conducted a learning project with the farmer to improve a problem. The farmer said: 'Most students come here and give us an answer, yours ask us questions with humility!' It is not only farmers that students get to think critically, since it is the students that have continually led programme developments by their feedback and questions: the theoretical base described in this paper followed the experiences. Student projects have become more complex and more deeply concerned with issues beyond the farm gate. Recent groups have worked with the National Farmers Federation in organizational development, helping farm families troubled by the so-called rural crisis, and with the Grain Legume Association on how to improve its role and functions. Such projects usually involve 'vacation' time work for the students, and create different relationships between Faculty, students and the rural community. This is consistent with the recent Government green paper on tertiary education (Dawkins, 1988).

The role of staff in the projects is often to 'model' the 'desired' response of students, but also to link experiences into underlying theory. Staff have moved from the traditional reductionist science model to an action research process model: researching with people (as clients) rather than researching on or on behalf of people. This has not been easy or comfortable for many, and has resulted in a degree of polarization in the Faculty. This tends to exhibit itself in the issue of workload, with staff committed to the new approach being busy, but coping, while others find the workload a major problem and are dependent on senior staff to set priorities. Staff operate as teams, and can no longer rely on their independent authority in a lecture setting. They are more accessible to colleagues and students, and need to carefully manage this access to prevent students being in their rooms all the time. However, staff are able to develop action research programmes with students and other agricultural bodies as mentioned above.

A metaphor that has developed to describe staff and student involvement in the process is that of 'learning to swim'. People are not thrown in the deep end and left to survive or drown! They are given instruction on the side. They see others swimming in the pool, and they are encouraged in when they feel able. Some start at the shallow end, where they can touch the bottom, but all have to get into the deep end. Some feel that the water is cloudy, so when they come in they find staff that they thought were swimming were really touching the bottom! Some students wonder who is teaching whom (or saving whom from drowning!). This use of metaphors and models is common in many aspects of our programmes, and helps us establish our theories-in-use (Argyris and Schön, 1978). Papers that we have written have described the models we have developed, and have helped us to pass on these ideas to others (e.g. Macadam and Bawden, 1985; Packham and Bawden, 1985; in addition to others cited earlier).

Another key reflection is how we have moved from an initial concern with the curriculum alone to encompassing, in addition, the outreach concept of locating students on farms. This concept itself has expanded to one of facilitating student interaction with the rural community. This led us to the facilitiation of action research (Reason and Rowan, 1981). Not only is this exhibited in how we educate, but also in how the programmes themselves keep developing. Such action research is itself a reflection of experiential learning, on which the programmes were originally based. Again this demonstrates how we have moved from anecdote to theory as we develop, and that is what we also demand of our students. This search for theory has now led us to focus on epistemology. Starting from a content-based programme we moved to one that considered process as well (Parker and Rubin, 1973). This has further developed to expose the different epistemologies of staff, and a critical review is occurring within workshops in the Faculty: we have come to realize that this is central to the way the Faculty approaches the servicing of the academic needs of our programmes. This debate is itself an example of how we operate, with a focus on the process of innovating, rather than the concept of innovation. The use of verbs, rather than nouns, in this way has been proposed by Checkland (1982) as an aid to creative problem solving and strategic thinking.

A final reflection is that the programme continues to evolve. All is not 'right' at the moment – we doubt it ever will be! The current focus is on the need to improve our resourcing and learning packages to better convey an understanding of science and technology. We are developing small bays to replace traditional large laboratories where students can get access to practical science work as the need arises. Examples include soil or feed analysis, plant identification, parasite monitoring, etc. The programmes are also extending outwards via the action research model. Links are forming with other institutions, and other courses are developing in the Faculty along similar lines to service needs other than agriculture. It is our hope that undergraduate programmes in social ecology will be on stream shortly to complement an existing graduate programme in this area.

References

Argyris, C. and Schön, D. (1978). *Organisation Learning*. Reading, Mass.: Addison-Wesley.

Bawden, R. J. and Valentine, I. (1984). Learning to be a capable systems agriculturalist. *Programmed Learning and Educational Technology*, **21**, 273–87.

Bawden, R. J., Macadam, R., Valentine, I. and Packham, R. G. (1984). Systems thinking and practices in the education of systems agriculturalists. *Agricultural Systems*, **13**, 205–25.

Bawden, R. J., Ison, R. L., Macadam, R. D., Packham, R. G. and Valentine, I. (1985). A research paradigm for systems agriculture. In Remenyi, J. V. (Ed.), *Agricultural Systems Research for Developing Countries*, p. 34. Canberra: Australian Centre for International Agricultural Research.

Beer, S. (1981). *Brain of the Firm*. Chichester: John Wiley.

Brundage, D. H. and Mackeracher, D. (1980). *Adult Learning Principles and their Application to Program Planning*. Toronto, Ontario: Ministry of Education.

Bruner, J. S. (1966). *Towards a Theory of Instruction*. New York: W. W. Norton.

Burgess, T. (1977). *Education after School*. London: Victor Gollancz.

Carlson, B., Keane, P. and Martin, J. B. (1979). Learning and problem solving. In Kolb, D. A., Rubin, I. M. and McIntyre, J. M. (Eds), *Organisational Psychology*, p. 39, 3rd edition. Englewood Cliffs, N.J.: Prentice-Hall.

Checkland, P. B. (1982). *Systems Thinking: Systems Practice*. Chichester: John Wiley.

Checkland, P. B. (1986). *The Politics of Practice*. Paper presented at the IIASA International Roundtable on The Art and Science of Systems Practice.

Dawkins, J. (1988). *Higher Education – A Policy Discussion Paper*. Government Green Paper, Canberra.

Dewey, J. (1910). *How We Think*. New York: Heath.

Duff, C., Ison, R. L. and Valentine, I. (1985). Acid soils: an example of problem based learning, In Boud, D. (Ed.), *Problem Based Learning in Education for the Professions* pp. 185–7. Sydney: HERDSA.

Emery, F. (1977). *Futures We are In*. Leiden: Martinus Nijhoff.

Emery, F. (Ed.) (1981). *Systems Thinking*, Vol. 2. Harmondsworth: Penguin education.

Heron, J. (1975). *Six Category Intervention Analysis*. Human Potential Research Project. Guildford: University of Surrey.

Kast, F. E. and Rosenzweig, J. E. (1978). *Organisation and Management: A Systems and Contingency Approach*, 2nd edition. New York: McGraw-Hill.

Kemmis, S. and McTaggart, R. (1988). *The Action Research Planner*, 3rd edition. Victoria: Deakin University.

Knowles, M. (1978). *The Adult Learner: A Neglected Species*, 2nd edition. Harston: Gulf Publishing.

Kolb, D. (1984). *Experiential Learning: Experience as the Source of Learning and Development*. Englewod Cliffs, N.J.: Prentice-Hall.

Kolb, D., Rubin, I. M. and McIntyre, J. M. (1983). *Organisational Psychology: An Experiential Approach*, 4th edition. Englewood Cliffs, N.J.: Prentice-Hall.

Lewin, K. (1951). *Field Theory in Social Sciences*. New York: Harper and Row.

Lundie-Jenkins, D., McKenzie, R. J., Blunden, S. R. E. and Molloy, H. D. (1985). The key role of off-campus experience in an experientially based learning programme. *Proc. 1985 HERDSA conf.*, Auckland, New Zealand.

Macadam, R. D. and Bawden, R. J. (1985). Challenge and response: Developing a system for educating more effective agriculturalists. *Prometheus* **3**, 125–37.

Macadam, R. D., Packham, R. G., Bawden, R. J. and Braithwaite, B. M. (1985). A system to educate systems agriculturalists: A case study in restructuring an academic organisation. *Proc. Australian Soc. Operations Research Conf.*, Adelaide, Australia.

Miller, A. (1985). Cognitive styles and environmental problem-solving. *International Journal of Environmental Studies.* **26**, 21–31.

Packham, R. G. and Bawden, R. J. (1985). Systems agriculture – An outcome of the Hawkesbury approach. *Proc. Conf. Principals/Directors of Agricultural and Horticultural Colleges of Australasia and the South-West Pacific*, Massey University, New Zealand.

Parker, J. G. and Rubin, L. J. (1973). *Process as Content.* Chicago: Rand McNally.

Piaget, J. (1952). *Judgement and Reasoning in the Child.* New York: Humanities Press.

Reason, P. and Rowan, J. (1981) *Human Inquiry.* Chichester: John Wiley.

Rogers, C. R. (1969). *Freedom to Learn.* Columbus, Ohio: Merrill.

Schön, D. (1983). *The Reflective Practitioner.* New York: Basic Books.

Spedding, C. R. W. (1975). *The Biology of Agricultural Systems.* London and San Diego: Academic Press.

Spedding, C. R. W. (1979). *An Introduction to Agricultural Systems.* London: Applied Science Publishers.

Tough, A. (1971). *The Adult's Learning Projects.* Research in Education Series, No. 1. Ontario: Institute for Studies in Education.

Turnbull, E. D. and Gamble, D. R. (1986). Economic concepts required by agriculturalists. *Proc. 13th Conf. Australian Agricultural Economics Society*, Canberra, Australia.

Vickers, G. (1981). The poverty of problem solving. *Journal of Applied Systems Analysis*, **8**, 15–21.

Vickers, G. (1983). *Human Systems are Different.* London: Harper and Row.

14

Some Critical Issues Related to Assessment and Accreditation of Adults' Prior Experiential Learning

Amina Barkatoolah

Experiential learning used in the sense of accrediting and assessing prior learning has a long and well recorded history deriving initially from the USA and the work of CAEL (see Chapter 1).

Barkatoolah explores developments in France that enable engineers without formal qualifications to gain access to the profession and formal qualifications. The developments derive from changes in the French and international economies as well as from the increased emphasis on the social justice aims associated with recognizing individuals for their prior learning. Barkatoolah confronts the paradoxes inherent in the processes of accreditation and assessment by examining three examples of practice. On the one hand, is the recognition that, in order to ensure the entry of 'rounded' professionals, the adjudicators are concerned to measure and evaluate behavioural and affective qualities as well as cognitive abilities in the candidate. On the other hand, Barkatoolah uses the analogy of job selection processes to show the factors that can militate against such an assessment being an impartial process. In particular, she raises issues concerning the following: the difficulty of measuring and forecasting some qualities; what is being measured, the outcomes or the person; the social and ideological predispositions of the candidate and adjudicators; and the asymmetry of the power relations. She considers how the broad aim of social justice may be undermined by a process which is still geared to employer or academically determined criteria of capability and personal competency, an issue also raised by Brah and Hoy (Chapter 6) and Criticos (Chapter 19).

Introduction

Job mobility, technological transformation and recent changes associated with the current economic crisis in France are causing individuals to seek recognition for learning they have acquired through their work and life experiences. This recognition is becoming a legitimate academic and institutional process. It comes either as an official accreditation (degree, diploma, credit for further training) or as a social process in career development.

Increasingly, adults consider recognition for their self-acquired competences as a measure of social justice. They have a self-image built on their experiences and, therefore, examining these experiences and evaluating them can be very important.

The concept of the recognition of prior learning (encompassing both traditionally acquired and extra-institutional learning) is of increasing importance in France. More and more institutions are becoming involved in assessing experiential learning. These institutions are acknowledging that individuals acquire valuable knowledge and skills in their work experience and through non-traditional learning. The question remains as to how, by delving into an individual's repertoire, they can untangle meaningful experiences? How can raw life experiences in the areas of work, leisure and education be subjected to manageable and acceptable forms of assessment and accreditation.

Generally, individuals are assessed either for further training or employment purposes on their educational attainments. The limitations of standardized testing procedures that focus more on cognitive criteria are now being acknowledged. Such tests tend to neglect behavioural and affective competencies, especially those related to attitudes and motivations, and the ways in which contextual factors influence our choices. As for commonly used psychological tests, they are suspected to allow more the identification of highly mechanical processes of learning and are, therefore, poor predictors of all-round performance and potential. But to date, there has been a certain caution about any new initiatives in the direction of assessing prior learning, due to the lack of a proper methodology and tools for evaluation. A need is felt, therefore, for a proper rationale and methodology for experiential learning for its recognition to be viable.

Recently, the Ministry of Social Affairs and Employment in France commissioned a research project (Meyer and Berger, 1985) to investigate the implications of current practices in this area. I was part of the team of researchers who worked on this project and this chapter deals with three examples of experiential learning assessment as they appear in three monographs which have resulted from this research (Barkatoolah, 1985a, b, 1987a). They are based upon an attempt to find out about procedures whereby the learning attained by an individual through work or life experience receives academic recognition by an official body, institutional recognition by an adult educational establishment or social recognition (in the workplace) for career development. I then address some of the wider critical issues arising from some of the procedures and processes of assessment currently in use.

Three examples of assessment and validation in practice

Some background information

The professional title of 'engineer' is under legal control in many European Common Market countries, namely France, Italy, West Germany and Belgium (but not Great Britain). In France, the title is under the strict control of an official institutional body, 'La Commission des Titres', which has laid down the required knowledge, skills and experience necessary for whoever is called upon to perform the duty of an engineer.

However, owing to a lack of qualified engineers, there is in France a widely-spread tradition of the so-called *ingénieurs-maison*: that is, high-grade technicians who carry out the function of engineers inside small- and medium-sized enterprises. It appears that 50 per cent of such 'engineers' practising in France do not actually hold a degree in engineering. The problem is that these 'engineers' are often not remunerated as such nor are they entitled to any form of recognition of their competence as professional engineers if they choose to change companies. For them, a degree will have definite desirable consequences in advancing them from their present situation which currently allows them no further career development.

As an answer to this problem, special procedures have been set up, especially in the continuing education sector, to enable these 'engineers' to attain an official and duly recognized title. The second experience described in this paper is an example of how such individuals can be admitted into a specially designed training course counting towards a degree after assessment of their experiential learning. In the first example, such adults can obtain the degree and title of engineer *solely* through the recognition of the competences acquired through work and life experiences. The third example shows how the recognition of experiential learning outcomes can facilitate career mobility.

The case of the DPE engineers (Ingeniéurs Diplomes d'Etat)

Since 1979, a special system has been established allowing self-taught adults to obtain the title of engineer after assessment and validation of their experiential learning. The basic entrance requirements are that candidates should be more than 35 years old and have 5 years or more professional experience.

In order to participate in this scheme all candidates must submit a file to the Ministry of Education consisting of the following documents:

- A curriculum vitae (C.V.) describing educational attainments, employment records, etc.
- Testimonials from employers showing the activities in which the candidate was involved and giving salary details.
- Copies of diplomas.
- Lists of publications and extra-professional activities.

After initial administrative procedures are completed, the candidate's file is sent to training institutions in the areas of the candidate's speciality to be examined by a jury of five persons: two faculty members and three qualified practising engineers (one of whom is a DPE engineer).

The candidate has to undergo an interview first and, if found suitable, has to produce a dissertation a few months later. The interview can last from 1 to 3 hours. The jury checks whether the competence, personality, human characteristics and general knowledge displayed are congruent with the predetermined profile of an engineer.

For the dissertation, the subject matter chosen must first be approved by the jury. It must focus on a relevant professional experience which shows evidence of the candidate's ability to achieve mastery of his or her professional field that goes beyond a mere technological adaptation. Another jury, this time at the national level, is summoned by the Ministry of Education to validate the assessment results of the first jury and to award the title of engineer.

It may be interesting to study some of the criteria that come into play during the whole process. At the very initial stage, a screening process is used for selecting the suitable files. Criteria such as age, the size of the business firm where the candidate is employed, the salary and position occupied, the educational background and work experience of the candidate are examined. Particular attention is paid to the size of the firm; though most of the candidates come from small- or medium-sized firms, they must show that their employment has given them the opportunity to gain a wide spectrum of competences deemed necessary to all qualified engineers. The salary will give additional evidence of these.

The nature, range and quality of work experience is examined. These are criteria that can provide information about the candidate's various abilities in, for example, project design and implementation, and his or her capacity as a team leader. The different stages of the person's career should demonstrate technical skills and the ability to improve and innovate.

The interview emphasizes two parameters: the personality and the occupational competences of the candidate. Dynamism, leadership, restraint, open-mindedness, and the capacity for interpersonal relationships are taken to be positive criteria.

In the assessment of occupational competences, points are subtracted if the candidate's present occupation is not highly technical. The same applies to over-specialization in a field, technical skills that are too narrow to have *market-value* (candidates must be able to 'sell' themselves easily), or a narrow scientific and technical background. On the other hand, early promotion, mastery of the main theoretical concepts related to the field, and the ability to come up with new solutions which would show the mark of an innovative spirit are regarded as positive points. Thus, during the interview, the whole life history of a person is scrutinized to discover the stock of knowledge, skills and attitudes accumulated.

The dissertation must show that the candidate has a command of the theory and practice necessary for their chosen field. A correlation is established between the scientific knowledge displayed and the technological background in which the candidate has evolved. This knowledge must be demonstrable in some form, should be at the level of achievement of an engineer in that field, and should imply a conceptual (theoretical) as well as a practical (experiential) grasp of the subject matter. Finally, it should be transferable to the world of work outside the candidate's specific job or setting.

This certification process would seem to be unique, in that a government ministry awards accreditation to candidates after they have been through a screening procedure.

An example from the CESI (Centre d'Etudes Supérieures Industrielles)

The case of the CESI is interesting because it shows how experiential learning can be assessed as the basis for admission into training courses. The CESI is a training institution that prepares adults for degrees in engineering. The Board of Directors includes, on a parity basis, representatives of five trade unions, two employers' federations and the business sector (e.g. Renault, Air France, IBM).

Instead of the usually programmed 5-year course, training at the CESI lasts only 2 years. One of the objectives is that teaching practice should focus to a large part on the work-based learning of trainees. Hence, admission is based on a selection process in which the assessment of prior learning from the field of work plays a major role. The basic requirements for admission are that all candidates should possess 5 years' experience in a professional activity, a cognitive knowledge comparable to the level of *baccalauréat* in mathematics and technical subjects, and a personality capable of adaptation and innovation.

The candidate's C.V. and another form which she/he has to fill in, provide information regarding their educational background, various activities undertaken, positions of responsibility held, etc. After this 'file' has been accepted, the candidate undergoes a series of tests in mathematics, physics, French and general knowledge about their technological background.

Particular emphasis is placed on the personality and the potential of the candidate. Several tools are used, based mostly on observation and judgement:

- psychotechnical tests,
- psychological tests and handwriting analysis, and
- interviews.

The psychotechnical and psychological tests are conducted by a psychologist who focuses on three areas: cognitive ability (e.g. problem solving, flexibility), personality traits and behavioural attitudes. The psychologist also assesses the candidate's dynamism, initiative, perseverance, stability, motivation, ability to adapt to new situations, restraint, and self-confidence. Assessors tend to regard these as the fundamentals of a mature and balanced personality.

A specific grid allows the psychologist to list both the weak and strong points of candidates' personalities and then make prognoses regarding their development. Using a similar grid to the psychologist, the graphologist then works on hand written samples provided by the candidates. The results of the two tests are then compared to see if there are any points of convergence.

Group interviews are another assessment tool. Trainers assess the behaviour of candidates and the extent of their influence on their peers, according to a predetermined checklist of meaningful behaviours. The data on a candidate's C.V. are correlated with the results of the psychological and psychotechnical tests to assess work experience.

The jury are presented with the test results and notes of recommendations from the psychologist and the graphologist. All candidates, admitted or rejected, are informed about the results of each test. Confidentiality forbids the file to be transmitted to the candidate's employers.

Experiential learning and the mobility system at SNECMA (Société Nationale d'Etude et de Construction de Moteurs d'Aviation)

To illustrate the issue regarding the recognition of experiential learning for mobility purposes, I have chosen SNECMA as my example. SNECMA constructs aeroplane and space engines for the French National Defence. The firm employs 26,000 people, of whom a relatively high proportion are engineers (13 per cent) and technicians. Recruitment is carried out according to a staff classification system (after a collective bargaining agreement) and, for each post, specific criteria have been determined.

At SNECMA there is great emphasis on internal mobility, special provisions enabling technicians to gain access to top executive positions. For this, a particular form of assessment is used, which consists of a dissertation and an intensive interview system. Assessment is carried out by a commission of nine members, all of whom are heads of divisions within the company.

After an internal preselection process, candidates are required to produce a dissertation on a subject closely related to their professional field. The dissertation should show that the candidate is able both to dominate their occupational sector and to contribute to it in an original way. It is a crucial item in the evaluation process and scores are determined by the eloquence of the work as much as by its substance. Personal information, such as autobiographical anecdotes, that are not in direct relation to the learning outcomes, are to be left out. These, however, are important during the interview, where the candidate's complete personal background is assessed.

The aim of the interview is to explore the range and nature of an applicant's competencies, command of their specialty, professional abilities, capacity for interpersonal relationships, ability to negotiate and to come to grips with new situations, motivation, cultural background, and leisure activities.

The modes of evaluation used at SNECMA are similar to those used with 'DPE' engineers. In both cases, similar criteria are employed to assess not only knowledge and ability, but also personal characteristics derived from behavioural attitudes.

Some key points

In all three cases there is an interweaving of different evaluation networks within the assessment procedures. There is, on the one hand, an educational principle according to which cognitive learning occurs through practical experience in the professional field and, on the other, an approach which requires biographical data and various fields of experience to be viewed in the light of an individual's personality, and social and cultural attainments. An attempt is made to take into account an individual's overall stock of social and cultural resources. Even though this approach is quite common as regards employment, it is entirely at variance with traditional evaluation procedures for the awarding of a degree.

What can be derived from these practices?

Though the aims and objectives of assessment in the three cases described in this paper are different, the procedures are similar.

In the three cases discussed, referentials are used for evaluation. These referentials – checklists of competencies drawn as expected learning outcomes – imply the existence of standards and criteria for evaluation. Some of these criteria are explicit, others rather implicit, but none the less a specific social prototype serves as the referential. In all three cases, there is no doubt that the evaluators are 'betting on the winner': the person they believe is going to be successful.

The assessment and validation of experiential learning thus performs the function of role assignment and the distribution of social status. In the case of SNECMA and that of the 'DPE' engineers, this function is obvious, in that of the CESI, identifying those who are apt to pursue studies with success implies ultimately the same outcome. In the case of SNECMA, evaluation initiates a decision for the attribution of a professional status and acts as a support to a staff mobility policy. For both 'DPE' and SNECMA, the assessment of experiential learning helps to allot a social certification. In the CESI example, the assessment of experiential learning serves as a predictor.

In assessing experiential learning, we are involved with a selection process. The fact that human beings who are part of a wider historical and social context are involved renders the encounter a complex, delicate and potentially political one. Opportunities can be denied or made available, depending upon a culturally determined set of criteria. An assessment is an act which aims at producing a value judgement, which will inevitably reflect the myths, prejudices and dominant assumptions that operate in the wider society.

From the three examples given, it is obvious that the tools used (intensive interviews, psychological tests, graphology, etc.) and the predetermined sets of criteria applied (leadership, initiative, personal effectiveness, entrepreneurial skills, etc.), also pertain to employment selection procedures. In fact, the assessment of experiential learning and recruitment procedures seem to obey one and the same law.

Other similarities exist between the two phenomena. In both cases, there seems to be a constant preoccupation to limit risks (albeit culturally determined), and hence the use of diverse instruments in screening individuals.

Another concern seems to link the two phenomena: that of foreseeing the development of behaviours. To analyse and evaluate the personality of an individual is a delicate task requiring humility – the employer or recruiting agent has to make a judgement about someone they do not really know. In selection for training, assessment consists of measuring an individual's ability to adapt and develop, also a concern of managers. In both cases an attempt is made to analyse an individual's personality by means of diverse tests, while remembering that human beings are multidimensional creatures and, therefore, they cannot actually be categorized scientifically.

Procedures in the assessment of experiential learning and recruitment stress the efficiency of the candidate and a 'functional approach'. Hence it is not surprising that there is a similarity in the language used. Such terms as 'attitudinal change', 'drives' and 'competencies', which are used in education, are also a part of a management's repertoire.

The assessment of experiential learning includes more than the evaluation of skills, knowledge and attitudes; it goes beyond the mere assessment of learning outcomes. As such, the whole process is imbued with a deep-seated ambivalence.

Any act of evaluation includes both a technical and a social aspect. It cannot be reduced to either one alone. It is a social practice with a definite aim of involving social agents entertaining, for a time, a particular kind of relationship in a particular social and historical context. In job selection, as much as in assessment for education purposes, we are involved with a process which brings together on the one hand an individual who has come to display his or her knowledge and self-worth – all that has been built up and stored during their life and work experiences – and, on the other, a set of individuals or a system whose task it is to assess candidates according to specific criteria. This gives rise to an asymmetrical, power-laden and culturally influenced situation, within which negotiation will inevitably be limited.

It is a fact that an individual is not judged, assessed or gauged in a vacuum. Norms and standards of performance have been carefully worked out beforehand, and procedures, tools, criteria and standards of performance are akin to those used in other contexts, specifically the recruitment for employment. If it is true that the assessment of experiential learning is closely related to a job selection process (the three examples given show evidence of this), then we are faced with a paradox.

In the United States, where the concept of the recognition of prior learning emerged nearly 40 years ago, the underlying rationale was (and still is) that of social justice (Barkatoolah, 1987b). It is seen as giving an individual recognition for all that they have learned throughout their lives, both personally and professionally.

In France, where the concept has recently surfaced, the same idea of social justice is upheld. The French term *reconnaissance des acquis* holds within this definition: the taking into account of all that has been acquired by a person –

that which has been learned from his/her personal and professional life experiences.

The question is, therefore, whether the fact that the assessment procedure bears a striking resemblance to the job selection process undermines the very basic philosophy and purpose inherent in the concept?

Who are the assessors and what are they evaluating?

Evaluators are those who wield the power to question the identity of an individual and allot a value to that individual. Evaluators are socially designated to perform their role using predetermined criteria, objectives, etc. Evaluation works under the assumption that individuals have within their personalities diverse sub-sets of abilities, potentials and motives which are the products of their life histories. The evaluator's role is to examine these sub-sets and rate them in a way that would lend scientific objectivity to the process.

In the same vein, we might ask ourselves what is being evaluated: the outcomes, the person or, indeed, the social context itself? It has been pointed out that the object of evaluation itself is often not very explicit. It is never very clear whether it is the traits and characteristics which construct a particular reality or the reality itself which is being assessed. Quite often, in fact, it appears to be the individual who is under scrutiny from a predetermined perspective. There seems to be a shift from the object of evaluation to the subject him/herself.

An epistemological problem is inevitable. In all evaluation processes, a number of determinants prevail: the situation of the evaluation proper, the evaluator's qualities, skills and awareness of his or her own cultural and ideological biases, and the wider social and historical context within which the assessment is taking place.

The way in which an individual does something determines partly what they are doing. The situation is influenced by their approach, attitudes, and values. A good example of this can be found in anthropology. When an anthropologist arrives in a village, she creates a different atmosphere from that when she is not there. What she sees all the time is the village with her presence. She must ask herself: what does this imply, what influence does it exert, and what kinds of modifications are brought?

In the assessment of experiential learning, will evaluators take into account all the implications of the evaluating situation? Will they be aware that their assessment could be prejudiced by their motives, impressions and values? Will they be conscious of the fact that because of all these, and also because of the kind of power relationship present, a particular situation is created and that this situation is far from neutral?

Finally, there is a moral and ethical issue present in the assessment of experiential learning. The fact that what is often being assessed is not a certain reality but an individual who is the agent (actor) of that reality gives rise to problems of a deontological nature regarding privacy (recruiters are well aware of these). As assessors of experiential learning are delving into biographical data, an individual's personal integrity may be threatened. Are all evaluators of experiential learning acquainted with the professional code of conduct necessary in the handling of very personal data pertaining to individuals? On what deontological basis can they justify their behaviour? How should they behave, so that candidates do not feel any interference in, or external pressure on, their personal life? Are candidates able to consult their record? Are they always allowed to see the results of their tests? What guarantees do candidates have about confidentiality in the transmission of results?

If the relationship between candidates and evaluators is asymmetrical, the communication is almost always unidirectional.

There are also cases where information is gathered about candidates without them being aware of it (e.g. handwriting analyses). It can even be argued that questions usually meant to produce information about the cultural background of candidates, their personal development, interests and values, might be destined to 'trap' them into giving information about their family life, political adherence, socioeconomic status of their parents, etc. – that is, violating their privacy.

Often, real individual characteristics are blurred in favour of personality traits the system considered appropriate at that moment. Such criteria currently used, e.g. leadership qualities, inventiveness, self-control, versatility, etc., are the present prevailing attributes of excellence and are all loaded with cultural connotations. Illustrating a kind of functional consensus between sociocultural norms and values and economic requirements, they reflect a certain conception of human beings and their relationship with the world.

Conclusion

This paper has attempted to point out, through the description of three types of practice, some critical elements related to the assessment of experiential learning. As changing jobs becomes more and more a necessity due to the loss and precariousness of employment, employer relocations, etc., assessment of experiential learning gives hope to people who are interested in changing or advancing their career.

Since the assessment and recognition of experiential learning is a new phenomenon, more needs to be learned about various evaluation modes and how they are influenced by the 'human instrument', who in turn is influenced by a wider social reality. As the evaluation process implies that work experience is to be carefully looked into, the instruments used have to bear some similarity with those used in the professional field for recruitment and job advancement, in order to ensure credibility. However, assessors ought to use them with caution so that they do not become tools of elimination. Assessment of experiential learning, while evaluating a candidate's ability, should also be able to point out the weaknesses, in order to suggest remedies for achieving the requisites for necessary professional certification or academic accreditation. This would make the approach constructive and different from a recruiter's elimination process. Assessors also ought to be aware of the implications underlying the use of a global approach for assessing experiential learning. In fact, many of them should receive proper training in that direction. Moreover, referential checklists of competencies should be more carefully drawn up so as to diminish the operation of subjective and sociopolitical biases. Therefore, more research needs to be carried out in this area.

References

Barkatoolah, A. (1985a). La reconnaissance des acquis en vue du titre d'Ingénieur Diplômé par l'Etat. In Meyer, N. and Berger, G. (Eds), *Etude à caractère documentaire sur la reconnaissance des acquis*. Paris: Université Paris VIII–Formation Permanent.

Berkatoolah, A. (1985b). Le C.E.S.I. (Centre d'Etudes Supérieures Industrielles). In Meyer, N. and Berger, G. (Eds), *Etude à caractère documentaire sur la reconnaissance des acquis*. Paris: Université Paris VIII–Formation Permanent.

Berkatoolah, A. (1987a). La Société Nationale d'Etude et de Construction de Moteurs d'Avions. In *Reconnaissance et validation des acquis: relevé de quelques pratiques*, issue No. 1. pp. 73–80. Paris: Université Paris VIII–Formation Permanent.

Berkatoolah, A. (1987b). Expériences nord-américaines en reconnaissance des acquis. In *Pratiques de formation–analyses*. Special issue. Paris: Université Paris VIII–Formation Permanent.

Meyer, N. and Berger, G. (Eds) (1985). *Etude à caractère documentaire sur la reconnaissance des acquis*. Paris: Université Paris VIII–Formation Permanent.

15

Experiential Learning and Professional Development

Annikki Järvinen

Jarvinen takes us through an evaluation of the application of the experiential learning process to the professional development of qualified nurses who are making the transition to become nursing educators. Recognizing the need for professionals to have a much wider range of skills and competencies, she designed and implemented the programme utilizing Kolb's learning modes of concrete experience, reflective observation, abstract conceptualization and active experimentation. The model of the course also provides the basis of the evaluation. This was aimed at measuring the students' feelings toward their course, through the use of diary assignments. Diaries enabled students to reflect on aspects of the programme and assignments and to consider their personal practice and approaches to learning how to learn. Her experience of adapting one course in a higher educational institution can be contrasted with that of Packham et al. (Chapter 13) where a whole institution took the experiential learning route. Nelson (Chapter 10) provides a further comparison with the application of a model that is designed to enhance the relevance of a higher education programme; i.e. personal and professional growth. Peterson (Chapter 16) provides an additional rationale for such programmes.

In spite of a steady growing interest in experiential learning in Finland, few educators have applied this innovative framework to higher education. Thus, it would seem that the study course 'Professional Development', which I designed on the basis of Kolb's (1984) experiential learning theory and have offered annually since 1985 at Tampere University, is the first systematic attempt in Finland (and probably in the whole of Scandinavia) to apply this framework of teaching and learning in university education. In this chapter, I shall analyse the course, its content, study forms and evaluation, all of which were designed with Kolb's experiential learning theory as the frame of reference.

In Finland, higher education at the undergraduate level consists to a large extent of programmes which qualify students for various professions. According to Schön (1983), the professions have become essential to the very functioning of modern societies. However, there are increasing signs of a crisis of confidence and legitimacy in the professions. The longstanding professional claim to a monopoly of knowledge and social control is being challenged (ibid.). This crisis is also reflected in higher education; in particular, criticism has been levelled against the professionalistic nature of education that is manifested in the 'hidden curriculum' as a ritualistic assessment of competence (see, e.g. Atkinson and Delamont, 1985; Haas and Shaffir, 1982; Järvinen, 1987). In my view, these problems accentuate the need for universities to find new ways to develop reflective practitioners who are capable of studying, evaluating and developing their own work. This is especially important in teaching practice (Peters and Postma, 1986; Macklin, 1981).

The process of professional development

Kolb's (1984) experiential learning theory of growth and development can be applied to the process of professional development by drawing parallels between the concept of learning and those of problem solving, creativity, decision making and scientific research. This model makes it possible to combine the study of education and work.

In the experiential learning model of growth and development, the human growth process is divided into three broad developmental stages: acquisition, specialization and integration. *Acquisition* extends from birth to adolescence and marks the acquisition of basic learning abilities (the concrete, reflective, abstract and active modes) and cognitive structures. *Specialization* extends through formal education and/or career training to the early experiences of adulthood in one's work and personal life, when certain modes are often emphasized at the expense of others – depending on the dominant contexts for learning and development. *Integration* is marked by the reassertion and expression of the non-dominant adaptive modes or learning styles (Kolb and Fry, 1975). In professional education we need to have both specialized and integrative goals.

> The aim is . . . to focus on integrative development where the person is highly developed in each of the four learning modes: active, reflective, abstract, and concrete. Here the students are taught to experience the tension and conflict among these orientations, for it is from the resolution of these tensions that creativity springs (Kolb, 1984, p. 203).

During the 4-year course, the students and I – as facilitator and researcher – analyse their development needs for the teaching profession, focusing in particular on their evaluation of themselves and of their own practice. The course commences in the students' first year and continues in the second and years 2 to 4 include several periods of teaching practice. In the following, I shall only describe the first stage of the process.

The course is part of a new, 4-year nursing education programme for students with specialized nursing qualifications, which started in 1985 at the Faculty of Medicine, Tampere University. The aim of the course is to support the students' professional development during teacher education and teaching practice. The students are specialized nurses with extensive work experience, studying for their Master's degrees that will qualify them to be nursing educators. I have been solely responsible for designing, running and evaluating the course, but all the teaching staff in the degree programme have given me their full support and encouragement.

In my view, university education should enable the prospective teachers to think reflectively. This we can only achieve through enhancing our self-awareness. We – educators and students alike – should become aware of the way we perceive, think and act, i.e. the way we learn. The aim is to touch our own experiences so that we can use them creatively.

The students are at the specialization stage: they have taken an occupational diploma, developed a strong professional identity and acquired extensive working experience. However, they are also in a state of change, having entered university as adult learners. For many, the course begins a process of perspective transformation, which:

> is a learning process by which adults come to recognize their culturally induced dependency roles and relationships and the reasons for them and take action to overcome them (Mezirow, 1981, pp. 6–7).

The first step in their learning process as prospective teachers is to become aware of their individual learning style and, consequently, to learn to develop all four of Kolb's learning modes: concrete experience, reflective observation, abstract conceptualization and active experimentation.

The course: 'Professional Development'

The course comprises 120 hours of study – 60 hours of seminars and 60 hours of independent study. The course starts in the spring term of the students' first year of study (Part I) and continues after the summer holidays in the autumn term of the second year (Part II). By the autumn term of 1987, 32 students completed the course.

The learning goals of the course can be divided into three categories: growth and creativity objectives, learning style objectives, and content objectives (Kolb, 1984).

1. *Growth and creativity objectives.* Students should:
   - be able to analyse their personal growth and development needs;
   - be able to assume personal responsibility for their actions and practice;
   - seek continuously to develop the evaluation of their own practice.
2. *Learning style objectives.* Students should:
   - be able to identify their own learning styles and approaches to problem solving;
   - seek to develop each of the four learning modes: active, reflective, abstract and concrete.
3. *Content objectives:*
   Part I
   (a) Experiential learning theory and problem solving.

(b) Interpersonal perception and communication as a basis for learning:
- practising and analysing self-perception and the perceptions of other people;
- giving and receiving feedback about those perceptions;
- evaluating effective and ineffective communication and ways of improving communication;
- analysing verbal and non-verbal modes of communication.

(c) Experiential learning model of growth and development and creativity.

(d) Creativity in the work community and adult education:
- planning a developmental programme for one's own work community;
- planning a programme for one's own personal development.

Part II

(a) Professionalism *vs.* professional personality:
- analysing the basic concepts and some research approaches.

(b) Work counselling:
- analysing certain theoretical approaches;
- participating in the work counselling sessions and evaluating these.

(c) Self-evaluation:
- producing self-evaluation methods jointly with other students (this section of Part II has not yet been implemented).

The working process and methods used were non-traditional: they were based on sharing one's own experiences with the group and reflecting and analysing them together. The methods for running the course were determined using Kolb's phases of experiential learning. The students:

1. Described their own problems from working life or completed exercises in self-evaluation, perception and communication (*concrete experience*).
2. Analysed the above exercises individually and in groups (*reflective observation*).
3. Studied articles on the topic and analysed them with their teacher and the other students in the group (*abstract conceptualization*).
4. Drew conclusions from the phases they had gone through and discussed new approaches in small groups and the whole class together (*second phase of reflective observation*).
5. Applied assignments at home and at work (*active experimentation*).

Several exercises and assignments were taken from Kolb *et al.* (1984).

The evaluation of the course

The first transition: From concrete experience towards reflective observation

The model of experiential learning provided the guidelines for choosing the methods for evaluation. I surveyed the students' immediate *feelings toward the course* during the penultimate session of Part I by asking them: 'How have you felt about this course and what are your feelings now? Describe your educational experience by using three or four adjectives.' This was an application of phenomenological response as developed by Willis and Allen (1978), which enables us to survey the feelings and experiences connected with the educational situation. Instead of giving the students a complete list of adjectives like Willis and Allen, I asked them to describe their feelings/experience in their own words. The adjectives were then compared with the list used by Willis and Allen (1978) and placed on their system of co-ordinates, in which the adjectives are rated on two dimensions: depression–elation and uninvolvement–involvement.

Of the adjectives used, 50 per cent could be situated in the quadrant of high levels of elation and involvement (e.g. 'satisfied', 'anticipatory', 'excited'). Nearly 50 per cent of them describe high levels of elation and average involvement (e.g. 'meditative', 'calm', 'liberated'). Only three adjectives used by the students can be located elsewhere, near the intersection of the axes ('neutral'). The students' specific comments on the course that were obtained through the questionnaires confirmed the results of this immediate evaluation. Their experience of the individual exercises and group assignments as well as team work were extremely positive. They cited the sharing of their feelings and experiences, and analysing them with the group, as very fruitful. They regarded the atmosphere as secure, and nobody reported feeling distressed or rejected. The students felt that the course had had an effect on their own lives, since all of them continued to apply or experiment with the exercises at work or at home after the course.

In the diaries kept during the work counselling sessions (Part II), the students recorded their feelings about the session where their own problem was dealt with, commenting on the group work and the practicability of the solutions suggested. The students reported that the group had even been able to deal with very serious problems, after they had got to know each other and grown used to working together. They found this stage hard and intensive but extremely rewarding.

It was useful for me to compare the diary I had kept as an instructor with the feedback given by the students. That the group of students grew increasingly coherent was clearly to be seen in all of our notes. My diary also enabled me to view the whole course as a continuous process of learning, and to be consistent with the working methods so as not to forget the central aims of the course.

The course proved to be at least as strong a process of experiential learning for me as it was for the students. My interaction with the students was very intensive during the course, but the small learning groups worked very autonomously. Consequently, the students regarded themselves as active participants in the learning process and the instructor as a facilitator and an organizer to whom they could turn when necessary.

The second transition: Towards abstract conceptualization and active experimentation

For the first essay assignment, the students could use a report distributed in the seminar, entitled 'creativity in the community and adult education' (Häyrynen,

1983). The assignment consisted of drafting a concrete plan for developing one's own work community (goals, participants, methods, schedule and evaluation). Sixty per cent of the students dealt with a work setting within the hospital or health centre organization, and the rest focused on educational institutions. About 50 per cent of the students stressed that the work community should analyse the values and preferences shared by the employees first, and then focus on developing the individuals' ability to cooperate and interact. The other 50 per cent analysed the employees' individual goals, communicative abilities and barriers to creativity, concluding their discussion by suggesting methods for developing collaboration.

The students succeeded better in defining the problem and drafting the operational plan than in conceptualizing the issues, which may be due to the concrete nature of the task given. The students regarded this assignment as very stimulating. The most interesting result is that two-thirds of the students reported that they had already initiated or were going to initiate this particular programme for development at their work setting. This clearly suggests that the process of experiential learning has become a part of their everyday lives.

The second essay assignment was set out as follows:

Draft your *personal goals and programme* for the development of the fields outlined below. Base your essay on the exercises you have completed during the course and on the discussions held at the seminars:

1. How would you develop your own skills of perceiving and communicating? Give a brief description of your present situation and your feelings towards it. State your goals for development. Describe the exercises and working methods you could use. Link these to your present job if possible. Construct a timetable and a concrete, realizable programme. Think of ways of evaluating the results; did you achieve your goals?
2. How would you improve your *learning style*? Describe the same aspects as above.
3. How would you like to develop your approaches to problem solving? Describe the same aspects as above.

The students considered this assignment difficult. Although they could have made use of all the exercises, analyses and articles that they had dealt with during the course, they did not utilize these materials sufficiently. One reason they gave for this was that it was such a long time since the exercises had been completed. Furthermore, they complained that the different sections (1–3) of the assignment seemed to have little connection with each other.

The most common barriers to the students' effective perception and communication as they saw it were stereotypes, inadequate control of emotions, and lack of active listening. To improve these, the students developed small-scale exercises for themselves, which could be implemented after each working day or week. Some had already tested these with their families or friends. The most difficult task for the students was developing the different modes of their own learning styles. These were charted at the beginning of the course by using the original version of the Learning Style Inventory developed by Kolb (Kolb *et al.*, 1984). Fifty per cent of the students identified themselves as assimilators, and the rest fell rather evenly into the divergent, accommodative and convergent learning styles. The result was unexpectedly heterogeneous, since in several studies nurses have in the main ranked themselves as convergers (e.g. Kolb and Fry 1975). One reason for this might be the tendency in higher education to stress the assimilatory learning style: when tested, the students may have given statements more consistent with this presumed ideal than with their real preferences. The assimilative style was also prominent in the students' approaches to problem solving; they felt that they should improve their ability to identify different problems and to consider alternative solutions in their work.

Each group presented a report on their work counselling sessions (Part II). All of the students had presented a concrete problem of their own work (explicitly stated as 'my problem') to which they wanted to find solutions together with the group. The problems were very personal ones, mostly connected with human relations. Half of the problems were about anxieties and fears in the nurse–patient relationship or the teacher–student relationship and the other half about cooperation with fellow practitioners. In the problem-solving process the students identified so strongly with each other, sharing and comparing their experiences, that it was hard for them to find any solutions. As was the case with the first essay assignment in Part I, those practitioners with a lot of nursing experience found it very difficult to shift from commitment to detachment, i.e. they experienced a tension between the concrete and abstract modes of learning.

Discussion

Applying the model of experiential learning to the content, forms of study and methods of evaluation of the 'Professional Development' course proved success-ful, from the standpoint of both motivating adult learners and linking their experiences of working life with theoretical considerations. When evaluating the course, the students reported that they applied and experimented with what they had learnt in an active and self-directed way in their own work, and had analysed critically the practices of their work community. It is apparent that the students have adopted the processes of 'learning to learn' and 'learning to reflect my own practice' as part of their everyday lives. There was a similar develop-ment in their readiness and ability to share their experiences with others, which is an essential stage of reflective thinking. The course has been, and continues to be, a significant influence in my own development. In particular, it has enabled me to grow in my role as a facilitator and to share my own experiences with the students. The results from their evaluation can be used to develop my own teaching role and approach on the degree programme and subsequent courses. The evaluation results can also serve as material for my follow-up study, in which I shall analyse the development of the students' goal-setting and self-evaluation during teacher education and teaching practice.

Finally, I believe that the fact that the students on this programme were themselves in a transitional stage motivated them to develop reflectively throughout the course. These processes helped them to understand their own personal and professional developmental needs. For example, they became very involved in the tasks of developing their own work community and analysing their own problems in the work counselling session: 'Transitions can be constructive experiences, if we have the will to create or accept marker events that produce just enough disequilibrium to ease the way' (Chickering and Marienau, 1982, p. 24). The active support and development opportunities provided by this experiential professional development programme not only helped the students through the challenges of their own transition, but the course also facilitated a process of 'perspective transformation' (Mezirow, 1981) for many of them. This most often develops as a series of transitions and 'becomes a major learning domain and the uniquely adult learning function' (ibid.).

The process of reflective thinking that was initiated during this course will be further analysed and supported during the periods of teaching practice. I find it crucially important that continuation and follow-up of this kind is maintained. This will encourage students to continue to develop their evaluation of themselves and their own activity, to enable them to become reflective practitioners in their prospective teaching jobs.

References

Atkinson, P. and Delamont, S. (1985). Socialisation into teaching: The research which lost its way. *British Journal of Sociology of Education*, **6**(3), 307–22.

Chickering, C. and Marienau, C. (1982). Adult development and learning. In Menson, B. (Ed.), *Building on Experience in Adult Development*. New Directions for Experiential Learning, No. 20. San Francisco: Jossey Bass and CAEL.

Haas, J. and Shaffir, W. (1982). Ritual evaluation of competence. The hidden curriculum of professionalization in an innovative medical school program. *Work and Occupations*, **9**(2), 131–54.

Häyrynen, Y.-P. (1983). *Luovuus työyhteisössä ja aikuiskasvatuksessa*. (Creativity in the work community and in adult education.) Valtion Koulutuskeskus B (21). Helsinki: Valtion painatuskeskus. (In Finnish).

Järvinen, A. (1987). Development of scientific and professional thinking of medical students. In Khattab, T., Schmidt, H., Nooman, Z. and Ezaat, E. (Eds), *Innovation in Medical Education: An Evaluation of its Present Status*. New York: Springer.

Kolb, D. A. (1984). *Experiential Learning: Experience as the Source of Learning and Development*. Englewood Cliffs, N.J.: Prentice-Hall.

Kolb, D.A. and Fry, R. (1975). Toward an applied theory of experiential learning. In Cooper, C. (Ed.), *Theories of Group Processes*. Chichester: John Wiley.

Kolb, D. A., Rubin, I. M. and McIntyre, J. M. (1984). *Organizational Psychology: An Experiential Approach to Organizational Behavior*. Englewood Cliffs, N.J.: Prentice-Hall.

Macklin, M. (1981). Teaching professionalism to the teaching profession. *The Australian Journal of Education*, **25**(1), 24–36.

Mezirow, J. (1981). A critical theory of adult learning and education. *Adult Education*, **32**(1), 3–24.

Peters, J. J. and Postma, L. (1986). The development of teacher behaviour: A balance between cognition and complexity. Paper presented at the 11th ATEE Conference on 'Research in Education and Teacher Training', Toulouse, France, 1–5 September.

Schön, D. A. (1983). *The Reflective Practitioner: How Professionals Think in Action*. London: Temple Smith.

Willis, G. and Allen, A. J. (1978). Patterns of phenomenological response to curricula: Implications. In Willis, G. (Ed.), *Qualitative Evaluation: Concepts and Cases in Curricular Criticism*. Berkeley: McCutchan.

16

Reducing Student Attrition: Towards a More Successful Learning Environment

Shari L. Peterson

Peterson examines the causes of the relatively high levels of attrition, particularly in the first year, of students attending colleges in the USA. Her concern is to counter these attrition rates. She cites the potential contribution that experiential learning-based curricular approaches can make towards this end. As with her colleague Nelson (Chapter 10), Peterson emphasizes the need for educational programmes to help students to integrate personal aspirations and career goals with educational plans. She argues that academic staff need to create and define the conditions for a learning environment in ways that are relevant to these aims. They also need to attend to 'teaching for learning': that is, enabling students to learn how to learn, which is at the root of the experiential modes she advocates. The chapter thus provides a challenge to the limitations of traditional forms of degree education which pay less regard to process than content. Contrasts may be made with O'Reilly (Chapter 9) and Horwitz (Chapter 7), who take experiential learning along routes which pursue greater student autonomy, and Packham et al. (Chapter 13) on institutional change.

This chapter can be read alongside Järvinen (Chapter 15) and Hutton (Chapter 4), who are also concerned with integration and development. The educational philosophy being advocated here may also be considered in the context of Wildemeersch's analysis (Chapter 5).

Introduction

One desire to which educators around the world will readily admit is for students to succeed. Because success means different things to different people, perhaps we, as educators, need to recognize that what students want from their educational experience and what we want for them may not always be the same thing. However, based on the proliferation of literature on the subject, one measure of 'success' which concerns all of the parties involved – institutional administrators, educators and students – is that of student retention.

Retention (retaining students in an institution of higher learning) is the opposite of attrition (losing students from an institution of higher learning). According to Tinto (1986, 1987), the primary goal of effective retention programmes should not be merely that more students are retained but that they be further educated. This view suggests that remaining in higher education is one thing; becoming educated may be another. Retention, therefore, is not the goal; becoming educated is the goal. Retention is not the end but rather the means to the end. Is it possible to provide an environment which is simultaneously conducive to retention and learning? I believe the answer to this question is 'yes', and I believe experiential components in an educational programme can play a major role in achieving that objective; for example, field trips, internships, and classroom activities that engage students in a number of ways.

A variety of interventions have proven successful in increasing retention, while promoting more effective learning. Many of those interventions are experiential in nature. Recognizing that students, educators and educational administrators each have objectives which reflect their own versions of educational success, experiential education seems to provide the link which connects those objectives.

This chapter suggests how experiential education can contribute to a more successful learning environment and reduce student attrition. Some views about attrition and retention will be reviewed, and some rationales for experiential education summarized. The chapter concludes by considering the future implications of the connection between experiential education and retention.

Attrition and retention

According to Levitz and Noel (1986), studies in the USA indicate that attrition is likely to be most severe after the first year of study, but it decreases by 50 per cent as each year passes. In community colleges, attrition is often even more acute between the first term and second term when rates of 60 per cent are common. These attrition rates have contributed to the fact that fewer than one in five adults in the USA holds a college degree. First 'impressions', therefore, appear to be critical. If an educational institution has as short a period of time as one term to influence students to persist, it seems reasonable that we should emphasize the first term in our efforts to retain students. Although these statistics are generalized and vary from institution to institution, the raw data are disturbing, particularly in the light of reduced birth rates. These are leading to current and future major declines in first-year enrolments in institutions of higher learning in the USA. Perhaps those in the educational setting should be more concerned about keeping the students they already have for economic reasons – moral reasons notwithstanding. For either reason, it seems ironic that some colleges and universities, while focusing on graduate education and research, state concerns about attrition and declining enrolments, but fail to acknowledge the relationship between attrition and the student's first-year experience. Unless an institution improves the quality of that initial undergraduate experience, particularly during the crucial first term, attrition rates are likely to remain high. High attrition rates among undergraduates will ultimately affect graduate-level enrolments. For institutions that are concerned – those that acknowledge the impact of 60 per cent attrition rates on society – what is to be done? Identifying some intervention programmes and practices that are linked to student success and student persistence is a starting point.

I believe that the heterogeneous students in American institutions in the 1980s have in common a keen interest in matters relevant to their careers. According to a study conducted by the Carnegie Foundation for the Advancement of Teaching, 90 per cent of US high-school students and 88 per cent of parents expect a college education to result in a satisfying career (Boyer, 1986). At the University of Minnesota, student surveys from both 1981 and 1986 show a plurality of students citing vocational reasons for attending college, nearly twice the number of students citing academic reasons. These studies reaffirm the testimonies I hear daily from my own students. It is not surprising that there are numerous studies to suggest that student persistence in the educational institution may be reinforced when, among other things, students have a career focus. For example, Astin (1975) found that there was a direct correlation between students having specific and definite career goals and the likelihood of their staying in school and graduating. Beal and Noel (1980) found that the most predominant reason that students dropped out was lack of career goals of any kind or indecision about what those goals might be. Those students who dropped out for that reason also had low educational aspirations. This conclusion suggests that there is a relationship between having career goals and formulating effective educational objectives. Experiential educators are probably not surprised by these findings, being committed to internships, field trips, and a host of career-oriented concrete experiences that facilitate student learning, but perhaps they are not as aware of their potential effect upon retention. However, many of us are aware of how such experiences help students to become more aware of their own life's objectives and career preferences, and enhance their confidence and determination to succeed.

Many traditional educators and institutions perceive career education and career preparation, including structured field placements as the sole domain of vocational schools or professional and business schools. The president of my own institution stated that students come to college for the 'wrong' reason, i.e. to get a job, and that they need to be convinced that the 'right' reason is to become educated. I do not share this view. Who are we to say that getting a job is a 'wrong' reason to come to college? I believe we should not only allow students their career focus, but even help them to find one, whether it be in business, science, or citizenry. Why? Because we know that having a career focus may help them to remain in higher education. If students persist, opportunities to help them learn how to learn in process as well as in content increase. Johnson (1986) refers to the value of an active, facilitative approach as a way of helping students to become learners, as opposed to becoming merely learned. He implies that the difference is this: a learned student has acquired the knowledge of 'experts' as it is already known, whereas the student as a learner is taught not only already known truths, but how to create new knowledge as well: 'The learner is his/her own theoretician – thus part of a flowing, self-expanding experiential cycle of learning' (Johnson, 1986, p. 140).

Educational goals need not be incompatible with career goals. According to most of the literature on career development in the USA, 'career' is not limited to paid employment, but rather takes on a broader definition whereby an individual attempts to integrate all of his or her various life's roles. A student, upon coming to college, might choose, for example, responsible citizenry or homemaking as a 'career'.

A colleague and I developed a Learning Model of Experiential Education (see Nelson, Chapter 10). This model (Peterson and Nelson, 1986) recognizes that decisions relating to personal aspirations, career goals and educational planning are interrelated and need to be treated as such. Decisions made in each of these areas need to lead the student in the same direction, and promote integration across all three. We posit that an experiential component in an educational setting (such as an internship or a field trip), provides the impetus for evaluating and analysing how the three components are related to one another. When students make educational decisions without having career goals in mind, they often choose courses randomly (Hillary, 1978). We suggest that career and educational decisions can be made more effectively when they are assessed from perspective of one's personal aspirations (Peterson and Nelson, 1986). It is, of course, possible that if one chooses not to get a salaried position, personal aspirations and 'career' goals, according to the broader definition, may be quite similar.

There is another 'personal' side to education as it relates to retention. Roueche and Roueche (1986) summarize the work on formal and informal interactions of students and teachers in and out of the classroom, and the extent to which they are positively associated with persistence and student satisfaction. This research suggests that personal interaction with the Faculty can encourage students to remain in higher education and thus reduce attrition rates.

There are many other factors besides having a career focus and opportunities for personal interaction with the Faculty that contribute to retention. For example, academic advice plays a critical role in any retention programme. This aspect of academic life is beyond the objectives of this chapter and intent of this book. What is suggested here, however, is the importance of providing students with a 'Faculty friendly' experience that accepts and encourages, not merely tolerates, their career concerns, as they begin planning their educational experience. In reinforcing the students' needs to have their career concerns recognized, we may give them the support they need to persist in our educational environment.

Before discussing the relevance of experiential education to reduce attrition rates and to improve the quality of the learning experience, we shall review some of the relevant aspects of experiential education theory that we have drawn upon in our own work, and development of the model.

Experiential learning foundations

Experiential learning is learning which actively involves the learner. Kolb (1984) describes the first stage in the learning cycle as coming from a concrete experience, and defines learning as the process whereby knowledge is created through the transformation of experience. This definition places the emphasis on the *process* of learning rather than on the outcome or content of learning.

This does not, however, exempt experiential educators from their responsibility for the *outcomes* of learning. Needless to say, as educators, we must be held accountable for the students' acquiring some content knowledge. Is it possible that content learning might occur more readily or to a greater extent in the context of process learning?

One of the areas in which experiential teaching departs in practice from traditional teaching is in the recognition that there are differences in the ways in which individuals go through the process of learning. According to Kolb (1984), learners learn better when the subject matter is delivered in a style consistent with their preferred learning style. These preferred modes of learning correspond to Kolb's description of learner types as accommodators, convergers, assimilators, or divergers. Accommodators prefer to have a concrete experience and active experimentation, and learn best from 'hands on' experience. Convergers combine abstract conceptualization with active experimentation, and learn best when provided with practical applications of concepts and theories. Assimilators use abstract conceptualization and reflective observation, and learn best when presented with sound logical theories to consider. Divergers combine the learning processes of reflective observation and concrete experience, and learn best when allowed to observe and gather a wide range of information.

Regardless of the fact that sometimes it might be helpful to adapt our teaching to the students' preferred style of learning, in traditional post-secondary settings, the student is most often expected to adapt to the traditional mode of teaching – lectures. Adapting to students' preferred learning styles has its benefits, but it is not a 'cure-all' and could be less than advantageous. The student could become so dependent upon the preferred learning style that valuable information presented in any 'foreign' style would be lost. I have witnessed such a phenomenon in my own institution.

The General College is a non-traditional, open admissions unit of a traditional research-oriented university. General College is more student-centred in that the Faculty place a high priority on teaching and skill development. Many in the Faculty use experiential methods and many of our students are 'accommodators' based on the Kolb scheme, learning best through active experimentation and 'hands on' experiences. Many of our students, having gained skills and experience in a college setting, take courses from and even transfer to the more traditional units at the University; but some students have difficulty adapting and some even fail in the 'traditional' university lecture mode. The challenge may be in convincing traditional educators to provide learning experiences which both accommodate differences in their students' learning styles, and provide opportunities to develop alternative styles of learning. Perhaps the real challenge is in preparing students for the realization that they are responsible for their own learning, including learning how to adapt to various other modes of learning. It seems to me that in helping students to learn how to learn, we are nurturing a more successful learning environment. Such 'process outcomes' are likely to outlast 'contents outcomes'.

It is no easy task to find a balance between supporting students as they learn how to learn, and challenging them to be responsible for their own learning. Knefelkamp *et al.* (1981) offer a possible solution and draw upon the work of many theorists when they describe a step-by-step procedure for providing that sensitive balance of challenges and supports in their *Practice-to-Theory-to-Practice Model*. In this model the Perry Cognitive Complexity Scheme is applied to the concept of experiential learning. Perry (1970) identifies learning stages in which the individuals progress through nine positions, from dualism to multiplicity to contextual relativism to commitment. Dualistic students expect that there is a right or wrong, a good or bad 'answer' to everything. They look to the 'authority' known as the teacher to provide the right or good answer and then they memorize it. These students see life as 'either/or' with no inbetween. As these students move to a stage of multiplicity, they begin to recognize that a diversity of opinion and values are legitimate, that right answers are not yet known, and that people are entitled to opinions if supported by evidence. They begin to see that the experts differ in their answers. Moving to the stage of relativism, students begin to analyse and compare the diversity of opinions, values and judgements of their sources of information and conclude that knowledge is qualitative, dependent on contexts. By the time students reach commitment, an affirmation, choice or decision can be made in the context of their awareness of relativism. In other words, they are free to draw their own conclusions versus their dualistic acceptance of one view as the only 'right' view. According to *The Practice-to-Theory-to-Practice Model*, challenges and supports exist as a function of:

1. The degree of structure in the learning environment.
2. The degree of diversity in the learning tasks.
3. The type of experiential learning (concrete/vicarious).
4. The amount of personalism in the learning environment.

These variables are to be varied according to the students' needs as determined by their level of cognitive complexity; thus the degree of each variable vascillates along a continuum. Defining and describing these four variables in more detail and offering examples of how to reinforce each, the authors suggest various learning environments which include an appropriate balance of challenges and supports. For students at particular stages in Perry's scheme:

> Students characterized by *dualistic* thinking for example, find *diversity* a *challenge* variable, learn best when able to utilize concrete learning experiences (thus, that is a *support* variable), find *structure* to be a necessary support, and prefer an environment in which *personalism* is present.
> Students characterized by *contextual relativistic* thinking, find *diversity* to be

supportive, that they can be their own *structure*, learn well in *vicarious* learning situations, and are comfortable with moderate degrees of *personalism* (Knefelkamp *et al.*, 1981, p. 30). [my italics]

Thus, what is support to one student may be a challenge to another, depending upon the stage of each student's cognitive development. Furthermore, to a dualistic student, diversity (perhaps in the form of requiring many different assignments) may be threatening, too challenging. Yet, as that same student moves through the stages of cognitive development, diverse assignments, once too challenging, may now be supportive to the student. If only one more student persists because he/she felt comfortable in a supportive, yet challenging environment, then educators might consider this reseach when designing course curricula.

Conceiving learning as a developmental process is not new. What is significant is the more recent recognition of the need to incorporate what we know about developmental learning into curriculum and programme design. Although, based on the few research studies in the USA, there is no clear outcome associated with applying developmental theories in the classroom, Sheckley (1986) recognizes the responsibility of the educator to promote integrative learning in the classroom by providing a developmental framework. We are responsible for providing opportunities for students to acquire information, but the acquisition of someone else's knowledge is not enough. We must also provide opportunities for them to interpret and integrate that knowledge according to their *own* ways of making meaning out of the experience. If we interpret and integrate *for* students, or fail to provide an environment in which students can acquire these skills for themselves, not only do we overchallenge them, thereby increasing the potential for withdrawal from the institution, but we also, perhaps even with greater consequences, fail to encourage their development beyond the dualistic stage of cognitive development. Being aware of the significance of facilitating a learning environment is not sufficient. This awareness has to be put into practice, even though the outcomes may be difficult to assess.

In her inspiring address at the 1987 National Conference of the American Association for Higher Education, Cross spoke critically of reform in colleges and universities that focus more on curriculum (outcome) than on instruction (process):

> While we talk easily of teaching *and* learning, we are generally uncomfortable talking about teaching *for* learning. I think we need to begin to talk boldly about what teachers can do to *cause* learning (Cross, 1987, p. 3).

In the speech, Cross highlighted some conclusions she has drawn from the research conducted over the past several decades. Of the three conclusions, two are basic tenets of experiential education:

1. When students are actively involved in the learning task, they learn more than when they are passive recipients of instruction.
2. Students generally learn what they practice.

The link

Focusing our attention on 'teaching *for* learning', and accepting the view that students have a need to be concerned about their careers, we could support that need by allowing students to use our educational institutions in the pursuit of their career goals, while at the same time teaching them how to learn.

Kolb (1984) found correlations between learning style and career interest. In his research, he found that there is a 'fit' between accommodators and careers in organizations and business and promotion such as administrators, managers and sales people; between divergers and careers in art, entertainment, athletics and social services; between convergers and careers in technology, such as engineers and physicians; and between assimilators and careers in information and science such as teachers, writers and researchers. Content and process concerns can be linked with career interests when considered within the framework of Kolb's evidence. Perhaps by addressing the relevance of the course content to career opportunities, teachers might also witness increases in 'content learning'.

Recognizing and developing the link between career pursuits and learning can help all parties – students, educators and educational administrators – to fulfil their personal objectives. The objective of the majority of American students seems to be to become educated so that they can succeed in a 'career'; the objective of the majority of educators seems to be for the students to learn the subject matter (content) as well as how to learn (process); and the objective of the majority of administrators, educators and students alike, hopefully, is for the students to remain in higher education (persistence) long enough (retention) for all of the above to occur. These objectives are neither contradictory nor mutually exclusive.

Conclusion

This chapter presents some ideas about how experiential education affects learning and how it might improve the persistence of students. I have also considered some theories of cognitive development, and what might be the result of applying such theories in the classroom. What needs further inquiry is the extent to which applying these theories, individually or in combination, actually does contribute to students' development and/or persistence.

Gordon (1985) suggests that a model programme be available to undecided students as they enter college that engages them immediately in an organized academic and career advising programme. My own work suggests that a structured first-year experience needs to include the following: an active learning environment that is geared to students' cognitive and developmental needs; opportunities to reflect on and integrate decision making with regard to personal aspirations, career goals and educational planning; a variety of experiential components; and a high degree of formal and informal interactions between the Faculty and the students (a specific example of this is described by Nelson, Chapter 10).

Tinto (1987) insists that if we want students to become actively involved in their own learning, *we too* must be involved in their learning. Accepting the importance of students' career concerns is a way of telling them that we are willing to get involved in learning that makes sense for them, not only for us. We can show a commitment to helping *them* to fulfil their objectives, not only our own. Most importantly, I believe that the various philosophies, theories and methodologies cited in this chapter provide a clear rationale for creating learning environments that make students responsible for their own learning, and enable them to progress developmentally while providing 'tools for success' according to their own desired outcomes.

References

Astin, A. W. (1975). *Preventing Students from Dropping Out*. San Francisco: Jossey-Bass.

Beal, P. E., and Noel, L. (1980). *What Works in Student Retention*. Iowa City: American College Testing Program.

Boyer, E. (1986). *College: The Undergraduate Experience in America*. Washington D.C.: The Carnegie Foundation for the Advancement of Teaching.

Cross, K. P. (1987). Teaching for learning. *AAEH Bulletin*, **39**(8), 3–7.

Gordon, V. (1985). Students with uncertain academic goals. In Noel, L. and Levitz, R. (Eds), *Increasing Student Retention*. San Francisco: Jossey-Bass.

Hillary, B. C. (1978). *Maintaining Enrollments Through Career Planning*. New Directions For Student Services, No. 3. San Francisco: Jossey-Bass.

Johnson, P. (1986). Help adult learners with process education. *Adult and Continuing Education Today*, **16**(18), 140–5.

Knefelkamp, L. L., Golec, R. and Wells, E. (1981). *The Practice-to-Theory-to-Practice Model*. Washington, D.C.: The American College Personnel Association.

Kolb, D. A. (1984). *Experiential Learning*. Englewood Cliffs, N.J.: Prentice-Hall.

Levitz, R., and Noel, L. (1986). Using a systematic approach to assessing retention needs. In Noel, L. and Levitz, R. (Eds), *Increasing Student Retention*. San Francisco: Jossey-Bass.

Perry, W. (1970). *Forms of Intellectual and Ethical Development in the College Years: A Scheme*. New York: Holt, Rinehart and Winston.

Peterson, S. and Nelson, M. (1986). Learning model of experiential education: A guide for decision-making. *Journal of Cooperative Education*. **22**, 16–28.

Roueche, J. and Roueche, S. (1986). Teaching and learning. In Noel, L. and Levitz, R. (Eds), *Increasing Student Retention*. San Francisco: Jossey-Bass.

Sheckley, B. (1986). Learning as a development process. *CAEL News*, **10**(1), 2.

Tinto, V. (1986). Dropping out and other forms of withdrawal from college. In Noel, L. and Levitz, R. (Eds), *Increasing Student Retention*. San Francisco: Jossey-Bass.

Tinto, V. (1987). *Leaving College, Rethinking the Causes and Cures of Student Attrition*. Chicago: University of Chicago Press.

17

Curriculum Development for Long-distance Internships: Some Principles, Models and Issues

Timothy K. Stanton and Dwight E. Giles

Stanton and Giles discuss their experience of devising and successfully implementing courses in US higher education in which either work- or community-based experiential learning (internships) are a significant component. They believe that one of the key struggles is to overcome Faculty reservations about the rigour of such programmes as compared to traditional campus-based courses where staff maintain involvement, supervision and control. In their experience, Faculties even question the legitimacy of internships near the campus. Internships at a distance, therefore, become even more problematic. Stanton and Giles explain how they have set up 'long-distance' internships in which students attain credit for their activities through participating in experientially based curricular structures which have the rigour of locally and institutionally based programmes. Their aim is to enable students to become more explicitly self-directed and in control of their own learning, and the Faculty to become better adapted to this change. They argue that this kind of fieldwork enables the student to move through increasingly complex levels of analysis from self through to the wider environment. Readers will find a useful comparison with the work of Packham et al. in Australia (Chapter 13) and Järvinen in Finland (Chapter 15). Effective communication between the Faculty and the students becomes a critical issue in such programmes. The authors are currently experimenting with electronic forms of linking the Faculty and the student over long distances, though they recognize the constraints of this facility. Their work is also taking place when Faculty travel budgets have been reduced and campus residential costs have increased. Readers may wish to consider this chapter alongside Brah and Hoy (Chapter 6), Wildemeersch (Chapter 5) and Salmon (Chapter 21). This chapter enables readers to consider wider issues of power and control with regard to experiential learning programmes in higher and continuing education, such as are raised in Chapters 1 and 22.

Current issues related to experiential learning through internship at US post-secondary institutions focus on the problem of Faculty oversight and quality control. In this chapter we describe our development of an interactive, group supervision curriculum for Cornell University interns who work and learn independently at locations far removed from the Ithaca campus. This curriculum combines 'andragogical' theory and practice drawn from adult education, established methods of 'field study' instruction utilized with traditional-age undergraduates, and new technologies. It enables the Faculty to provide from afar the facilitation of learning and internship supervision normally only given in internship programmes with placements near the sponsoring campus. As a case study, this curriculum serves as an effective response to Faculty and institutional concerns that interns do not learn effectively unless instructors are close by and available for continuing support, guidance and supervision.

Background

Support for and supervision of students' learning through internships, field studies and practica[1] appears to be increasing within US post-secondary education. Faculties are becoming familiar with research about a process of experiential learning, described by Kolb (1976, 1984) as a 'learning cycle' of action, reflection, conceptualization and active experimentation. This form of active learning has been identified as being complementary to classroom learning in helping students attain educational goals related to career development, cognitive and moral development, social responsibility, and competence in subject matter.

The National Institute for Education Study Group on Excellence in American Higher Education recommended in 1984 that college Faculties increase their use of internships and other forms of carefully monitored experiential learning. Numerous other commissions and reports (Boyer, 1986; Kaston and Heffernan, 1984; American Association of State Universities and Colleges, 1986) have identified the importance of internships and called on institutions to increase opportunities for student involvement in such programmes. The debate today appears to be focused less on whether this form of experience-based learning has a place in the curriculum and more on where it should be based and on how it can be effectively facilitated and evaluated. Of special importance to this debate are the issues of Faculty involvement and quality control when students undertake internship learning a great distance from the sponsoring institution.

Through the work of researchers, Faculties and associations of practitioners, such as The National Society for Internships and Experiential Education (NSIEE), a set of principles of good practice for 'experiential teaching' has evolved. These cover areas such as: preparation for experiential learning; effective facilitation and assessment; working sensitively with community

1. Practicum/a, as the Latin root suggests, are field experiences that focus on professional practice – such as the practicum requirement for social work. The term is sometimes used interchangeably with other experiential education terms, but more precisely it refers exclusively to activities that are explicitly focused on pre-professional practice.

organization partners of experiential learning programmes; and building institutional support (Stanton and Howard, 1981, Kendall *et al.*, 1986). Examples of effective internship, field study and preprofessional practica courses and programmes abound on a variety of college and university campuses.

However, a closer look at programmes which appear to have become institutionalized within the academic fabric reveals that most academic staff place students in communities adjacent to or near the sponsoring institutions. Local internships enable students to continue their affiliation with campus life, take other courses, and otherwise maintain contact with friends and institutional supports. Additionally, there are usually opportunities for local interns to participate in a fieldwork seminar that allows them to view their field-based learning in a comparative framework. Perhaps, more importantly, 'local' field or internship placements ensure that there can be on-site Faculty supervision of students' experiential learning, which in turn assists the sponsoring programme in gaining academic accreditation and Faculty involvement and respect. Nevertheless, even at institutions where local internship programmes have become successfully established, there remain questions about the legitimacy and substance of learning gained by students through internships or field studies undertaken beyond the proximity of their campuses.

For example, at Stanford University, there has been at least a 20-year struggle to build institutional, academic support for internship learning. Programmes have come and gone with the Faculty as a whole remaining unconvinced of the merits of this form of education. However, in spite of this scepticism, which is common for US research-oriented universities, a small number of departments have developed and maintained internship and practica courses, and interest in experience-based learning is growing. Some Faculties are now assigned to teach courses, which utilize local community-based field placements. In response to a recent upsurge in student interest in public and community service, an additional department has established an academically accredited 'internship supervision' seminar for students participating in internships with local government and human service organizations in the San Francisco Bay area. To enable students to undertake 'substantive' internships in Washington, D.C., and engage in and receive credit for related academic learning, Stanford has established a 'campus' in Washington, which will enable the resident Faculty to guide students' experiential learning and ensure its academic quality.

Even at an institution like Stanford, which is traditionally reluctant to accredit internship learning, there is growing acceptance of the educational importance of internships. Nevertheless, such acceptance appears only to be given when the Faculty have on-site, continuing supervision of participating students. Efforts to enable students to gain credit for long-distance internships arranged independently meet much greater resistance, with the following explanation often being given: how can we give credit for an activity which takes place beyond Faculty oversight and control? As Stanford's Washington campus indicates, the real issue is not distance from the campus but distance from the Faculty. This issue is 'solved' when the Faculty moves off-campus with students to 'an off-campus campus'.

Varieties of long-distance experiential learning programmes

A review of the varieties of long-distance internship programmes indicates that most have addressed the problem of Faculty oversight and, ultimately, quality control, similar to Stanford. They move either the students, the Faculty, or both to the field site. These programmes may be divided and categorized as 'sponsored', 'residential' or 'independent'.

Sponsored programmes are those established in a location to serve students coming from institutions in other locations. Usually they are organized around a curricular theme. They place students in internships, supervise their learning, offer seminars, and evaluate and assess students' work-related and academic performance. The programmes operate under contract with the student-sending institutions and have their staff function as Faculty surrogates for the home campuses. Examples in the USA include The Washington Center and The Great Lakes Colleges Association's Philadelphia Center, both of which provide supervised internships for students from a variety of colleges and universities. A major attraction of these programmes has been the urban and governmental internships they provide that are not available at students' home campuses, many of which are located in rural areas.

Residential programmes often resemble sponsored programmes in practice, and are also located in the USA and abroad. However, they are normally sponsored and operated by a single institution for its students only, and often have a more narrowly focused curriculum. Within this category fall such programmes as Cornell's Human Ecology Field Study Programme in New York City, Stanford's overseas studies campuses, and Cornell and Stanford's Washington 'campuses'.

Independent programmes are those that sponsor students' experiential learning away from campus independently. The original cooperative education or 'sandwich' programmes, such as that at Antioch University, exemplify this model. An individual student travels to an independently arranged placement for a term or longer, with little or no continuing supervision from the Faculty or staff at the home campus. Some institutions, such as Antioch or Beloit College, require these 'co-ops' or 'sandwich' programmes as graduation requirements. However, 'co-ops' often carry no academic credit.

As this listing indicates, Faculty supervision and academic quality issues in long-distance internship programmes have traditionally been expressed in terms of proximity (by moving the Faculty to the site – residential; or utilizing the surrogate Faculty – sponsored), or they have been avoided by not awarding credit, or by relegating the academic supervision to when the student returns to campus. While each of these programme-types meets certain institutional and student needs, none seems to provide for a continuously supervised curriculum with academic credit for students away from campus and not in sponsored, residential or 'off campus-campus' programmes.

Thus, experiential educators, interested in supporting and enabling students to undertake internship learning away from campus, face the challenge of developing experiential learning curricular structures which function effectively over long distances and which replicate the quality and intensity of Faculty supervision available through local programmes. They must address Faculty concerns that students do not learn when the Faculty is not close by and available for support, guidance and supervision. In order to address these concerns within the framework of academic quality traditions and with respect for the learner-centred objectives of experiential education, a reformulation of the issues of distance and communication must be attempted.

We describe a curriculum which we have developed and used for the past 7 years with long-distance interns at Cornell University's College of Human Ecology. It is based upon two basic criteria we identify above, namely:

1. There must be an opportunity for continuous Faculty supervision.
2. Students must be able independently to choose off-campus sites that are at a distance from campus and not part of a structured on-site programme.

After we present this curriculum, we discuss the issues involved in its development and applicability to other institutional settings.

Case study: The individualized long-distance learning curriculum

The New York State College of Human Ecology is one of several colleges, both statutory and endowed, that make up Cornell University. The stated purpose of the college is to prepare students for 'careers in human problem solving', and this applied social science focus is reflected in its six academic departments: Consumer Economics and Housing, Nutritional Sciences, Textiles and Apparel, Human Service Studies, Human Development and Family Studies, and Design and Environmental Analysis.

The College's field experience education programmes, which are labelled 'field study', take two distinct forms. In the first group are the traditional practicum courses, which are based in departments and designed to provide pre-professional training or 'participation' in a student's major. All of these courses take place in the Ithaca area within travelling distance of Faculty sponsors. For example, the Social Work Practicum course enables students with this major to work as interns in human service organizations under the supervision of professional social workers.

The second form of field experience available to students is offered through the Field and International Study Programme. These courses are open to all students on an elective basis. Their curricula address the concept of 'human ecology' and strive to broaden students' academic experience, challenging them to gain an in-depth, multidisciplinary understanding of modern urban society through active participation in organizations and structured reflection and analysis of their experience.

Until 1980 the courses in this second type of programme offered students internships either locally, in the Ithaca area, or through a residential programme in New York City. The residential programme was co-ordinated and instructed by an on-site Faculty member of the programme, who resided in the

New York area. In this type of programme a student majoring in social work might have a placement in a financial services firm in New York City. Her academic work would focus on the industry, on issues raised in an urban setting, and on broader social, political and economic forces that shape the urban context.

At that time students who had participated in the programme, and others seeking to join it, began discussing the need for a third form of field study, one that would enable students to undertake internships independently in locations other than Ithaca or New York City and focus on topics other than those addressed in the other two courses. In response to this request, we and our Faculty colleagues in the programme began developing this third option. Our goal was the application of the field curriculum developed earlier to an individualized, self-directed field study away from campus. Supervision would be group-oriented, i.e. one Faculty member would supervise several students. However, each student's field study would be individualized around the student's articulated learning objectives and placement activities. Of course, there would be no traditional field seminar or on-site Faculty supervision. Criteria for acceptance of students accepted into this third form of field study were that they be able to undertake independent, self-directed field learning away from campus, and that their learning objectives and needs not be those met by the regular course offerings.

The conceptual foundation of this curriculum is derived, in part, from Knowles' model of objective-centred, self-directed, 'andragogical' learning (Knowles, 1975, 1978, 1980). In this long-distance curriculum the learner must not only articulate learning objectives but must further be self-directed in and self-responsible for achieving these objectives. She must identify and choose an internship placement that meets her learning objectives and then negotiate with her prospective placement supervisor and campus-based faculty sponsor[2] to produce a three-way agreement on her objectives and their fulfilment.

Of course, the other partners in this form of off-campus education – the Faculty sponsor and the field supervisor – also have objectives. The role of the student is to assert her own learning objectives in the context of the structured reflection demanded by the curriculum and the tasks required at the field organization, and to monitor and assess her performance in light of these objectives. The role of the Faculty sponsor is one of working to enable the student to meet her learning objectives, facilitating her reflections and self-evaluation, challenging her to be critical, and helping her connect her conceptualizations arising from her experience to relevant theories and knowledge.

The structure of the curriculum is based on Kolb's (1976, 1984) model of an experiential learning cycle. The curriculum helps students to move through a cycle of concrete experience, reflective observation, abstract conceptualization and active experimentation, both in pursuit of their individual learning and the

2. Faculty sponsor here refers to the Faculty member who agrees to serve as the student's 'course instructor', officially allowing the student to register credit for her internship learning, providing learning guidance and readings, and in most cases assessing and grading the students' work.

course content objectives. While this process is quite easily (or relatively so) accomplished in programmes and courses where there is a field seminar, the nature of the interaction in this independent long-distance learning is different. Structures which support the curriculum's content objectives in human ecology in lieu of a seminar include (approximately ten) regular written fieldwork analysis assignments (Stanton, 1981). These assignments ask interns to reflect on their internship-based experience and observations around specified curricular questions, theorize about their reflections in light of relevant assigned readings, and draw conclusions which can then be tested in the ongoing internship. To enable interns to articulate, monitor and assess progress toward their individual learning objectives there are: learning plans; continual written (critical incident journals) and telephone dialogue between the intern and Faculty sponsor; comparative conversations among interns (by phone, letter or site visit); self-reflective dialogue with oneself as an intern – both through regular assignments; and a final self-evaluation. These are the means for enabling the Faculty member and student to develop and maintain a dialogue around their separate sets of goals and objectives, to monitor their performance, and to assess progress at the end of the semester.

Engaging in this independent, cyclical learning process is a disciplined effort, which demands and enhances interns' abilities to learn how to learn. In a final evaluation of his internship learning, one of our students wrote:

> Self-directed learning is a lot more difficult than I imagined. I had thought it simply meant doing things by oneself . . . What I didn't realize is that it asks so much of you. Not so much of you in arranging a schedule or planning a paper but in getting to the core of your feelings and desires. Asking questions which often don't come up in class like, 'What do I want to learn and how do I go about it?' . . . Self-directed learning requires the student to profess not to others but to himself . . .

The format of the curriculum is adapted from the ethnographic approach to data gathering in anthropology and conceptualizes the experience as field study in the classic anthropological sense. The internship is the mode of participation and the curriculum is the structure of the observation. The interns are trained in participant observation methods before leaving campus and are asked to prepare the fieldwork analysis assignments (FAAs) as organizational ethnographers. As described above, these assignments take interns through the action/reflection dynamic of Kolb's learning cycle engaging them in a kind of 'conversation with the situation they are trying to understand' (Morgan, 1986, p. 337). Thus, by the end of the internship, through the pursuit, monitoring and assessment of their own experience and through completion of the curricular FAAs, each intern develops a series of chapters expressing a critical evaluation both of the place that was the site of their internship, and of their performance while there.

Although the case study we present here has a curricular content specific to the academic focus of the Cornell programme, we would argue that this curricular structure will support different content concerns, which would then provide reading content and fieldwork analysis assignments. As a matter of fact, we have developed many more FAAs than we use in a given semester; choice of inclusion depends upon Faculty interests, students' learning objectives, and dynamics of the placement site. Stanton is developing a long-distance internship curriculum in public policy based on this model at Stanford. One way we might describe this curriculum is a structure which enables students to meet individualized learning objectives within a Faculty-defined context of content and skill goals..

A critical element in this structure is communication among participating interns as well as communication between the interns and their Faculty sponsor on campus. Over the years we have instituted different forms of this inter-learner communication that function much the same as a field seminar in the other types of internship programmes. These have included having interns visit each other (in person, by phone or by letter), newsletters containing excerpts from interns' journals and reports, and assignments for interns to interview each other so as to highlight comparisons between experiences and organizational settings. Currently, Giles is using 'Circulation Reports' that are sent to campus by each student and then sent out as a packet to the entire intern class every 10 days or so. As the semester develops, these reports become more interactive as students respond to each other and to the issues raised in previous reports.

Principles

Several specific principles can be derived from this example that are relevant in curriculum development for long-distance internship learning:

1. The student-intern must accept the role of and learn how to perform as a self-directed learner.
2. The curriculum must utilize the field experiences of all students in ways that are both individualized and generalized.
3. The curriculum should move the student-intern through increasingly complex levels of analysis, e.g. self, work group, organization, community, and the macro-environment. We call this the helical model of curriculum progression.
4. The placement supervisor has a crucial role in monitoring and supporting the student's learning objectives as well as mentoring him around the organization's tasks.
5. Regular communication is crucial and needs to be structured between the off-campus intern and Faculty sponsor, between sponsor and field supervisor, among interns, and where possible among groups of interns and the Faculty sponsor(s).
6. The Faculty sponsor must cede control of the learning experience to the student, becoming a coach to the student in taking responsibility for success or failure (a novel experience for most undergraduate students and faculties), and in using the Faculty member effectively as a mentor, teacher, adviser, counsellor, and assessor of the growth and learning achieved (the student becomes an adult learner).

Issues

As we have illustrated the case and formulated the principles, the major issue becomes one of structuring communication between interns and the Faculty, not one of distance from campus or, ultimately, even distance from or lack of control by the Faculty. This issue is even more crucial when interns travel across international borders, which may further complicate and hamper communication (we have begun to apply this curriculum to student internships outside of the USA).

Our principal communication modes have been the mail, telephone calls, and site visits where possible. The heart of the curriculum is a schedule for both the intern and the Faculty sponsor to correspond with assignments and feedback. As we know from basic learning theory and our own experience, feedback needs to be timely and interactive to be most effective. To enhance the timeliness of the feedback and to ease the difficulties of long-distance communication, we have begun to develop an electronic curriculum that utilizes personal computers in the field, electronic communication networks, and the university mainframe computers. While we use existing hardware, software and network capabilities, this represents a new application of this technology to internship curricula. Presently, we are concentrating on the transmission of documents (assignments and feedback) in both directions. In the near future we plan to implement interactive modes of network conferencing that will include all interns in a given semester and the Faculty instructor in a regularly scheduled electronic seminar. Interns will also be able to exchange electronic 'circulation reports' among themselves on a regular basis. Other possibilities include an electronic site visit with the intern, placement supervisor and Faculty sponsor as well as supervisor conferences. The results of this electronic interaction will not only be faster and more effective communication, but ultimately increased academic learning by interns. Interactive, timely feedback will enable interns to better integrate Faculty comments into development of fieldwork reports and their final paper.

This curricular model, then, redefines the issue of academic quality assurance in long-distance internship learning, from one of proximity/distance and Faculty control to one of structuring and enhancing communication in a way that honours students' needs to have distant internships and that respects the university's desires to have the Faculty monitor and supervise internships. The gains to students are substantial in this model in that geography is no longer a major constraining force in their choice of internship sites. There are, however, institutional costs and commitments that are crucial if this curriculum is to succeed. The institution must support the communication function by allocating Faculty time and material resources such as the telephone, postage and, where possible, computer and electronic networking capabilities.

One challenge in this curriculum that we have faced as instructors, is the need to learn a new mode of learning facilitation. We and our interns, lacking immediate, affective cues that signify intellectual achievement and emotional understanding, must learn to rely on the clarity of our written communication. Therefore, in proposing this model for adaptation to other settings we note that this is one curriculum option among several, and that it is not promoted as ideal for all students. Many students want and need direct contact with their Faculty and peers. It is also important to consider that this curriculum is part of a larger sequence of experiential education offerings at Cornell where, as noted above, internship students are trained in ethnographic methods and self-directed learning skills through a required pre-field preparation course (Whitham and Stanton, 1979; Giles, 1986).

The potential contribution of such a curriculum is that it enables students to undertake increasingly distant internships that need not be supported by costly residential programmes or Faculty travel budgets. Its major requirement is that communication must occur on a regular and timely basis. To date, we have not discovered any real outside limit on time between intern–Faculty communication efforts, but we have found it difficult to maintain a schedule of feedback when post time has exceeded 10 days. For this reason, electronic communication is an exciting addition to this curriculum. It is also a potential constraint, if it can only be utilized in those situations where electronic resources are available.

The authors now reside on the opposite coasts of the USA. As an experience in practising what we teach, we have written and revised the chapter electronically. This has enabled us to have an instant and interactive exchange of ideas, feedback and critique. From this we have learned, experientially, the power of effective communication in learning at a distance.

References

American Association of State Universities and Colleges (1986). *To Secure the Blessings of Liberty*. National Commission on the Role and Future of State Colleges and Universities, Washington, D.C.

Boyer, E. L. (1986). *College: The Undergraduate Experience in America*. Carnegie Foundation for the Advancement of Teaching. New York: Harper and Row.

Giles, D. E., Jr. (1986). Getting students ready for the field. *Experiential Education*, **11**(5), 1–8.

Kaston, C. and Heffernan, J. (Eds) (1984). *Preparing Humanists for Work: A National Study of Undergraduate Internships in the Humanities*. Washington, D.C.: National Endowment for the Humanities.

Kendall, J., Duley, J. S., Little, T. C., Permaul, J. S. and Rubin, S. (1986). *Strengthening Experiential Education Within Your Institution*. Raleigh, NC: National Society for Internships and Experiential Education.

Knowles, M. (1975). *Self-directed Learning: A Guide for Learners and Teachers*. Chicago: Association Press/Follett.

Knowles, M. (1978). *The Adult Learner: A Neglected Species*. Houston, Texas: Gulf Publishing.

Knowles, M. (1980). *The Modern Practice of Adult Education: From Pedagogy to Andragogy*. Chicago: Follett.

Kolb, D. A. (1976). *Learning Style Inventory: Technical Manual*. Boston: McBer.

Kolb, D. A. (1984). *Experiential Learning*. Englewood Cliffs, N.J.: Prentice-Hall.

Morgan, G. (1986). *Images of Organization*. London: Sage.

National Institute of Education (1984). *Involvement in Learning: Realizing the Potential of American Higher Education*. Washington D.C.: US Government Printing Office.

Stanton, T. K. (1981). Discovering the ecology of human organizations – Exercises for field study students. In *Field Study: A Sourcebook for Experiential Learning*. London: Sage.

Stanton, T. K. and Howard, C. (1981). Principles of good practice in postsecondary education. *Synergist*, **9**(3), 16.

Whitham, M. and Stanton, T. (1979). *Pre-field Preparation: What, Why, How?* New Directions for Experiential Learning: Enriching The Liberal Arts Through Experiential Learning. San Francisco: Jossey-Bass.

Part 4

Transforming and Empowering

4. Perspectives

How is it possible to teach the educators how to learn from others outside the institution? We learn a lot just by listening to other peoples' experiences, that are different from our own. Education is poor in culture. And it knows little about the culture of other people.

Experiential learning can be exploited to good effect to make people feel that they are participating in change. But the issue for me, the difference between a 'survivalist' and a 'transformational' approach is, are those programmes doing anything to challenge the structures? Or are they only obscuring the fact that the real oppression continues?

For me the relationship between experiential learning and social change is personal. I think because I work towards social change in everything I do, I usually feel isolated in that role, but when I meet with others who are trying to do the same thing, I begin to feel connected. As a black woman living in the West, I am so used to separating my own personal growth from my professional growth. Feeling connected to others is a rare experience, and really important to me.

In most of Africa and South America, experiential learning is part of the life blood of transforming society – it is involved in challenging those very institutions that perpetuate the agony of our current situation, and I think for us in that part of the world those are the things that are most crucial.

I think experiential learning is a result of social change and also a cause of social change. I think society is facing a major revolution, and it is clear that education has not changed, but there is far more mobility of workers, of different kinds of knowledge. It is not possible to find the full range of skills and values we need in our formal system. People are trying to find this learning outside the system. In different social classes and cultures. Experiential learning becomes a tool for not just technological change, but also social and cultural change.

18

Facilitating Learning for Adults Through Participation: Some Observations from Tanzania

K. J. B. Keregero

Keregero takes us through a government-sponsored rural development project in Tanzania. The project specifically aims to counter the traditional 'top-down' approaches to rural development which are noted as having been unsuccessful. Experiential learning approaches are used in a conscious 'bottom-up' process, whereby 'animators' or facilitators and villagers are both treated as 'knowing subjects'. Contrast with Criticos (Chapter 19) and Serrao and Jensen (Chapter 20) the respective roles of facilitators, the extent to which 'top-down' approaches are avoided and how wider political agendas of each are interpreted. We have found there is often difficulty in ensuring participatory, bottom-up experiential learning in institutional, government or radical sponsored 'in the community' projects, in making the leap from intention to reality. Keregero is also in the middle of a project, using experiential methods within a social change programme which seeks to enable the community to engage in their own development out of poverty. A contrast with Salmon's concern with personal stance enables readers to consider some of the issues raised in Chapter 22.

Introduction

There is no question that rural development is very much required in Tanzania. The issue has usually been how to bring it about. Over the years, the top-down concepts of rural development and education have been criticized as leading humanity into passivity. Consequently, the need for development and educational initiatives which are human-centred, with human beings as both the means to, and end recipients of, the benefit derived from the development process, has been very much encouraged. As observed by Hall (n.d.):

> Development is more and more seen as an awakening process, a process of tapping the creative forces of a much larger proportion of society, a liberating of more of a person's efforts instead of a 'problem' to be solved by the planners and academicians from afar.

Just as planting a dead seedling in the ground will result in nothing more than a lifeless stick that will ultimately wilt, development that is based on free handouts, directives and imposed prescriptions or ready-made answers will eventually fail due to its inability to respond appropriately to the winds of change. Hence rural development has become more a concern for learning and human development than a mere desire for modernization and wholesale technology transfer. According to Nyerere (1973, p. 60):

> People cannot be developed; they can only develop themselves. For while it is possible for an outsider to build a man's house, an outsider cannot give the man pride and self-confidence in himself as a human being. Those things a man has to create in himself by his own actions. He develops himself by what he does . . . by making his own decisions, by increasing his understanding of what he is doing, and why; by his own full participation.

Thus the greatest challenge we now have in attempting to facilitate self-sustaining development in Tanzania is how to empower villagers so that they can increasingly become effective actors in activities intended for their own development. Helping people to change from a stance of 'waiting to be told' to one of 'acting because it is the right thing to be done' calls for an educational process that ensures active participation and guarantees system adaptability, continuity and sustainability.

A question that has become quite central in most well-intentioned rural development efforts directed at human development is: 'How can individuals, particularly adults, be assisted in dealing more effectively with problems and situations that affect their own lives in their communities?' In this chapter I shall discuss the efforts that have been made, on a pilot scale, to facilitate experiential learning for adults at various levels through participation in learning activities intended to bring about rural development. They are based on the proposition that learning occurs as a result of the activities in which the learner engages. Such activities constitute the various experiences to which individuals have to be exposed during the learning–seeking process. The proposition underscores the observation that only active interaction with the real-life environment has a better chance of contributing towards effective learning for adults.

Rural development projects that utilize educational means necessarily involve participation of some sort by individuals seeking to learn and those responsible for facilitating learning. Thus, the idea of facilitating learning for adults through participation reflects an orientation towards increasing the extent of involvement or interaction by adults in the learning process. Experience in Tanzania has revealed that the higher the degree of participation by adults, the greater has been the likelihood for effective learning and development to occur. Through a project utilizing the concept of participation in the choice, formulation, execution and assessment of development activities, adults have been enabled to improve their skills, attitudes and knowledge substantially.

Participation and experiential learning: an overview

Margaret Mead once said: 'All changes should be introduced with the fullest consent and participation of those whose daily lives will be affected by the change' (Mead, 1955, p. 289). Her observation is very much in line with the following working definition of participation:

> . . . what gives real meaning to popular participation is the collective effort by the people concerned in an organized framework to pool their efforts and whatever other resources they decide to pool together, to attain objectives they set for themselves. In this regard, participation is viewed as an active process in which the participants take initiatives and take action that is stimulated by their own thinking and deliberation and over which they can exert effective control (ACC Task Force on Rural Development, 1978).

With this definition we can also identify passive participation as the involvement of people in actions or tasks that have been formulated by others and are, in fact, controlled by others. This kind of participation becomes unacceptable. Unless initiatives are adapted through deliberation by the people concerned and made their own, in the final analysis they will not be effective.

In a discussion of a rationale for involvement of people in programme development, Boyle (1981) notes that the literature on participatory activities presents a variety of reasons and justifications for involvement. According to Boyle, participation arises from the need for:

1. Educating people and facilitating understanding, consensus and wise decisions.
2. Securing consent and legitimacy.
3. Enabling the identification of better data about people's needs and problems.
4. Providing social therapy – an opportunity for the disadvantaged to engage in decision making and counteract their alienation.
5. Providing a means to alter the power structure.
6. Facilitating the teaching–learning process.
7. Mobilizing resources.
8. Facilitating the exercise of initiative, creativity and self-reliance of individuals.

Looked at from this perspective, therefore, participation enhances experiential learning as it provides an opportunity for individuals to engage in activities that can lead to their learning. As pointed out by Jarvis (1987, p. 164): 'experiential learning seems to be restricted to a particular type of learning that either involves participation or emotive involvement'. This view concurs with that of Dewey (1938), that all genuine education comes from experience and that all learning has an experiential basis. Jarvis thus concludes that: 'Learning always commences with experience, and the process of transforming that initial experience is the process of learning' (Jarvis, 1987 p. 164).

The notion of experiential learning as held by Jarvis is in line with that advanced by Chickering (1976, p. 63) as 'the learning that occurs when changes in judgements, feelings, knowledge, or skills result, for a particular person, from living through an event or events'. The definition is further amplified by Coleman (1976, p. 50) who distinguishes instructor-induced learning (information assimilation) from experiential learning as follows:

> Much of the learning that takes place in class proceeds through instruction, in which information or knowledge is transmitted from an instructor to the learner, while much of the learning that takes place outside class proceeds through acting (or in some cases, seeing another person act), and then experiencing or observing the consequences of action.

Coleman goes on to say that in everyday parlance, information assimilation is often contrasted to experiential learning by describing the latter as learning through trial and error or learning in the school of hard knocks.

Thus experiential learning extends the notion of learning beyond the formal classroom and reflects the notion that anything worth knowing does not always have to be taught. Learners could simply be given the opportunity to discover it for themselves. Participation essentially creates opportunities for interaction with real-life situations and offers meaningful learning experiences. It enables people to get involved, to do something with others and take action that has been jointly agreed upon. By engaging in purposeful activities through a process of participation, learners are likely to reduce trial and error experience. Participation, therefore, provides for systematic opportunities for experiencing and, hence, learning from real-life situations. Lindeman (1956) provides a useful illustration of this point:

> Learning which is combined with action provides a peculiar and solid enrichment. If, for example, you are interested in art, you will gain much more if you paint as well as look at pictures and read about the history of art. If you happen to be interested in politics, don't be satisfied with being a spectator: participate in political action. If you enjoy nature, refuse to be content with the vicarious experiences of naturalists; become a naturalist yourself. In all these ways learning becomes an integral part of living until finally the old distinction between life and education disappears. In short, life itself becomes a perpetual experience of learning.

Participation provides opportunities for individuals to engage in meaningful learning experiences, or what Tyler (1949) refers to as interaction between individuals and the external conditions in the environment to which such individuals have to react. Through participation, individuals can be actively involved in thinking, feeling and acting in relation to specific problems and needs in their real-life environment. This is what Rogers (1969, p. 5) terms significant or experiential learning and describes its features thus:

> *It has quality of personal involvement* – the whole person in both his feeling and cognitive aspects being *in* the learning event. It is self-initiated. Even when the impetus or stimulus comes from the outside, the sense of discovery, of reaching out, of grasping and comprehending, comes from within. It is

pervasive. It makes a difference in the behaviour, the attitudes, perhaps even the personality of the learner. *It is evaluated by the learner* . . . Its essence is meaning. When such learning takes place, the element of meaning to the learner is built into the whole experience. (emphasis added)

Therefore, the idea of organizing learning experiences for individuals through participation is defendable.

The project

This approach has been applied in a pilot project called Planning Rural Development at Village Level (PRDVL). The project can best be described as a government effort towards accelerating production, improving efficiency of resource utilization and fostering greater participation of villagers in decision making. At this pilot stage, the PRDVL project covers 30 villages in three districts: Iringa Rural District in Iringa Region, Kilosa District in Morogoro Region, and Mpwapwa District in Dodoma Region. The Government of Tanzania co-ordinates and mobilizes its own resources at various levels as well as assistance from other organizations to support the project. UNICEF and ILO have actively supported the government for this purpose over the last few years.

The overall goal of the PRDVL project is to identify the planning and implementation needs of villages in order to develop and test a methodology for the promotion of participatory, self-sustaining rural development initiatives in Tanzania. The government is expecting to receive recommendations from the project so that useful results may be adopted and replicated in other parts of the country. In order to provide policy guidance, the project has a Steering Committee which meets at least twice a year, in one of the project villages. The Steering Committee also links the project with critical national institutions, and serves as a channel through which the project communicates with the government. PRDVL activities are closely guided by a Project Advisory Committee which serves as the executive organ of the Steering Committee. The Project Advisory Committee assists the project team in ensuring a scientific approach in the identification, assessment and analysis of problems and needs at village level. It also provides a forum for critical analysis and discussion of findings from work in villages and generally functions as a resource group, providing expert advice on the conceptualization, design, development and execution of the project's methodology. Members of the Project Advisory Committee, which I chair, are appointed on the basis of their professional capability and personal interest in the project, rather than as representatives of their institutions.

The practice of facilitating learning through participation

PRDVL project activities are undertaken collaboratively by a group of scientists from institutions of higher learning, government staff at various levels and by villagers. This kind of mix ensures a proper understanding and articulation of the needs, problems and constraints to development in the project villages.

Methodology

The project utilizes what can be termed participatory research-cum-action methodology. This combines investigation into problems and issues concerning the life and environment of a selected target group and concurrent corrective action through collaboration with, and participation of, members of the target group. The key feature of the methodology is the participation of members of the target group as equal partners rather than mere objects of research and action.

The participatory approach to rural development is at the core of the ideology of socialism and self-reliance espoused by Tanzania. It is indeed the basis for the strategy for rural development through the use of villages as nuclei for self-reliant initiatives. The Villages and Ujamaa[1] Villages Act of 1975 provided a framework for the participatory approach nearly 20 years ago. Unfortunately, this approach was not quite grasped at the beginning, as most rural development functionaries preferred quick results through top-down approaches.

However, based on the experience and lessons of the immediate past, there is increasing preference for bottom-up participatory rural development approaches. Consequently, there is adequate political goodwill and support for these projects. The PRDVL project is, therefore, well received and supported by government and has great potential for being expanded on a larger scale in the country, particularly in terms of its methodology.

In order to facilitate participation, members were encouraged to form their own special interest groups. These participatory organizations, as they have come to be known, serve as instruments for collective action, and a basis for collective reflection and analysis. The groups are formed around operations chosen. As of December 1986 there were 37 such groups formed (Table 18.1). The groups are managed by members themselves and serve as a means for collective, creative initiatives.

Table 18.1   People's participatory groups

Enterprise	No. of groups	Membership
Agriculture	30	330
Tea/Coffee Shop	1	10
Shop	1	5
Carpentry	1	10
Blacksmith	1	10
Brick-laying	1	8
Tractor operation	1	22
Tailoring	1	3
Total	37	398

Source: PRDVL Quarterly Reports.

1. Ujamaa literally means 'socialist'.

How learning is facilitated

Most rural development projects have traditionally utilized what Freire describes as the banking concept of education, which is characterized by the teacher–student contradiction. According to Freire (1974), this contradiction is stimulated and maintained through the following attitudes and practices:

1. The teachers teach but students are taught.
2. Teachers are supposed to know everything while students are presumed to know nothing.
3. Teachers are supposed to think while students are supposed to be thought about.
4. Teachers choose and enforce their choice and students comply in turn.
5. Teachers choose the programme content, and the students, who were not consulted in the first place, adapt to it.
6. Teachers become the subject of the learning process while the students become mere objects.

The banking concept is top-down and manipulative and has increasingly demonstrated failure to achieve sustained rural development outcomes. It assumes that there must be a trainer before learning can occur. Consequently, the PRDVL project espouses a dialogical approach which is bottom-up in nature. At the core of the learning process is the animator who, as a starting point, has the task of breaking the subject–object dichotomy in order to encourage active interaction. According to Freire (1974), this implies:

1. Demythologizing reality.
2. Encouraging dialogue as a basis for facilitating learning.
3. Enabling learners to be critical thinkers rather than objects of assistance.
4. Making learning a continuing endeavour that reflects the transformational character of reality.

Thus in the PRDVL project, animators play a role which is different from that of traditional teachers or trainers. Animators operate by creating an alternative relationship in which the villager and the animator are perceived as two knowing subjects. This is different from a relationship whereby the villager is perceived as an object to be acted upon by the animator, who is supposedly the knowing subject. This alternative orientation is based on the increasing realization that both the animator and villager have rich intellectual traditions, the former being rooted in formal education and the latter in real-life experiences and practices (Tilakaratna, 1985).

In order to stimulate the necessary interaction at village level, the animator carried out several functions, including:

1. Engaging villagers, their leaders and other functionaries in a learning process in their own real-life environment.
2. Sharing knowledge and experiences with villagers in a process of learning together.

3. Guiding villagers in an active process of thinking and discovery and carrying out specific actions in relation to identified problem situations.
4. Working with villagers in formulating, carrying out and assessing outcomes of suitable development activities.
5. Assisting villagers in building a capacity to undertake and manage collective activities.

A key aspect of the animator's role is the horizontal sharing of ideas with villagers. The animator strives to stimulate the critical awareness of villagers in order to ferret out their intellectual capabilities. In the words of Tilakaratna (1985, p. 13):

> This interaction sparks off a certain chemistry – the poor are stimulated to initiate a process of scientific enquiry into their life situations (poverty). The poor move away from their sensory perception of, and fatalistic beliefs about, their poverty into a conceptual and analytical framework which enables them to relate their poverty to the social reality around them.

In order to ensure effective interaction between animators and villagers, contact with target groups is made possible through farm visits, home visits, group meetings and group activities. The animator's work schedule is generally flexible and patterned around the convenience of villagers.

Preparation of animators

Preparation of animators for work with villagers has essentially been patterned along the principle that learning occurs as a result of the activities engaged in by the learner. Animators have been given the opportunity to learn by interacting with villagers and participating in solving their real-life problems. The first step in the orientation of animators for the job was a 6-day workshop. Through group discussions with fellow participants and resource persons, animators were enabled to reflect critically on the knowledge, experiences, attitudes and skills that they already possessed. After the first workshop, the animators went back to their assigned villages to work with villagers and collect socioeconomic data. There has since been a series of 3- to 7-day workshops every 3 months, held on a rotating basis in each of the three project districts.

Emerging experience has revealed that animators interacted well with villagers. This made it easy for them to gain acceptance and engage in effective dialogue with villagers and their leaders. In part, this was a result of group learning activities in which the animators were involved in sharing and being exposed to collective reflection and analysis of experiences with their colleagues in a participatory learning effort. A major outcome of the initial orientation of animators was their ability to examine and analyse the socioeconomic situation of the project villages. By working closely with villagers, animators were able to identify priority problem areas which needed action and, as a result, assist villagers in developing small-scale projects, utilizing most of the resources from the villagers themselves. Thus the learning process for animators is closely linked with their activities in the field.

The animation process: A case example

In order to illustrate the role of the animator and the animation process in general, I will describe the formation and operations of a carpentry group, one of the groups listed in Table 1.

The carpentry group is in Kimamba Village, Kilosa District. When the animator for this village took up the job, she interacted with as many people as possible in order to gather information and gain further insight into village life. She soon broke communication barriers and facilitated the formation of a group of 10 people, all men, who were interested in undertaking carpentry as a way of generating income. Of the 10 group members, only 3 had good skills and knowledge in carpentry. Through a process of dialogue, the animator and group members were able to think critically about their situation. After identifying carpentry as a possible way of generating income and improving their standards of living, they were able to:

1. Formulate their goals.
2. Establish their operational mechanisms, including the election of leaders for the group.
3. Identify constraints to the effective establishment and implementation of income-generating activities.
4. Formulate ways of dealing with identified constraints.

The major constraints identified from the very beginning of the project were a lack of working capital, tools and a proper workplace, and inadequate carpentry skills on the part of seven members of the group.

The question of working capital had been initially exaggerated by group members in anticipation that the animator was a benefactor. They expected her to give money to them. On the contrary, the animator discussed the question: 'How best could you improve your standards of living through carpentry with maximum self-reliance?' In addressing this question, under the guidance of the animators, group members soon realized that they could raise initial working capital through contributions from their own meagre resources, utilize tools owned by three of their colleagues, and construct a temporary working shed at the residence of one of their colleagues. In short, members learned through dialogue that the means to achieve their goals were largely in their own hands. After a short period of time, the group were able to make tables, chairs, beds and stools.

The products were of a reasonably high quality, and the group soon became known all over the village. As the volume of business increased, new needs arose, including improving the skills of the other members who were not carpenters; attaining more funds to invest in the project in order to handle more orders; gaining a larger market that would enable them to generate larger incomes; and finding a better and more secure working place. The animator assisted the group to make their working place an actual laboratory for learning. Through contact with the Member of Parliament for that constituency, she was able to secure a building that was once used as a community centre but had been out of use for a number of years. The group moved into the spacious building where they now work and display their products. The three skilled members of the group are now training the rest of the group in carpentry skills through apprenticeships. The workplace, therefore, provides an opportunity for teaching by showing and learning by doing.

Recently, the Member of Parliament provided some seed money to the group to boost their activities. Through dialogue, the animator has sensitized group members towards the use of credit facilities. Arrangements have already been made by the PRDVL project management to provide a revolving fund to the group as a starter. It is expected that, with time, the need for more money will drive the group into borrowing from credit institutions.

The animator's contribution as a go-between and catalyst in this project has been remarkable, and includes efforts to secure the present workplace, initiation of on-the-job learning opportunities for members without skills in carpentry, and the provision of access to a revolving fund and credit facilities. Recently, the animator managed to secure a contract for the group to make 400 school desks for the District Council.

In order to keep the group in harmony, the animator visits the members regularly and discusses the progress of the project with them. She has assisted in creating self-governance in the group. Members hold their meetings regularly and have learned to deal with their problems without much intervention by the animator, except in situations that necessitate her input. The group leaders have in fact become animators in their own right and this provides opportunity for the project animator to work with other new groups. The animator has been well accepted by the group. During discussions, they no longer regard her as the 'expert who knows everything' but more as an encouraging companion who enables them to think critically on their situation in order to generate useful and self-reliant courses of action. It is even more promising, considering that the animator, who is a young woman, and the group members, who are all male adults, interact so harmoniously and cooperate so closely. Both the animator and group members are quick to admit that they are engaged in a process of endless learning about one another, about their group activities and about their work environment as a whole.

Observations about the project

Although the PRDVL project is still in its early stages of development, a number of observations pertinent to experiential learning through participation can be cited.

Villagers involved in the project have begun to show interest and practice in investigation, critical questioning and analysis of their own situations. They have begun to see the benefits of collective analysis and implementation of results. Also, as a result of self-enquiry and analysis under the guidance of animators, villagers have been able to formulate and implement a number of projects intended to improve their standards of living. The following are a few examples:

1. A group of skilled and semi-skilled carpenters has been formed. Several other members without skills but with an interest in carpentry have also joined the group. The group not only serves as a training ground for its members but also produces such items as furniture and other wood products for the village market. They have expressed desire to sell products outside the village as well.
2. A group of blacksmiths has been formed. One member who is quite skilled trains most of the other members. They can now produce metal charcoal stoves, buckets, shovels and simple hoes for use at village level. The group faces a shortage of raw materials and has managed to survive by using scrap metal sheets from old vehicles and unused containers.
3. A small group of tailors is beginning to form and is involved both in training members in tailoring as well as making clothes.
4. A fairly large group of farmers have come together and is engaged in the cultivation of maize and groundnuts. They are currently being guided through learning experiences to enable them to appreciate and adopt recommended husbandry practices. The group has bought a tractor on a cooperative basis and uses it on its own farm and hires it out. They have had to grapple with issues concerning tractor scheduling, maintenance and book-keeping.

Villagers involved in the project have learned how to organize their own groups, conduct meetings and follow-up on issues that require attention by others. All groups have, on their own, elected their leadership and maintain their own schedules of group work. Already there are indications of the emergence of group members who have developed abilities to organize, animate and mobilize others. These individuals will be the logical successors of the current animators. This means that villagers are gradually developing a capacity to serve as their own animators as the official animators gradually withdraw.

The animation process has demonstrated that programmes for learning through participation cannot be rigidly prestructured. While the need for a working framework within which learning takes place is emphasized, there must be adequate flexibility to accommodate and respond to the needs and problems identified by villagers and animators. However, through the animation process, we have been able to confirm earlier observations that villagers by and large grapple with problem-oriented real-life situations. This requires an appropriate problem-oriented learning approach rather than the traditional subject-oriented one.

When starting, interaction between villagers and animators concentrated on their experiences and knowledge, with no attempt to introduce anything new. This approach gives participants the feeling of dignity, particularly as it involves them directly in the learning process, instead of alienating them from the problem-solving equation. The greatest achievement attained is the increased level of awareness on the part of participating villagers and staff. Through regular interaction, the participants have become increasingly aware of their priority needs and problems, and have come up with very creative approaches towards solving their own problems. Kiponzelo Village in Iringa District, for example, came up with estimates for fertilizer requirements for the farming season of 1986 on the basis of needs identified through animation. This was the first time estimates had ever been made for such requirements.

One of the expectations of the PRDVL project was its ability to spread its effect to other non-project villages. There is evidence to show that this is beginning to take place. Recently, a non-project villager from a neighbouring village managed to organize a group of fellow villagers based on the approach used at Nyabula, one of our project villages in Iringa District. In addition, it has been agreed that the animation process be used in providing on-the-job training for some village health workers assigned to the Iringa Nutrition Programme.

Critics of participatory learning approaches using dialogue argue that:

1. Most villagers know little or nothing about their development, let alone innovations identified as necessary for improving their living conditions. As such it is difficult to conduct effective dialogue with participants who are disadvantaged right from the start.
2. The animation process tends to be very slow and, therefore, expensive. It is, therefore, not a suitable approach for a country whose development needs and problems tend to dictate to people to 'run while others walk'.
3. Animation as a whole requires more abilities, knowledge and attitudes than are currently possessed by many village functionaries and local leaders.

The first critique is simply a misconception of learning and the role of the animator as an educator. Dialogue is itself a learning process for villagers and animators as they encounter real-life situations and struggle to discover together critical problems, needs and alternative ways of dealing with them. The second critique is allayed by past experience which has demonstrated that simplistic and quick-fix techniques imposed on villagers have not contributed adequately to sustainable development. The last critique is the real challenge for the PRDVL project, to prepare and develop individuals who will be well qualified to articulate and actually practise animation. Here, the project has arranged for periodic workshops for animators to facilitate regular interaction and exchange as well as visits to project villages of their colleagues to learn 'by seeing and doing'; regular short-term training programmes for animators; and the launching of a newsletter for animators and a project summary sheet for villagers, to facilitate documentation, exchange and dissemination of real-life experiences from the field.

I have attempted to link the notion of participation with that of experiential learning. One of the arguments advanced is that participation creates opportunities for interaction with real-life situations and, therefore, offers meaningful learning experiences. Observations from a rural development project which utilizes a bottom-up participatory approach have been presented, indicating that such participation has potential for facilitating learning for adults.

References

ACC Task Force on Rural Development (1978). *Report of the Third Meeting of the Working Group on Programme Harmonization.* UNIO/62(c) paragraph 9. Rome, 26 January.

Boyle, P. G. (1981). *Planning Better Programs.* New York: McGraw-Hill.

Chickering, A. W. (1976). Developmental change as a major outcome. In Keeton, M. T. and Associates (Eds), *Experiential Learning*, pp. 62–107. Washington, D.C.: Jossey-Bass.

Coleman, J. S. (1976). Differences between experiential learning and classroom learning. In Keeton, M. T. and Associates (Eds), *Experiential Learning*, pp. 49–61. Washington, D.C.: Jossey-Bass.

Dewey, J. (1938). *Experience and Education.* London: Collier Macmillan.

Freire, P. (1974). *Pedagogy of the Oppressed.* New York: The Seabury Press.

Hall, B. L. (no date). Creating knowledge: Breaking the monopoly. Working Paper No. 1. *Participatory Research Project Working Papers*, Toronto.

Jarvis, P. (1987). Meaningful and meaningless experience: Towards an analysis of learning from life. *Adult Education Quarterly*, **37**(3), 164–72.

Lindeman, E. (1956). *The Democratic Man.* In Gessner, R. (Ed.), *Selected Writings.* Boston: Beacon Press.

Mead, M. (Ed.) (1955). *Cultural Patterns and Technical Change.* New York: The New American Library.

Nyerere, J. K. (1973). *Freedom and Development.* Dar es Salaam: Oxford University Press.

Rogers, C. R. (1969). *Freedom to Learn.* Columbus, Ohio: Charles E. Merrill.

Tilakaratna, S. (1985). The animator in participatory rural development: Some experiences from Sri Lanka. *World Employment Research Working Paper.* Geneva: ILO.

Tyler, R. W. (1949). *Basic Principles of Curriculum and Instruction.* Chicago: University of Chicago Press.

19

Media, Praxis and Empowerment

Costas Criticos

This chapter, written from a South African perspective, seeks, politically, transformational alternatives to apartheid education through an experiential learning philosophy and approach. Criticos addresses these wider issues within the context of a formal education setting and in his programme through which he works with community 'change agents'. Experiential learning is a democratic process involving 'facilitator' and 'participant'. They are seen as co-workers in learning – the meanings of which emerge as human and unmechanistic within a clear political framework for social change. He poses critical questions for those in Western capitalist countries who use experiential learning for purposes that simply make the existing society more 'efficient' in coping with changing economic conditions. He also challenges those who work in higher and continuing educational settings whose work with the community becomes simply another means of imposing and maintaining their expertise. Keregero (Chapter 18) and Serrao and Jensen (Chapter 20) also aim for a more democratic relationship between facilitator and learner. Criticos also points to the dangers of the experiential learning approach being co-opted by 'educational dominators' in societies where education is traditionally in the hands of the experts. His concerns complement those of Wildemeersch (Chapter 5) and Brah and Hoy (Chapter 6).

Contrasts may be made with others working in institutional settings such as Nelson (Chapter 10), Stanton and Giles (Chapter 17) and Peterson (Chapter 16); and with Salmon (Chapter 21), O'Reilly (Chapter 9), and Wylde (Chapter 11) who stress the importance of personal meanings as a basis for empowerment.

Apartheid education denies many of the goals regarded as essential by democratic and open societies. Most notably, apartheid education fails to prepare learners for work and life as autonomous adults. Worker, church and progressive organizations have attempted to counter the effects of apartheid education with alternative education programmes. The programmes encompass both alternative contents and methodologies. Their underlying strategy is not simply to dismantle apartheid education, but to replace it with a democratic learner-centred model.

In this chapter, I will attempt to show that experiential learning, which is a popular method, offers an appropriate strategy for alternatives to apartheid education. Furthermore, experiential learning has a crucial role to play in post-apartheid education.

One aspect of education which is severely limited for blacks is the area of media education and the training of media practitioners. This limitation functions to deny media production skills and resources to black communities. The Media Attachment Programme (MAP) based in the Department of Education at the University of Natal was initiated in 1984 to address these problems. The problems manifest themselves either as communities striving to produce oppositional media or individuals who have for a variety of reasons been denied access to formal media training. I first encountered these problems in 1982 when I joined the University as Head of the Audio-Visual Centre. In this position I was frequently advising young people about study and careers in media. The people who sought my advice were mostly adults who had encountered enormous barriers to further education; barriers raised because of their race, education or opposition to the State. In addition to this advisory role I was frequently asked to assist community organizations with the production of media resources. The centre's limited resources and the inadequate and indeed inappropriate provision of media training in a country of increasing State repression militated against the worth of our advice or assistance.

Frustration over my inability to respond to these needs led to the radical solution of using collaborative production processes to solve community media problems. A production team is composed of a facilitator, participants with training needs and community members with production needs. The production process, tediously slow by Western commercial standards, is concerned with more than the product – it is concerned intimately with a process that develops production skills and a product 'owned' by the community.

Essentially, the training takes the form of an 'attachment', in which the roles of teacher and learner are redefined as facilitator and participant, working in a democratic relationship. The programme embodies open-entry, negotiated curricula and outcomes, and democracy and sensitivity to participant, facilitator and community development.

Participants included independent oppositional producers, community workers and postgraduate students. MAP accommodates those participants who would be refused entry to formal study, as well as those participants who, because of their location within the culture of resistance, have been denied access to State and commercial facilities.

The methodology of this programme was not preceded by a lengthy period of research or an understanding of the rich potential of experiential learning but came about in a natural and naive way. The critical and theoretical period came much later when I attempted to understand why this experiential methodology worked. The crucial breakthrough came with a changed perception which made connections between the training and production needs originally perceived as discreet problems and unrelated to the educational crisis.

The South African educational crisis

A number of myths operate to cloud the understanding of the nature of the present crisis in South African education. These myths are that the crisis is purely centred on education, that education is neutral, that the crisis is recent and that issues centre on the unequal provision of education. What then is the nature of the crisis?

The educational crisis has a history coincident with the history of the Nationalist Government. It has, however, only manifested itself publicly with the 1976 Soweto disturbances. From this point onwards, the crisis became public and has deepened to the extent of a low-level civil war which is contained in the Black townships through the deployment of troops in these areas and with the repressive controls of the general State of Emergency. The crisis facing black education is part of a general crisis facing the Nationalist Government and capital.

In the last decade the crisis has become evident by the rapid growth of labour movements, community organizations and political movements. The crucial developments include the formation of the NECC (National Education Crisis Committee), COSATU (Congress of South African Trade Unions) and the UDF (United Democratic Front).

The most common myth held by both whites and blacks is that black education is different because it receives only 10 per cent of the amount spent on white education (per child). Black education is in fact different from white education by design. Apartheid has designed black education so as to ensure the subjugation of black communities. The most influential document in relation to black education was a pamphlet on education issued by the Institute for Christian National Education. This document, which preceded the Nationalist Government coming to power in 1948 and apartheid education, set the pattern which has directed State thinking and legislation to this day. The principles which established the pattern are spelt out in the final article of Part II of the pamphlet (ICNE, 1948):

> Article 15: Native Education.
> The white South African's duty to the native is to Christianize him and help him on culturally. Native education should be based on the principles of trusteeship, non-equality and segregation; its aim should be to inculcate the white man's view of life, especially that of the Boer nation, which is the senior trustee . . .
> . . . Native education should not be financed at the expense of white.

What is visualized in this pamphlet is a 'non-education', a training which has conspired against the disenfranchised to fulfil the apartheid ideology. Parmanand (1987) uses the term 'non-education' because he believes the provision of schooling for blacks does not ascribe to true education. He elaborates:

> Non-education has from the beginning been used as a political weapon against blacks. It has by design perpetuated the lowly status of blacks and

sublimated status of whites. By commission it has *inter alia* indoctrinated rather than educated us in a white man's history, almost succeeded in convincing us that white is right, humiliated us into a denial of our own humanity, dignity and worth.

Youngman (1985, p. 156) gives us an international perspective, using a Marxist analysis of education, to explain the universal phenomenon of differential provision of education:

> The expansion of capitalism has invariably been accompanied by the expansion of educational institutions designed to contribute to reproduction by developing the differentiated intellectual capabilities required by the labour market and engendering the ideology and social practices which legitimate the social order.

In South Africa, as is in other capitalist states, there is a principal determining contradiction between capital and labour. What is unique to this society is the dominant contradiction in which all whites have political freedom, while blacks, especially Africans, suffer national statutory oppression (Mkatshwa, 1985). These contradictions are explicitly and arrogantly confirmed by J. N. Le Roux, a 1945 National Party politician who suggested that:

> . . . we should not give the Natives any academic education. If we do, who is going to do the manual labour in the community? (Parmanand, 1987).

This then is the context of black education and the current struggle. The slogans no longer call for more books or equal education. The call is for education for liberation and empowerment of the people. The 1985 slogan 'Liberation now, Education later' has given way to 'People's Education for People's Power', which clearly advances education as a site of struggle for social transformation.

Alternatives to apartheid education

We have shown that the crisis in black education cannot be isolated from the economic, political and social character of South Africa. By the end of 1985 the endemic violence in townships had caused approximately 250,000 black students to drop out of school.

At the beginning of 1985 there were 25,584 black (African) students enrolled in the final year of secondary education in urban schools. From this enrolment, 24,231 students registered to write the end of year exams and of these only 10,523 wrote the exams. In the end, only 4897 passed the exam with 1327 getting a high enough mark to apply for a place at a university. This represents a meagre 19 per cent of enrolled students who passed the exam and 5 per cent who are eligible to apply for entry into a university (Hartshorne, 1986).

As a result of the severity of the crisis and the outcome of meetings between the SPCC (Soweto Parents Crisis Committee) and the ANC in Harare, the SPCC organized the first National Consultative Conference. This was in

December 1985 at the University of the Witwatersrand. At this conference, attended by 162 progressive organizations, the foundation for the National Education Crisis Committee (NECC) was laid. The keynote address by Father Smangaliso Mkatshwa has become the reference for debate centred on the nature of People's Education:

> The theme of the conference is 'People's Education for People's Power'. This theme makes it quite clear that we do not want just any type of education. People's education is a devastating indictment on Apartheid slave education. The call is now for education for liberation, justice and freedom. It is a demand for full participation in all social structures (Mkatshwa, 1985).

The conference delegates passed a number of resolutions on 'People's Education' which have defined the character of the struggle for 'People's Education'. These include:

- Elimination of capitalist norms of competition.
- Encouragement of collective input, critical thinking and analysis.
- Empowering of workers to resist exploitation.
- Promotion of correct values of democracy and non-racialism.

The NECC and other organizations have worked on programmes and strategies to fulfil these resolutions. The NECC has been active through committees commissioned to rewrite school texts to present people's perspectives rather than capitalist, euro-centric views. The most active committees have been those working on the rewriting of the English and History textbooks.

In January 1987 the most severe school-related restrictions were added to the general State of Emergency. The views of the NECC were declared 'subversive' and NECC programmes, alternative texts, clothing carrying slogans and any writing related to People's Education, were banned. Convictions related to these latest restrictions carry a maximum penalty of £4500 sterling or 10 years in jail (Sidley, 1987). More recently (February 1988), the NECC and 16 other educational, cultural and worker organizations have been banned.

The theory and experience that informs and underpins the NECC and most alternative organizations is socialist pedagogy and the experience of national liberation movements. Socialist pedagogy embraces the resolutions of People's Education and is directed towards the ultimate goal of social transformation. One of the fundamental characteristics of education in newly independent states involved in national reconstruction, involves a critical reflection on the past. This includes discovery of the roots of social injustice and inequalities (Mayani, 1975), and finding ways to remove them before proceeding with human development.

Khotseng *et al.* (1986) refer to this stage of the pedagogy as 'unveiling' the reality of the oppressed which then proceeds to recreate new knowledge through which people discover themselves as its 'permanent creators'.

Mblinyi (1977) projects her experience of Tanzanian education to other settings in her checklist of liberating education. The list below abbreviates her more complete list to the most fundamental indicators of liberating education. Such education should:

- Provide mass education based on proletarian ideology.
- Remove contradictions between mental and manual labour.
- Democratize school and relationships.
- Promote cooperative forms of work.
- Promote student creativity and self-confidence.
- Promote problem solving and critical thinking.

The practice of liberating education in different settings is manifested by a few universal characteristics. These practices include a link between work and knowledge, democratic learning relationships and the integration of the lived experience of the learners. Clearly these characteristics challenge the traditional didactic expert mode of teaching and yield a different form of education. Youngman (1986) proposes nine principles which inform a Marxist approach to adult education. These principles yield the characteristics stated earlier and indeed provide a guide to action for liberating educators.

I now wish to identify the role of experiential learning in alternative programmes. Youngman's (1986, p. 96) sixth principle on praxis is most useful to us:

Principle Six
The specific determinant of consciousness is praxis, or activity. Human activity involves purpose and intention, and knowledge arises and deepens within a continuous process of activity, conceptualization and renewed activity. Praxis takes place within situations transmitted from the past but can change these situations and create new ones. Thus people are conscious agents of social change within the constraints of historically constructed objective conditions. All praxis is essentially social.

This cycle of activity and conceptualization is crucial and forms the cornerstone of most educational programmes, but especially those involved in national reconstruction. Mudariki (1985) states that most of the problems inherited by Zimbabwean educators stem from the division between mental and manual labour. He sees the link between mental and manual work as one of the major areas of class struggle in establishing a socialist system. It is through the mental–manual link that knowledge is created (Hall, 1978).

Youngman (1986, p. 59) cites Mao's essay *On Practice* as providing the clearest expression of the Marxist approach to praxis:

Practice, knowledge, again practice and again knowledge. This form repeats itself in endless cycles and with each cycle the content of practice and knowledge rises to a higher level. Such is the whole of dialectical materialist theory of knowledge and such is the dialectical theory of knowing and doing.

This interest in praxis is central to our debate on experiential learning, learning which builds on the learners' resident experience and through critical reflection reconstructs experience. For Freire (1985) an education of this nature demands commitment and determination to pursue the rigour of the mental–manual cycle: a cycle which moves from the concrete context of facts and relationships to theory, where the concrete is reflected on and analysed, and back to the concrete 'where men experiment with new forms of praxis'. Freire regards this cycle as radical conscientization which rejects the capitalist mode of 'banking' education (depositing knowledge into empty heads) in favour of an education which he describes as problem posing.

In this section I have attempted to identify the forces which influence the nature of alternative educational programmes in the South African education crisis. Experiential learning as practised in progressive movements has a transformative character which has responded to the educational crisis. Experiential learning is concerned with knowledge building and conscientizing as opposed to knowledge preservation and transmission. Western views of experiential learning are more loosely defined and are often used interchangeably with practical training. My own view is that experiential learning is radical and transformative and it is for this reason that experiential learning has become a popular method in the midst of crisis.

My own personal definition of experiential learning is: *from experience, through experience, to experience*. This definition is a simple variant of Youngman's sixth principle which underpins my work and the methodology of the Media Attachment Programme.

Media attachment programme

As the social crisis in South Africa deepens, censorship and the banning of media opposed to the State increases. The State has come as close as it can to thought control with its repressive media curbs. The most severe restriction is Proclamation 224, published in the Government Gazette of 11 December 1986. This proclamation prohibits the making, publishing or importing of a 'subversive statement'. 'Subversive' is defined as any activity which documents unrest or draws attention to the State of Emergency. The presence of blank spaces and obliterations in newspapers gave some indication of the extent of censorship. This is now regarded as 'subversive'.

It is in this climate of repressive media controls and distrust of mass media that the alternative media have grown (Tomaselli, 1985). There are similar parallels during the events that led up to the overthrow of the Marcos regime in the Philippines. Dionisio (1986), points to the role that small media had during the most repressive period after Martial Law in 1972. Using 'group media' in the form of cooperatively produced newsletters, videos and slide productions, etc., the small media 'ate through the thick silence which was the dictatorship's strongest protection'. One of the most significant developments on the small media front was the 'Betamax revolution' which circulated copies of community productions and foreign documentaries related to Ninoy Aquino's assassination on 21 August 1983. At the time there were approximately 1 million VCR households (Dionisio 1986). Other observers claim that without the small media and later the people's control of the big media, Marcos would not have been ousted.

In South Africa, small media are being employed by a variety of progressive educational bodies, labour movements and church groups. It is in this climate of the growing use of small media to deny state propaganda that the Media Attachment Programme (MAP) came into being. MAP, which is based in the Department of Education, University of Natal, was founded in 1984 in response to requests for media production and training problems by community and educational organizations. Initially, the production and training problems were tackled separately, but our inability to make any meaningful contribution to either problem led to a radical reformulation of the strategy.

The strategy is based on the principle that the solution emerges from the unification of the two problems initially perceived as separate. On the one hand, we had requests for production services and, on the other, we had requests for training. MAP is essentially the bringing together of communities which require media production and participants (learners) who wish to develop production skills. These skills are then learnt in an experiential manner during the ensuing production.

The name Media Attachment Programme refers to the relationship between the participant learning production skills and the facilitator. The participants and facilitator are co-workers who work cooperatively on community media problems.

There are a number of areas which are crucial to the effectiveness of the programme. These include entry requirements, learning dynamic, certification, community developments and the University setting.

Entry requirements

All the participants have concluded their formal schooling and have some work or post-school experience. Preference is given to participants who have strong motivations to pursue a career in community-orientated media and cannot pursue a formal full-time course. The reasons for participants avoiding formal courses includes their ideological stance, lack of funds, educational level and other personal domestic reasons. The number of participants that can be accommodated simultaneously depends on the number of facilitators available and the number of production tasks outstanding. Up to now I have been the only full-time facilitator, although I have been assisted by past participants and other volunteers for short periods. The majority of our participants have been white, despite an affirmative action policy to support aspirant black media producers. One reason for this is that many media posts in progressive organizations are still held by whites.

Two forms of attachment are possible – either a 'term' or a 'task' attachment. In the 'term' attachment, a participant stays on the programme for a fixed period and may complete a variety of tasks during that time, Whereas a 'task' attachment does not have a fixed duration as the participant remains on the programme for as long as it takes to complete a specific task. Since we started the programme, there has been a tendency to select the 'task' attachment as there is reluctance to leave a production before it is finished.

Learning dynamic

The learning dynamic takes place within a team of co-workers who will solve community media problems cooperatively. The team which always includes the facilitator and a representative from the community has a variable number of participants depending on the participants' prior experience and the nature of the problem. 'Impi Yombango', a recent production on violence in the rural areas of Natal was commissioned by the Catholic OMI order. The video shows that apartheid and the earlier colonial legislation facilitates and fuels violent territorial battles for scarce resources. This form of violence called 'Faction Fighting' (Impi Yombango) is used by the state to describe the revolutionary struggle in townships and ascribe this to primitive tribalism. The production team included three participants in addition to the facilitator and the client. Each of the five co-workers has a functional role which is democratically negotiated to satisfy individual learner needs and the cooperative task needs.

The facilitator has an additional role to the co-worker role. The facilitator attempts to guide the choice of functional roles and the participants development in each functional role. The learning is experiential and follows the cycle of practice and knowledge referred to earlier in a dialectic relationship. This cycle (Fig. 19.1) has been described as the 'Dialectic' Learning Cycle (Criticos and Beard, 1986, pp. 149).

In the early stages of production the facilitator may play an active and prominent role because of the participant's (co-worker's) limited experience and knowledge. The extent to which the facilitator plays a major role is entirely dependent on the initial abilities of the participants. In the 'Impi Yombango' production one of the participants was a professional video editor and another

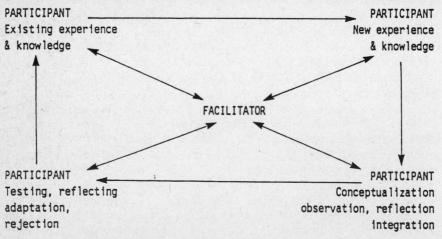

Figure 19.1   The 'Dialectic' Learning Cycle.

had extensive research experience. At the two crucial periods the facilitator relinquished his role as facilitator to the participants who had resident skills that were required. The facilitator and participants therefore exchanged roles following democratic decisions to facilitate the maximization of individual learning and completion of the task. The better facilitator is not one who has wide experience and expert knowledge but one who is skilled in facilitating the co-workers' development through praxis. The facilitator must:

- Facilitate cooperative work.
- Guide the choice of roles during production.
- Guide group decisions via democratic process.
- Guide the production process to execute production to the client's (community representative) brief.
- Guide the production process to maximize each individual participant's learning.
- Provide regular opportunities during formal planning meetings and informally for critical reflection of past experience.
- Contextualize production processes within the social history and aspirations of the community client.

From this list it is clear that facilitating skills are more valuable than expert production skills. The learning does not take place exclusively within the production process. When the production demands skills that cannot easily be elicited in the production the facilitator guides the participant to short courses or readings which proceed in parallel with production. The most common example of this is the development of computer literacy and word-processing skills. Word processing is a valuable skill during the research and scriptwriting stage and a large number of participants have attended short courses in order to apply these skills in the production.

It is often the case that a participant who has set out to develop a specific skill (such as video editing) discovers a much stronger interest and pursues the development of this skill. The clearest example of this occurring was the case of a participant who learnt computer skills for scriptwriting a training programme on obstetrics. The participant pursued the development of greater proficiency in computer work through additional short courses, self-study and practical assignments related to MAP projects. This person now works as a freelance computer consultant undertaking computer literature searches, database development, translation and word processing.

From the previous account it is clear that the learning process, 'curriculum' and methods are not predetermined, but determined dynamically during the process of production. The only 'known' components of the enterprise is each participant's individual learning objectives and the group's task in relation to the client's brief. The learning dynamic which manifests itself as the co-workers pursue this brief results in knowledge in a natural way. However, this 'natural' way is full of risks and messiness, i.e. it is human as opposed to mechanical.

Contestation and critical debate are essential features of our methods. What this means is that the transformative experiential learning methods used by MAP are not predictable and reliable. They are, however, appropriate and valid methods which demand a great degree of motivation on the part of the participants and facilitator. In all the cases of conflict that have arisen during production the cause could be traced to impatience with the democratic process and the slow pace of work while the other participants develop skills. Ironically, we have also been faced with progressive organizations which espouse democratic process and a post-apartheid vision but are intolerant of our slow process-orientated methods. These organizations often suggest: 'Get on with the job. You are the professionals.' Our position has been to refuse work on these terms as it is essential that the organization (client/community) is represented and active in the process of cooperative production:

> We believe that human consciousness and knowing emerges out of activity and engagement. Its contents, pre-theoretical, remain related to activity in diverse ways. This means theories and ideas continually interact with human activity from which they spring. In other words, the relationship between consciousness and activity is a dialectical one – activity produces ideas, which in turn produce new forms of activity (Criticos and Beard, 1986, p. 150).

Community development

Community development is not used in a Western sense of developing 'primitive communities' to Western standards. MAP regards community development as the process of development and acquisition of community objectives, that is objectives identified and 'owned' by the community. As stated earlier, MAP is the development of media skills through the praxis of solving community media problems through democratic process. Our concern for community needs is best illustrated by comparing our methods with that of a commercial production team. A commercial team is composed of a number of specialized experts: scriptwriter, producer, camera person, sound engineer, etc. This team is organized in such a way as to produce a finished product in an efficient manner – to 'produce the goods' – a finished product in the hands of the client for maximum profit. The production process is surrounded by mystery and complexity in order to maintain the producer's expert status. The producers are concerned with the product and not the client or their aspirations. Invariably, therefore, the client receives a product which is not 'owned' by the client/community. The product has made them poorer and has reinforced the powerlessness of the subordinate community. Furthermore, the product is usually produced from the Western filmic tradition which repeatedly employs coding which reinforces the white hegemony through confirmation of societal contradictions (see earlier reference to Mkatshwa, 1985).

Commercial approaches to production are not unlike the traditional university approach to client communities. The academic and the host institution often see themselves as the experts dispensing knowledge to clients and, rarely, as co-workers. The traditional expert operates in a paternalistic manner, often reinforcing the contradictions which constitute apartheid. Figure 19.2 illustrates the different relationships between university and community.

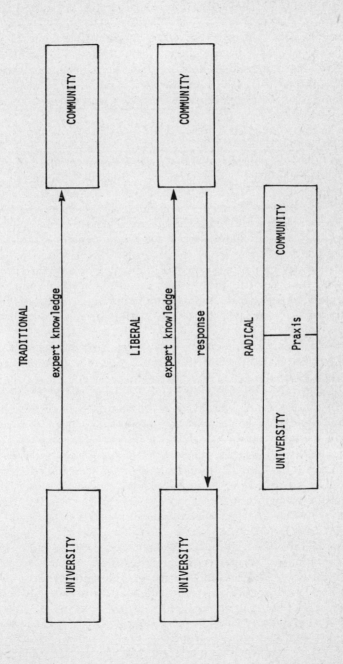

Figure 19.2 University and community relationships.

In the *traditional relationship*, the university dispenses knowledge in a 'top-down', expert manner. In the *liberal relationship*, the university pays some attention to community perceptions, but maintains the expert/non-expert gap. The *radical relationship* is one in which the university allows community perceptions to transform the university through praxis. It is in this group that we locate MAP.

The making of 'Philani', a documentary on the Kwa Thintwa School for the Deaf, is an example of this radical relationship. Kwa Thintwa School is a school for deaf Zulu children. The school is situated in Inchanga (a rural district on the outskirts of Durban). The state provision of resources is inadequate to meet their needs and the school sought our assistance to produce a video programme for fund-raising purposes.

The school, through its representative, played a major role in the production. They were directly involved in the research and scriptwriting and they had selected the key players for the programme. Furthermore, because we had open-ended objectives we were sensitive to community needs that had not been stated specifically as objectives. No professional (expert) staff were used in the production, the narrator was a university projectionist and the music was composed and performed by an illiterate messenger. The narrator and musician developed new skills and self-esteem in addition to earning additional income.

Kwa Thintwa School 'owns' the programme as they were co-workers in the production. The praxis of the mental–manual cycle and the structure of MAP facilitates the occurrence of the radical relationship. The cooperative engagement of university and community in a community media problem produces transformative tools and transforms both university and community (De Sanctis, 1975).

A professional production team may well have produced a product with higher technical quality, but they would be unlikely to be sensitive to the educational and development needs of the production team and community. The crucial distinction between our production methods and 'professional' methods is that MAP is engaged in the *process* of cooperative production of community-identified objectives, and the professionals produce *products* for the client.

The MAP methods are similar to the *fotomontaje* methods which promote learner and community initiatives rather than the educator initiatives. O'Gorman (1978) writes on the fotomontaje approach during her work with Federcao de Oragos pora Assistencia Social e Educational, a Brazilian organization which promotes participative education and social intervention among marginal rural groups.

Fotomontaje, which fulfils the principles of conscientization, aims at helping participants to portray their own lived experience in order to reflect critically on it and thereby transform the experience. The material includes all forms of audio and visual materials which document the social contradictions of the depressing conditions in the barriados (slum settlements).

O'Gorman sounds a warning about radical philosophies being co-opted. She challenges some of the manifestations of Freire's conscientization principles in which educators now see conscientization as one of their many 'methods'. She sees this distortion as the essential meaning of conscientization being 'subverted and used as surreptitious educator domination'. Experiential learning and, specifically, the MAP methods will be co-opted by educators and trainers who locate themselves within the culture of oppression. These educators who seek to maintain or reform apartheid cannot use these methods as neutral techniques as they encompass a critical character and are concerned with knowledge building as opposed to transmission. They will therefore have to degenerate experiential learning to the level of practical training or risk being challenged by their learners.

Certification

A radical transformation of the practice of training media producers which includes open-entry, cooperative work, democracy and a negotiated curriculum, suggests a radical approach to the area of certification. Certificates of performance in competition with fellow students and the educator through an examination are inappropriate in a methodology which rejects competition. However, the reality of work demands that the participants have some form of certification.

The problem of certification was solved by giving the role of validation to the community. The community then validates the abilities of the participant by accepting the completed media solution. In practice, this means that MAP provides a certificate of service which describes the amount and nature of work experienced during the participant's attachment, and lists all the programmes produced by the participant. The participant may now seek work with a portfolio of completed work and a certificate of service rather than an examination result. This idea comes from the practice of employing artists who convince employers of their abilities by showing a portfolio of their past work. For these reasons we do not issue a traditional certificate, but rather employ portfolio certification.

Conclusion

It is still too early to comment on the performance of MAP against other methods of training media producers. After 3 years of experience, it seems as if we must continue along this path. The small number of students who have completed their attachments have secured posts as media producers or coordinators in progressive organizations in competition with candidates who hold formal academic media qualifications.

I believe that this model of learning can be applied to any area of academic work. The application will inevitably challenge the structure and contradictions resident in educational institutions such as power relationships, examinations, certification and curriculum. However, I believe that these methods can be employed within a traditional university and within a formal university degree course. The Department of Contemporary Cultural Studies (University of

Natal) has implemented a production module in their honours course which was administered by MAP. In addition to this department, we have had enquiries from other educational institutions who expressed interest in experimenting with the MAP model.

We have shown that experiential learning, as applied in alternative programmes, is popular and appropriate to transformative practice. Experiential learning, the cornerstone of the MAP method, has particular relevance to South Africa, where differential education has produced people who confirm the White hegemony. In essence, MAP challenges the practice of apartheid education and produces transformative tools.

References

Criticos, C. and Beard, P. (1986). The University of Natal Media Attachment Programme. In *Excellence in Teaching and Learning in Tertiary Education: Conference Proceedings*, Stellenbosch, University of Stellenbosch.

De Sanctis, F. M. (1975). Towards a social university. *Prospects*, **5**(3), 405–14.

Dionisio, E. R. (1986). Small media, big victory. *Media Development*, **33**(4), 6–8.

Freire, P. (1985). *The Politics of Education*. London: Macmillan.

Hall, B. L. (1978). Continuity in adult education and political struggle. *Convergence*, **11**(1), 8–15.

Hartshorne, K. (1986). African matric results. *Indicator SA*, **4**(2), 54–8. Durban: Centre for Applied Social Studies, University of Natal.

Institute for Christian National Education (1948). Pamphlet, February 1948. Johannesburg (Unpublished).

Khotseng, B. M., Matlou, M. D. and Mahlomaholo, M. G. (1986). The pedagogical character of the struggle. In *Critique–Vision–Strategy: Conference Proceedings, Kenton 1986*, Johannesburg, University of Witwatersrand.

Mayani, Y. H. (1975). The TANU educational concept in the context of adult education. *Literarcy Discussion*, **6**(1), 27–44.

Mblinyi, M. (1977). Basic education: Tool for liberation or exploitation? *Prospects*, **7**(4), 489–503.

Mkatshwa, S. (1985) Peoples education for peoples power. In *Proceedings of The First National Consultative Conference*, Johannesburg, University of Witwatersrand.

Mudariki, T. (1985). Adult education and the world of work – The case of Zimbabwe. *Education with Production*, **3**(2), 51–60.

O'Gorman, F. (1978). Conscientization – Whose initiative should it be? *Convergence*, **11**(1), 52–9.

Parmanand, S. K. (1987) The politics of education in South Africa. Paper presented at *Conference of the Professors for World Peace Academy*, Johannesburg, 1987 (unpublished).

Sidley, P. (1987). Botha insists there will be no black alternative. *Times Educational Supplement*, 9 January 1987.

Tomaselli, K. (1985). Progressive film and video in South Africa. *Media Development*, **32**(3), 15–17.

Youngman, F. (1985). Adult literacy and the mode of production. *International Journal of Lifelong Education*, **4**(2), 149–61.

Youngman, F. (1986). *Adult Education and Socialist Pedagogy*. London: Croom Helm.

20

Learning Through the Heart:
A Woman-to-Woman Approach

Tara Serrao and Phyllis Marie Jensen

This chapter, set in South India, is about the oppression of the Lambani tribe. In particular, it focuses on the oppression of the women of that tribe and how they are being empowered with the support of women from Christa Sharan Social Development Society. Access to the means of overcoming oppression is not easy for the Lambani women or for the women members of the Society who seek to support them. Here is an example of experiential learning that is conceptualized only after a long period of active involvement and is, therefore, pertinent for those who move from theory first. The Society workers would not try to instruct the Lambani women, they would only listen to and share their experience with them. The key is in a phrase the authors use themselves in trying to understand where the Lambani women were 'coming from': in any situation the subject matter of discussion was determined by 'the activity of the moment' (their phrase). Thus the relationship was based upon the personal stance of the women and the relevance of context. Serrao and Jensen enable us to consider how seemingly small changes can persistently erode at the roots of oppression even though much remains to be done. With this example there is a crucial link with Salmon (Chapter 21), who asserts the need for practitioners of experiential learning to understand the personal stance of the learner. The chapter provides a useful contrast with the other chapters on social change written by men in Part 4: Keregero and Criticos (Chapters 18 and 19). For us this chapter also offers a contrast to more 'top-down' interpretations of experiential learning as a force for social change.

Learning through the heart is a method of experiential education that arose in development work in rural India where teaching women in groups was not possible. This was due to the fears of the Lambani people as well as work demands on the women and cultural constraints on their activities.

The Lambani people

The Lambani are a former nomadic hunting and gathering tribe believed to have come to the Rajasthan State in Northern India from Asia Minor many centuries ago. More recently, the Lambani were brought to the southern states by the British who valued their forest tracking skills.

After Indian Independence, legislation was passed forbidding hunting in the forests and therefore, the traditional way of life of the Lambani, foraging from the land, was no longer possible. Lacking land of their own, these poor, outcaste and almost untouchable people (in India, caste prejudice and social proscriptions are still strong), began to wander from village to village in search of food, shelter and work. They lacked the knowledge of agricultural practices, methods of building construction and servant work, the only forms of employment available to the unskilled. Even these types of work were not always available, and when they worked they were badly paid and hired and fired at will. If they protested they were driven from the villages. Hungry and used to a life of foraging, they often just took what they needed. They soon became branded as thieves.

Some Lambani resorted to borrowing money from landowners for the necessities of life. When they were unable to repay the original loan and the exorbitant rates of interest – up to 500 per cent – either they or their children became bonded labourers (this is a form of slavery in which one or more years of work without wages is taken in repayment for a financial debt). Bonded labour is illegal in India because it is an economic arrangement that is virtually impossible to conclude: while working without wages, money is still required to pay for existing needs, i.e. food, shelter, clothing and health care. To pay for their continuing needs, the period of labour is extended.

To remedy this situation, the government gave land to the Lambani so that they would have a place to live. However, the land was stoney, arid and waterless. Nevertheless, they constructed shelters out of mud and palm thatch and lived in camps called *thandyas*. These were separate from, but still close to, other villages.

Each Lambani *thandya* had a leader, a Panchayat, whose role it was to settle arguments. Women used to participate in this process, but as the Lambani gradually adopted the attitudes, beliefs and behaviours of the local people, women were even forbidden to approach the Panchayat with a complaint. The case was heard and decided by men who later informed the women of their final decision.

Some of the other, less desirable aspects of the local culture were also adapted by the Lambani – they began to drink alcohol, to chew betel nut, to loiter and many became bootleggers for want of other work. They soon developed a reputation for laziness and untrustworthiness.

Because they were looked down upon, they did not identify with their heritage and over the years much of their own culture has been lost. There is evidence that the Lambani were originally a matriarchal society and dowry payments were unknown. Although dowry is currently forbidden by law, it has been adopted by many of these people. Formerly, women had had positions of power in the community and could mingle freely with others, but this too has changed. Also, each young girl was expected to stitch her own wedding garment which was elaborately decorated with silver beading, silver embroidery and mirror work, but these skills are rarely seen today. However, they did retain their own language, as well as a love for music and dancing. Whenever they gathered together they began to sing, old songs and new, for they have a wonderful ability to improvise, translating immediate experiences into song. At festivals they have been known to dance all night. The women and men dance separately, and the latter do a stick dance called *Kolaata*.

In India, religion is generally inherited and rarely do individuals change their religion. Politically and practically the Lambani are Hindus, although they have retained many of the beliefs and superstitions of their animist ancestors. They believe being Hindus gives them status, whereas it actually lowers their status by entangling them in the caste system. Caste is almost synonymous with the type of work ascribed. This has become so much a part of the self-definition of the Lambani that they have not questioned their position, even though they are of almost the lowest caste. In Karnataka State, the Lambani are listed as members of the Scheduled Caste, in other states they are listed as Scheduled Tribes.

The development organization

A Catholic priest, Father Joe Mary Lobo, in Kadur Parish in the District of Chikmagalur, 215 km north-west of Bangalore, the state capital of Karnataka, was disturbed by the poverty he saw around him. With the assistance of the Catholic Relief Services, he began an American aid programme for feeding school children, orphans and the aged. While immediate relief was paramount, it became obvious that this kind of help would not eradicate poverty, but would only create dependency. What was needed was a programme to promote self-reliance, cooperation and, hopefully, self-respect.

Much welfare work in India has been undertaken by the Church, but Father Lobo felt that love and compassion for the poor was not the exclusive property of the priests and nuns. He wanted to train lay people and hoped that the villagers themselves would eventually take on leadership roles and extend their knowledge and skills to neighbouring villages. It was felt that 'a man educated is a man educated, but a woman educated is a family educated'. As a result, the emphasis was on training women in development work, because they were able to work with women and children (due to cultural constraints, this is not possible for men).

In 1978 a registered society was set up comprised almost entirely of lay people, half of whom were women. The organization was called the 'Christa Sharan Social Development Society': *Christa Sharan* means 'Christ at your service'. It was located in the town of Birur, 6 km from Kadur. Father Lobo obtained permission from his Bishop to leave parish work and devote himself full-time to rural development among the Lambani and other poor people.

Five Lambani settlements were originally chosen for the initial programme on 'Mother and Child Health Education', which was funded by the Canadian Catholic Organization for Development and Peace (CCODP). Since then, 20 other villages have been included and funding bodies in Canada and Germany have supported the work. The initial programme was begun with the assistance of one trained development worker who enlisted the help of 20 enthusiastic women, 18–20 years of age.

The initial programme had three main goals. The first was the eradication of malnutrition through a change in the existing dietary habits of the Lambani. They had been eating *ragi*, a local cereal crop rich in calcium and iron, plus a variety of pulses (lentils, peas and dried beans), but no fresh vegetables. It was hoped that the establishment of kitchen gardens would provide fresh produce. The second goal was the prevention of communicable diseases through the immunization of children under 5 years of age; the promotion of personal hygiene through bathing and an alternative to the existing practice of open defecation; and the setting of standards of cleanliness both inside and outside the homes and communal areas of the settlements. The third goal was for children to attend school regularly.

Early difficulties

Father Lobo and Project Co-ordinator Tara Serrao, began work with a total staff of 20 social development aides and office workers. The first task was to train the development aides to teach the village women about health and nutrition.

In India people are usually very hospitable and curious and the Christa Sharan workers expected to be greeted with civility and interest. What they encountered was suspicion, hostility and overt rejection. In some instances, stones and dirty water were thrown at them. The Lambani were afraid of the development workers. They thought the women had come, as others had previously from the hospitals, to carry out a sterilization programme. They also misinterpreted geological surveys, undertaken for well-digging, as preparations to seize their land. There were rumours that the women wanted to entice the village boys into marriage and other stories that the children would be stolen and sold to the Americans. Many thought that the Christa Sharan workers would try to convert them to Christianity. Fearing the loss of illegal bonded labourers, the landlords magnified the existing fears of the Lambani.

Added to these difficulties was the problem of how to bring the women together. Except for official gatherings, religious festivals, and births, marriages and death within the families, the Lambani women did not meet together. There were stolen moments of gossip, but cooperative groups and informal gatherings did not exist. The women were not allowed to leave their settlements, and thus they considered the development workers as strangers or foreigners even, who did not know or understand their traditions.

Gaining support

The development workers found this situation very difficult to accept and so they began to ask themselves a number of questions. Why had they come? What were they trying to do? What did they expect to achieve? Were their methods correct? What could they do to gain acceptance? What kinds of change were needed?

At first the development workers walked to the villages, but with the gift of 12 bicycles, they began to ride, often 20–30 km a day, in all kinds of weather. It was considered scandalous for women to cycle and it soon became dangerous on the roads because the male drivers of bullock carts, motorized vehicles and bicycles would not make way for them. In some villages the bicycles' tyres were punctured. This soon turned out to be a blessing in disguise. The persistence of the development workers, despite the abuse heaped on them for breaking traditional values, evoked a sympathetic response on the part of the Lambani women. Slowly, they began to talk. In doing so, another set of problems was revealed.

Initially, the development workers cycled to the villages in groups for safety and moral support, but by coming in groups scared the Lambani. Therefore, workers began to split up into groups of two at the outskirts of a settlement, and then part company once they had reached the village.

Since group education was not possible, because the village women would not gather together for the purpose of instruction, the development workers began to talk to them, one by one. They found that the Lambani women, unlike school children, simply would not accept what the development workers were trying to teach them. The Lambani were set in their own ways and they had their own causal explanations, and believed illness to be a result of the displeasure of the Gods. In order for any development work to take place, what was needed was a change in the attitudes of both sides. The more time the development workers spent with the Lambani, the more they began to realize that these people – illiterate, presumed lazy, unable to earn money or to spend it wisely – were in fact very clever. Once the development workers came to respect and appreciate the Lambani, they found that they opened up their hearts: love of the people was the only way that development work could proceed. Thus, developmental education became a process of 'learning through the heart'.

In the woman-to-woman approach, the workers visited the Lambani women individually in their houses, and even tucked up their sarees and helped them in the fields: planting, reaping, picking chillies, or digging peanuts. In each situation they tried to understand the Lambani method and then, instead of instructing the women, they would share their knowledge with them. The subject matter was determined by the activity of the moment.

If a Lambani was breastfeeding, the workers would speak of the importance of breastfeeding and introduce weaning foods. Previously, the Lambani women breastfed for 2–3 years and would not feed infants anything else except supplemental cows' milk. If a woman was cooking, nutrition and the importance of vegetables would be stressed: workers even helped to plan and create kitchen gardens.

Superstitions surrounding childbirth prevented pregnant and lactating mothers from consuming certain foods. Papaya, an excellent source of vitamin A, was believed to cause abortion. During the last months of pregnancy food was withheld, as it was thought that a regular diet would result in an oversized foetus and delivery would be made much more difficult. With encouragement from the development workers the village women improved their diet. If a woman was milking a buffalo, a worker would sit with her and talk about milk, meat and fish, and the importance of protein in the diet. If a child was ill, the worker offered her services and slowly succeeded in motivating the mother to have her children immunized.

The diffusion of knowledge

The women who cooperated with the development workers began to understand that caste is not God-given, but made by people, and that women and men are equal human beings and should have equal rights and opportunities. This information made them bold and willing to challenge traditional practices, and those who had originally ostracized them, now began to envy them.

The former attitude, touted in the phrase, 'I take care of mine and the Gods take care of others', had prevented cooperative action and concern for their neighbours. But with their new attitudes, the Lambani women began to share their new knowledge with others. They encouraged their neighbours to come out of their homes, to walk to the fields with them and to come to regular meetings. Thus, group instruction became possible: flash cards, flannel graphs, posters, songs, story telling, puppet shows, slides, movies, street theatre and role playing were all utilized. Some of the younger married women who had never had the opportunity to go to school began to learn to read and write.

The women learned that they must fight for their rights or that they would never be liberated from the oppression found in their families and community. To accomplish their goals, they formed women's clubs called Mahila Sangha. *Sangha* means to come together and to stick together for a common purpose. With this organization and a new perspective they shared their knowledge and skills. Soon kitchen gardens became a common feature in target villages, and vegetables became part of the staple diet. Both personal hygiene and sanitation, in the home and village at large, improved beyond expectations.

When the development workers had started going to the Lambani settlements, they found that the women were restricted in their freedom of movement. These restrictions were imposed after puberty, because it was feared that young girls would be 'spoiled' by a man before marriage or defiled afterwards. Mothers with married sons ruled all the other females in the household and did not trust them to leave their houses or to talk to other women, and they required that they be accompanied when going to the fields to work.

Through education and cooperative action in the sanghas, women, and mothers-in-law especially, gained a new respect for themselves and for other women. Relationships within families soon began to improve. The women forbade their menfolk to drink alcohol, quarrels became fewer, and more children were sent to school on a regular basis. The women began to take responsibility for their lives beyond their immediate environment. They demanded their right to borrow money from the banks and used the money to buy cows and goats. They began to earn their own money and even opened group savings accounts. Having developed self-confidence and a curiosity for learning, the sangha women became more bold and even took their grievances to top government officials. When their demands were not met, they threatened a *Dharna*, or a sit-in.

Not only did the sangha women begin to travel to the local towns by bus, they made plans to visit larger centres, like Bangalore, Kolar, Dharwar and Mangalore. To these cities they travelled by train, and took courses in agricultural methods, animal husbandry and social forestry. They met with representatives of other development organizations and other villagers from other programmes and gained new ideas for future projects.

Men's and children's sanghas

Seeing the changes in their homes and villages accomplished by the women, the men too began to gather together and formed men's sanghas. The men's and women's sanghas then began to meet together for larger cooperative projects in animal husbandry, housing and irrigation. Precooperatives, called the 'Co-responsible Societies', have come into existence to train women and men in cooperatives and credit unionism. In this education for cooperative action, Christa Sharan was greatly helped by the Cooperative Union of Canada.

The children too have begun to form sanghas. Initially, they were set up for the purpose of studying together and learning to work cooperatively. Now one children's sangha has begun to collect the money given to them for sweets, and with these savings they plan to open a small shop. They have also organized interschool activities, including singing, games and athletics.

With the cooperation of the women's and men's sanghas, there has been an important financial change in the system of village justice. Previously, the money levied in a fine became the property of the Panchayat; now the money becomes the property of village funds to be used for communal purposes.

Diffusion to other villages

The first five settlements chosen for social development were the poorest in the area. Seeing the changes in the people and the improvements in their villages, others began to request help from Christa Sharan. Requests and support have also come from the Zilla Parishat, the district-level, development administrative body.

Ten years after they began, Christa Sharan workers are now sharing information with people in 20 villages. Members of the women's and men's sanghas of the original five settlements have been recruited to help their neighbours: the Lambani have become a confident and resourceful people again.

These changes have not taken place without reaction from those who had profited by their exploitation of the Lambani. In the early days of social development with the Lambani, the opposition reached almost militant proportions, but in recent years it has become more subtle. Threats are still made, however, to Christa Sharan workers. The stalling of bureaucratic processes and the temporary loss of necessary documents in local offices have also been known to occur.

Matters not directly addressed

Because of the fear of conversion to Christianity, some social practices arising out of the religion of the Lambani have not been addressed directly. First, is their belief in astrology. No ceremony will take place without the stars being consulted and no marriages are arranged without matching the horoscopes of the intended bride and groom. There are a number of bogus astrologers, palm readers and match-makers who demand large sums of money for their services.

Second, is the practice of slaughtering and sacrificing a goat at each house during festivals. In order to do this, many Lambani go into debt, but to some degree this practice is becoming less frequent.

Third, is the isolation of women while menstruating or after childbirth. During the former the woman is not allowed inside her house, and her mother-in-law or husband assumes the household tasks of cooking, cleaning and childcare. Originally, this practice served a useful purpose in giving women a rest from household tasks. Today, however, they continue to work hard in the fields while menstruating and they are denied the comforts of their homes during this time.

Believed to be unclean following childbirth, women are secluded either in a part of the house or in a small temporary shelter outside. In one village the shelter was outside the village boundary, and the hut was so small that the new mother was unable to stand up. She was dependent upon others to bring her food, though because her shadow is also considered unclean, the food was left at the village boundary. There was little, if any, communication. Before the Christa Sharan workers came to the villages, mother and child could be isolated for up to 2 months, regardless of the weather or their health status. It is thought that much infant mortality and ill health is the result of such practices. In recent years, this isolation has gradually decreased to a few weeks. Since notions of purity and danger are part of the Lambani religion, it is felt that further changes in this practice must come from the people themselves. Perhaps a more scientific understanding of health and illness will accelerate this process.

Fourth, is the problem of the education of female children. The percentage of children who attend school regularly has increased from 20 to almost 80 per cent, but girls are routinely taken out of school when they reach puberty to protect their virginity. An increased respect of women and trust in the behaviour of boys and girls is necessary before girls can be fully educated.

Future plans

There are many children whose families are too poor to supply the food, clothing and books necessary for schooling. To remedy this, Christa Sharan has requested the government to lease 10 acres of land to them for a nominal rent.

The intention is to set up a residential training centre for unschooled children. Training for economic independence will be offered according to individual choice: agriculture, carpentry, animal husbandry, poultry raising, stitching and typing. This plot of land is also meant for the use of men and (especially) women of various villages to meet for discussions, training camps, seminars and other activities which go to help rural development.

In Karnataka State there is a new system of local government called the Mandal Panchayat. It is comprised of elected representatives from the villages, one-third of whom are supposed to be women, but these numbers have as yet not been met. To be able to benefit from the full potential of this body, it is imperative that the villagers understand and be trained to participate in the democratic process. To do this a system of representation within the villages is being set up. This group will learn how to determine local needs, establish priorities, plan projects and make their requests known to the Mandal, which must approve projects before implementation. Once this standard of independence has been achieved, the Christa Sharan workers will be available for consultation, but will focus their energies on other villages.

21

Personal Stances in Learning

Phillida Salmon

Practitioners of experiential learning will recognize Salmon's view that learning is highly particular to the learner. For her, the 'personal stance' of a learner is a crucial but neglected part of what we define as learning. But personal stance also has implications for the 'teacher' or practitioner. We, as teachers, cannot separate what we know from what and who we are and what and how we teach. Unlike the conventional understanding of learning and teaching, the notion of personal stance helps us to see that content is not 'out there', independent of the learner and the teacher.

Learning for Salmon has necessarily to do with change. Learning as experiential means that change is not just social or academic; it is also personal. It can be both empowering and difficult. Salmon takes us through an educational project she has been engaged in as an evaluator which emphasized the development of what Salmon regards as the crucial goal of experiential learning, i.e. understanding – understanding that is firmly located in the learner's experience. This is not a neutral issue. She suggests that a deeper understanding of the many dimensions of our experiencing, within the wider social context, empowers. Such personal empowerment, for Salmon, can lead to action. She is critical of the current tendency to equate the development of personal qualities and skills with empowerment and experiential learning.

This chapter is placed in this section because we endorse her view that understanding that is integrated in the way she suggests can bring about a change in the learner's personal stance. This in turn can enhance our capacity for personal agency in relation to the major social issues of the epoch. Otherwise, we are merely passive recipients of the status quo. Wylde (Chapter 11) provides an example of how her personal stance influences her interactions as a learner. Wildemeersh (Chapter 5) is also pertinent in respect of the potential of experiential learning for empowering and changing. A comparison may be considered between Salmon's ideas in relation to those of O'Reilly (Chapter 9) and Brah and Hoy (Chapter 6). Finally, readers may wish to examine an unwitting instrumentality inherent in some chapters which, albeit, do seek to extend the opportunities available to learners and enhance understanding.

In this chapter, I suggest that we may be able to understand learning more fully, and thereby set up better learning opportunities, if we think of the learning process in rather different terms from the ones we generally use (see Salmon 1988). Taking the metaphor of personal stance gives a different meaning, not just to learning, but also to teaching, which, as teachers, we think about less often than we should. Because personal stance refers to the positions which each of us takes up in life, this metaphor emphasizes aspects of experience which go deeper than the merely cognitive, and which reflect its essentially relational, social and agentic character. In this, it offers a view of learning as a vehicle for social change.

For many people, the vast literature on learning offers little real enlightenment. What they know as learning, in their own first-hand experience, is hardly encompassed in the currency available. Conventional accounts offer only the most limited definitions: 'Learning' must be clearly distinguished from feeling, from practical engagement, from intuitive, in-the-bones knowing. It is, of course, these separations which advocates of experiential learning are most strongly concerned to reject. The very term *experiential learning* insists that there can be no fundamental distinction between what is personally understood and what is personally, intimately experienced through living. This in turn demands the acknowledgement that human learning is highly particular; the usual generalizations about the processes of education will not do.

But, as yet, I do not think we have gone very far in understanding how it is that individual learners actually come to construct their own unique material. This may be because the *material* of learning has traditionally been viewed in different terms from those that define the learner. As advocates of experiential learning, we do not seem to have done much to change this. To do so may mean thinking very differently about the whole question of learning. It is here, I believe, that the concept of personal stance is a useful one.

What is distinctive about this concept of learning is that it gives paramount importance to the personal positions of learners. How we *place ourselves*, within any learning context, whether formal or informal, is fundamental. This is not just a matter of 'attitude', in so far as it defines our own engagement with the material; it represents the very stuff of learning itself. It is through the stance we take up in any situation that we give our own distinctive meaning to what it involves. For example, it is critical how we position ourselves towards our 'teachers' in any educational setting. This is what governs the limits and possibilities of our engagement together, what shapes and defines the material we construct out of that engagement.

In the talk I gave at the conference, out of which this book has emerged, I used an experiential introduction to the concept of personal stance. I asked all the participants to attend to their perception of me, as a particular person standing in front of them. What kind of person, on this preliminary acquaintance, did I seem to be? I invited them to note down, for their eyes only, what kind of person, provisionally, they would define me as being. Then I asked them to think about these perceptions as referring to their own personal stance towards me.

The privacy of these judgements was guaranteed. But had I invited the conference participants to share them, there would, of course, have been much diversity in the kind of dimensions referred to. There I stood, a single focus for each person's perception. But where some people might have defined me in terms of my social identity – my race, gender, age or social class – others might have considered my professional competence or orientation. For others still, my relations with the audience might have been the focus, or perhaps my relationships outside. Some people's perceptions might have been directed to my own feelings – my hopes, anxieties, my sense of the meaning of what I was presently undertaking. On one level, all this could be said to be about me. I had, after all, made myself the focus; these descriptions would have described me. But more fundamentally, as I suggested, these perceptions were about the personal stance of each perceiver.

The context of this talk was a broadly formal one: a keynote address, to be followed by a discussion, in an academic lecture theatre. Its purpose was, in a sense, quite traditional: to introduce certain ideas, certain ways of seeing things, to people who had not previously viewed them quite like that. Here was one version of that familiar set-up – an official learning situation. Yet, as everyone there would almost certainly have conceded, all contexts, even formal learning contexts, are personally experienced. Our concern in this conference was with what it is that comes to be constructed out of that experience.

Anyone in the position of 'learner' to another person's 'teaching' must necessarily approach the task through some kind of apprehension of the 'teacher'. The delicate act of 'reading' someone is, I would suggest, a way of implicitly placing oneself towards that person. Let us imagine that one member of that audience defined me as a middle-class, middle-aged, white woman. For this perceiver, the categories are likely to be highly significant, to carry important connotations within our learning encounter. My social identity, defined like this, involves expectations as to the curriculum I am to offer. My ideas on experiential learning – the topic of my address – are going to be those of a person whose life experience (as a white, middle-class, middle-aged woman) will influence what she does and does not see as issues. The perspectives I take, the interests I have, the concerns I am alive to, will be fundamentally affected by my social position. To the audience member who looks at me like this, my words and behaviour are 'read' in a highly distinctive way. These connotations govern her interpretations of what I say, frame her understanding of my curriculum. Even if her initial expectations turn out not to be entirely accurate, but need some modification, the terms of this perception are likely to remain dominant; they constitute the basic ground of our 'teacher–learner' encounter. And what they essentially represent, I would say, is a distinctive position towards me and the material I am engaged in presenting.

If we need to consider the personal stances of *learners*, this concept is surely just as important in thinking about *teachers*. Teachers and teaching are, perhaps, less often the focus for writers and practitioners concerned with experiential learning. When they are at issue, it is often as *facilitators facilitating* learners. I think these terms are quite unhelpful for understanding what happens between teachers and learners. They conjure up images that are highly generalized, with none of the particularity of identity and experience granted to learners. They suggest only rather bland connotations – personal qualities of empathy, warmth and genuineness – without offering any real explanation of what actually takes place in the process of teaching. Such concepts may at best gloss over, and at worst actually obscure, what happens when people teach.

When, as teachers, we teach other people, what are we really doing? In teaching, whether formally or informally, we set out to convey what we know, what we have experienced. We cannot come to know any aspect of the world without taking up a particular kind of stance towards it. We place ourselves towards the situation and, through that placing, that positioning, we experience it in a particular way. What we understand is inseparable from the position we have taken up. And when we try to communicate our knowledge, we necessarily convey our own position, our own stance towards it. This means that, as teachers, we do not just pass on a curriculum; we actually represent, even embody it. Knowledge – understanding – is no more separate from teachers than from learners.

Yet the distinction between people and what they know is probably even more common in the consideration of teaching than it is when learners are in question. For me, this is clearly illustrated by a study carried out by Walden and Walkerdine (1985). Although these women writers do not discuss their work in these terms, what they present seems to exemplify exactly what I have described. The study arose out of a general concern, among many people in education, over the lack of competence of girls in the spheres of maths and science. It is now well documented, for instance, that despite their relative superiority in the early primary years of schooling, girls have, as a group, fallen well behind boys by the mid-secondary stage. One remedial strategy among educationists, has been the appointment of women teachers of maths and science. This has been seen as a way of reversing the development of incompetence on the part of girls by providing role models of female competence.

It was this situation that Walden and Walkerdine set out to examine. They chose to study a number of British women maths teachers, in both primary and secondary schools, by sitting in on their lessons and talking with the teachers and their pupils. Out of these observations and interviews an interesting picture emerged. In the first years of primary school, things generally went very well; the teachers, whose girl pupils made excellent progress, felt confident and satisfied. In the later primary years, there was some falling off; the teachers felt, and apparently were, much less successful in their teaching, and seemed unable to forestall girls lagging behind in maths. By the secondary stage, things were worse still, with a marked decline in the performance of girls, and a general lack of confidence on the part of their teachers. As Walden and Walkerdine found, these women teachers were, as time went on, often caught up in a vicious circle. For all their good intentions, when actually faced with children past their first years of schooling they tended to judge the boys in their class as more able in maths than girls. Many of these women expressed a sense of uneasiness about their role. So lacking was the confidence of some of these teachers that, if challenged in lessons, they would sometimes defer to their male pupils. Not surprisingly, both boys and girls in these teachers' classes generally maintained and lived out the traditional stereotype of female incompetence in mathematics. Somehow, the remedial strategy had backfired, and women maths teachers had communicated the very message they had been appointed to negate.

In discussing these educationally disappointing outcomes, Walden and Walkerdine considered two aspects of the situation of women maths teachers. The first concerns the changing content of their school maths curriculum. When children are initially introduced to maths in school, it is typically in the context of activities such as weighing ingredients for cooking, or measuring materials for sewing. This early content is as stereotypically feminine as that of later years is stereotypically masculine: the activities of mechanics and engineering. If we think of the position of a woman teacher, it is obvious that her relation to these two kinds of curriculum is very different. Whereas in teaching the first sort of content she is presenting ideas relating to her own 'proper domain', the second kind of material is not, stereotypically, her business at all, but that of men, and, potentially, of her male pupils. Even though, as a woman maths teacher, she is likely of necessity to have moved well beyond such simplistic constraints, the classroom world where she does her teaching operates its own philosophy about gender. To most adolescents at the secondary stage, women maths teachers are probably experienced as anomalous: people who have moved outside their own sphere, not really at home in what they teach, operating only a borrowed authority.

Such messages, as Walden and Walkerdine suggest, are heavily underlined by the whole institutional structure of schools. In the secondary system, status and gender are of course closely interlinked. Just as, in the maths curriculum, the early years are those of the 'feminine' domain, so women are overwhelmingly in charge of the infant stage of schooling. But this begins to change as age progresses and, by the secondary stage, the positions of institutional power are almost always held by men. This is the case all the way through the school structure. Not only do men rather than women occupy the role of head teacher, even at the ancillary level, the typically male position of caretaker carries much greater authority than does the typically female position of cleaner, for example. And, most crucially, for the question of maths teaching, it is men who vastly predominate over women as teachers of the two high-status subjects – maths and science. All this cannot but act to contradict, implicitly but powerfully, the legitimacy of a woman maths teacher.

I think we should see this complex situation as essentially a matter of personal stance. As Walden and Walkerdine show, it is very difficult in our society to be both a woman or a maths teacher in school. The stance of being a woman may prove, for many people, impossible to integrate with that of being a maths teacher. The attempt to reconcile the two incompatible stances may only result, as in many of these teachers, in an inner-sense of conflict, dissonance and contradiction. For all these teachers' hopeful intentions, the message of unease gets communicated; such women are the living demonstration for their girl pupils of the conviction that, ultimately, 'all this is not for us'.

The anti-sexist strategy which underlies the appointment of women maths teachers makes no connection between people and what they know. It assumes that women can acquire 'masculine' kinds of knowledge, and then present it to girls, thereby reversing age-old stereotypes. But, as this study clearly demonstrates, the overcoming of sexist limits is not so simple. This may sound completely defeatist; but I am not, as I hope later to convey, suggesting that we should fatalistically accept the sexist, classist, racist, ageist constraints on opportunity and experience which abound in Western society. What I want to argue is that we have to think differently about both learning and teaching, and to work for social change through modes which acknowledge the complexity of these processes.

In the conventional understanding of learning or teaching, *content* is viewed as essentially 'out there', independent of the persons of both learner and teacher. Because of this, there is typically quite a massive disregard of the inescapably personal meaning of every curriculum. Practitioners of experiential learning are, of course, united in challenging this neglect of the personal in the case of the learners. But about teachers and their practice, there is something of a silence. Yet, for me, the idea of personal stance is as important in considering teaching as in thinking about learning.

My own experience of formal teaching has been mainly in a British academic context – specifically, in university departments of psychology. In this context, it is common practice for lecturers to be allocated particular areas of the syllabus on the basis of broadly defined 'expertise' and 'interest'. Having worked as a clinical psychologist for 11 years, I have usually been given the spheres of 'personality' and 'deviance', rather than, for instance, those of 'psycholinguistics' or 'cognitive development'. This means that, as a lecturer, I am expected to convey 'the literature' within these areas. This is typically defined as giving the students a map of the terrain, defining the directions of published work, the landmark studies, the position of recent work in the field, and so on. If I do this as I am expected to do it, I need to present a range of material towards which I stand in widely differentiated ways. Some of the studies of personality and deviance I describe are real anathema to me; they involve attitudes and practices that do violence to the humanity they are supposed to be studying. Others seem only extremely boring: much time and effort is expended on essentially trivial questions. A few studies arouse my ardent interest; I dwell on them with real excitement and a sense of hope. Yet, in this context, it is not my own, quite distinct positions that I am supposed to be teaching; on the contrary, my task is to present 'the material', as fully, clearly, and dispassionately as I can.

What kind of impact does such academically correct teaching make on those who receive it? To put it mildly, this situation cannot make for very effective teaching. Where someone stands in part estranged from the material they offer, it is that estrangement which will surely come across. Teaching is, perhaps, the invitation to others to take up, at least provisionally, one's own personal stance. How learners actually experience that invitation – as an exciting promise, or as a hollow exercise in bad faith – must be a matter of their teachers' own real positions towards the message they profess. Though we may seek to disguise our real stances, the boredom, repugnance and secret reservations, cannot but be communicated to those who hear us. I believe for the women maths teachers I have described, it was their own private contradictions which, unwittingly, they put across. The stances these women took up in presenting their maths curriculum in secondary schools were irreconcilable with that deepest, most basic stance of all – their gender. But, conversely, where teachers carry a particular conviction, a special inspiration, it is through the inner resonance of the material with their deepest feelings, their most fundamental understand-ings. It is surely no accident that good teaching is so often defined as a matter of integrity.

What is at issue in any learning has necessarily to do with change. The concept of learning as *experiential* makes clear that significant change is never just academic; it always has personal ramifications. But, just as the term facilitator suggests facility and ease, we do, I think, often gloss over the difficulties and complexities involved in real personal learning. In the context of working as a clinical psychologist with troubled, searching people, I have long been aware of how hard it is to achieve a radical change of position within personal life. And the situation of psychotherapy clients is really that of any learner writ large. For all of us, significant personal change is difficult, and sometimes so profoundly disturbing, that it is strenuously resisted. This is particularly true, I think, of precisely those kinds of learning to which advocates of experiential modes are most committed. Learning that is personally empowering, that can lead to social change, is, by the same token, learning that is initially unsettling, even potentially threatening.

My own thinking about all this has been as an evaluator for a curriculum development project. This project, which ran from 1983–6, was funded jointly by UNICEF (UK) and the Health Education Council; its highly able and committed research officer was Lesley Smith. The aim was to develop materials relating to childhood which would counter traditional stereotypes (Smith, in press). On one level, the project set out to widen the range of young people studying childhood beyond the usual group of 'non-academic girls'. On another level, materials were to be developed which would act to make explicit and to challenge the many kinds of social oppression affecting children and young people. Six particular dimensions were seen as crucial to understanding childhood: race, gender, socioeconomic factors, the world-wide dimension, the historical dimension and the marginalization of certain social groups. The curriculum, entitled 'Dimensions of Childhood', was to lend itself to work with young people, aged 16–19, in a wide variety of institutional contexts, including youth work settings, further education, sixth form colleges and Youth Training Schemes.

In no sense was this project aimed at merely academic understanding. On the contrary, the need for experiential kinds of learning was implicit at every level. Most of the young people concerned would have already left school and be 'out in the world'; their involvement with the materials, if it occurred, would be on terms very different from the didactic institutional modes of traditional school-ing. Since the project set out not just to pass on theoretical concepts, but actually to foster the potential for social change, the learning it offered had to be of a very personal kind. This meant that the young people concerned, together with their tutor, had to put themselves, their lives, their social engagements, at the forefront of their considerations, instead of leaving personal matters outside the door, as in so much official education. This was, of course, both potentially exciting and potentially threatening.

In accordance with these goals, the 'Dimensions of Childhood' curriculum was constructed in ways that would encourage and support real personal involvement. The learning progressed through two broad stages. In the first of these, each of the six dimensions was introduced, using experiential modes such as games, role play, life-lines or work with images. The second stage entailed the working out, and carrying through, of some kind of personal enquiry into one or more of the dimensions. Unlike traditional research projects, this was neither a solitary nor a personally detached endeavour. The young people worked in small groups, sharing and reflecting together on their feelings and intentions, before carrying out the enquiry, alone and in pairs. The outcomes were similarly mulled over within the small group in the context of interested and thoughtful personal support, before being shared with the wider group.

Part of my role as evaluator was to consider the whole question of how this learning was to be assessed. Issues of assessment are of course very tricky where experiential learning is concerned. This kind of learning, potentially so significant and so empowering, can easily be marginalized if it remains uncertificated. On the other hand, the wrong kinds of accreditation, by defining learning goals in inappropriate ways, can effectively trample under foot the fragile, delicate growth of experiential learning. Fortunately, the wind of change has now begun to blow through the previously closed and secret fields of British official certification. And one of the new forms of assessment, the Certificate of Pre-Vocational Education (CPVE), seemed at first to represent a promising avenue for accrediting the 'Dimensions of Childhood' curriculum.

The declared philosophy of CPVE rests on three assumptions. The first is that the learning at issue is practical rather than academic; what people can do, in real-life contexts, is the issue, not what they can present as abstract ideas. The second assumption concerns the function of assessment, which is to guide future educational programmes, rather than to make a statement about achievement so far. For this reason, assessment is defined as formative, rather than summative. In the last assumption, how learning comes to be assessed is to be the outcome of the negotiation between learners and tutors, rather than representing an imposed and unchallengeable judgement on the part of the tutor. These assumptions seemed in the closest possible accord with the experiential learning philosophy which underpinned our curriculum.

Like most accounts of experiential learning, the CPVE rationale abjures reference to intellectualized concepts. Where, in conventional forms of assessment, it is *understanding* which is typically seen as the focus, CPVE and other experientially oriented forms set out to find another kind of currency. What are they left with? In practice, there are two sorts of terms in usage. Either personal qualities are made the objective of learning: i.e. confidence, autonomy or the ability to work with others are the focus of assessment. Or else, as in CPVE, learning is defined as the development of personal, practical or social skills, and it is on these that assessment is centred. Both these forms of currency avoid referring to anything which might over-intellectualize experience. They are each about what people do, rather than what they say. Both sound very down to earth, and equally accessible to tutors, young people, parents, employers, or 'the man in the street'.

But, for all the laudable aims that lie behind them, both these kinds of terms are, I think, deeply problematic. To make the development of personal qualities the goal of learning is surely to introduce, however unintentionally, a hidden agenda. Though confidence, autonomy and cooperativeness may seem quite straightforward – unexceptional 'good qualities' – perhaps the situation is not really so simple. Because these ways of behaving are generalized from a highly particular kind of situation – that of the learning encounter – important differences are glossed over. Qualities such as confidence or cooperativeness, if they mean anything, are the expression of wholehearted personal investment and solidarity in the situation – something that may not characterize the relative guardedness and reserve of many young people in educational settings which, however experiential, are necessarily politically unequal. Nor are these qualities as straightforward as they look. All definitions of certain ways of behaving as desirable are culturally relative. Those that make up the objectives of existing forms of assessment tend to incorporate particular values; they elevate the liberal virtues of being polite and forthcoming, and what has been called the 'good citizenship complex'. Rough edges – perhaps a rather important asset at times? – are disallowed. Under the cover of apparent neutrality, these goals do, I think, operate a quite objectionable kind of normative pressure.

All this is just as true, in different ways, for the second kind of learning goal: that of skills and competences. The development of communication skills, for instance, is seen as helping young people acquire a real-life competence which can only enhance their personal opportunities. Side-stepping theory, advocates of such a goal would simply point to 'the facts': this young woman, previously unable to present herself in job interviews, has now secured good employment. But the apparent common sense of this argument is, I think, quite spurious. Taking 'what works' as the criterion for defining learning is, necessarily, reifying the present status quo. And where does that leave the possibility of learning for social change?

As I see it, we have to reject both personal qualities and social skills as definitions of experiential learning goals. And this surely brings us back to understanding. Unlike either of the other two kinds of currency, understanding locates the arbitration of experience within learners themselves. You cannot speak with authority as to your own possession of personal traits, because these are really about the reactions that others have to you. And the test of your skills does not lie within you; your competences need to be tested out in ways that others can judge. But only you can say whether you have come to understand something that was previously obscure. Yet, though the concept of understanding brings back the proper subjectivity to experience, it does not, as it is usually used, carry all the vital connotations which make experiential learning potentially so different from traditional academic practice. It is here that the image of stance can, I think, help to enlarge and revitalize what we mean by understanding. I will try to illustrate this in the context of the 'Dimensions of Childhood' curriculum.

In its characteristic usage, within traditional kinds of learning assessment, understanding refers to something entirely intellectual and cognitive: knowledge in the head rather than in the heart or in the bones. It represents the kind of apprehension which is neutral and detached, which is governed, not by personal commitment, but, on the contrary, by abstract and generalized principles of rationality. This is probably as remote as it could be from the learning which most believers in experiential modes are seeking to bring about. In this philosophy, what is at issue is a new way of knowing, intuitive and felt, which, in being lived out, widens personal choice and social agency. If any one has flushed out what this might mean, and offered a possible model of practice, it is surely Paulo Freire (1972a,b, 1974). Crucial to his ideas is the assumption that people can achieve empowerment only through a grasp of the themes that are critical to the current social epoch. To come to be capable of acting on, rather than simply being subject to, social events, requires a very particular kind of understanding. Essentially, as I would like to put it, it entails adopting a different kind of position towards things.

The 'Dimensions of Childhood' curriculum does, I think, exemplify, potentially, what it could mean to develop an understanding that is personally empowering. The critical themes of our own social epoch are defined by its six dimensions. And the ability to grasp these dimensions – to know them, not just intellectually, but as arenas of one's own potential agency – surely calls for the development of a special kind of understanding.

I do not think that either of the other two kinds of concepts are useful here. The formulation of learning as personal qualities, or as skills and competences, fails to allow for what is really crucial – enlarging the sphere of potential social agency. This is because, unless we *understand* our own situation, we cannot begin to act on it. If most young people remain trapped in oppressed and oppressive life-contexts, it is through an inability to define what makes them so. Personally empowering learning needs to offer new ways of making sense of personal situations. Young people, like all of us, have no chance of escaping the stereotypical understandings implicit in their local life-worlds, unless they can acquire new concepts that make genuine, intuitive personal sense. I think, therefore, that the real potential of a curriculum like that of the 'Dimensions of Childhood' is that it offers certain crucial concepts, allowing possibilities of new ways of thinking about, and *placing oneself towards*, one's own life-situation.

The acquisition of potentially empowering understanding is certainly not a simple process. For all that young people 'know', from daily, often painful, experience, about the kinds of oppression on which the 'Dimensions of Childhood' curriculum is centred, the actual *concepts* of racism, heterosexism or marginalization are likely to be strange and difficult. At one level, the task is that of widening social vocabularies. But, of course, the learning must go beyond merely enabling young people to talk glibly in a new terminology; the concepts need to be grounded in lived experience, local situations, personal choices and possibilities. As in all forms of experiential learning, the 'Dimensions of Childhood' curriculum uses first-hand learning modes, requiring learners to acknowledge and share material that is highly personal. Again this is far from being an easy, comfortable process. Yet we have a model of practice, the development of this very special sort of understanding in the work of the Women's Movement. Through modes that affirmed the deepest, least articulated kinds of personal experience, women have worked supportively together to arrive, finally, at a new formulation of potential agency – personal is political.

Obviously, new understandings, like those of the Women's Movement, entailing new personal stances, do not happen all at once. Perhaps three different stages are involved. The first of these involves an affirmation of first-hand personal experience – an articulation of what may so far have been only implicit. Knowledge-in-our-bones, understanding-to-be-lived-by, must underpin our explicit understanding if this is not to be sabotaged. A purely top-down, intellectualized account can only result in the kind of academic sterile learning that experiential learning practitioners are so strongly concerned to reject. The first part of the 'Dimensions of Childhood' curriculum, emphasizing work with drama, images and drawing, is aimed at eliciting and affirming just this kind of intuitive 'knowledge'. I would see this stage as one of consciousness-raising, in which it is vital to acknowledge and validate what cannot and should not yet be put into coherent verbal form.

The next stage can, I think, afford a greater reliance on verbal modes; it is a stage in which more explicit formulations need to be made. But again, as I see it, this is by no means the end of the process, only a step on the way. When we encounter a new concept, we cannot all at once make it our own; we rely instead on second-hand formulations, to be tried on for size. In the 'Dimensions of Childhood' curriculum, young people are asked to plan an enquiry which they will carry out into one or more of the six dimensions. In defining this enquiry, they are likely to resort to formulations of the dimensions which are not first-hand or original, but taken from the tutor, the mass media, or someone they have heard talking. It seems to me very important that this intermediate and necessary stage is allowed, rather than demanding that learners produce an original perspective from scratch.

But it is a different matter once an enquiry has been carried through. Because putting at issue a socially vital dimension necessarily entails adopting a personal stance towards it, the experience allows a first-hand engagement with the ideas involved. In the 'Dimensions of Childhood' curriculum, the personal feelings and assumptions underlying the young person's enquiry are the subject of sharing and reflection in a supportive small group. This means that the young learners come to develop a greater awareness of their own personal stances, and that of their 'subjects' towards the dimension involved. How do I, as a young white, working-class girl, stand towards the black and Asian people I am interviewing? What do they really feel about the topic of race with which this enquiry is concerned? How am I reading their response? What can they tell me, and what cannot they say? What does all this mean for my position towards the issue of race, and what do I need to rethink? Grounded as the dimension has become in first-hand experience – first-hand agency – it can now be reformulated in genuinely personal and thereby potentially empowering terms.

This example, in which I have tried to flush out the meaning of personal stances, has involved a particular kind of learning on the part of young people. But I see this concept as applying equally to older learners – and, indeed, to people struggling with personal issues who are not generally defined as learners at all. And if learning entails the trying out, provisionally, of a new stance, then teaching entails the public living out, wittingly or unwittingly, of what such stances may mean personally.

Finally, if we read the whole process of learning in this way, we are, I think, not likely to over-simplify what is involved in achieving that ultimate goal – learning for social change. For as I have argued throughout this chapter, there can be no possibility for reworking the social order so long as new learning remains unintegrated with the deepest levels of understanding. Only if, through knowing the world differently, do we come to change our own personal stance towards it, can our learning be genuinely empowering, allowing an extension of personal agency within the current social order.

References

Freire, P. (1972a). *Pedagogy of the Oppressed*. Harmondsworth: Penguin.

Freire, P. (1972b). *Cultural Action for Freedom*. Harmondsworth: Penguin.

Freire, P. (1974). *Education: The Practice of Freedom*. London: Writers and Readers Cooperative.

Salmon, P. (1988). *Psychology for Teachers: an Alternative Approach*. London: Hutchinson Education.

Smith, L. (in press). *Dimensions of Childhood* (working title). London: Health Education Council/UNICEF.

Walden, R. and Walkerdine, V. (1985). *Girls in Mathematics*. Bedford Way Papers. London: Institute of Education.

Part 5

Looking Forward

5. Perspectives

When I found that this very natural process of learning is being institutionalized, I feel a little bit angry. What is happening? The majority of people learn
everyday from their reality, but feel isolated. OK, there are people who are
sincere in their attempts to struggle with looking at things from a different
perspective. But what worries me is that this is becoming very much a classroom
kind of thing. Trust in experiential learning by the wider society will disappear
and that is the main worry I have. But equally, we can help each other to see our
work from a different perspective. It is difficult.

We are dealing with experiential education as if it were an alternative and
perhaps I am speaking to the converted but, in my estimation, the reason why
younger students are going through an experiential learning process, the reason
why there are higher education institutions that are adopting this approach is
because it is fundamentally better. That is one of the reasons why I am very
concerned that we do not see this as a fringe movement.

Experiential learning can empower people, and change their role as learners
from one of being recipients in a learning situation to one in which they take
control of the process. This means they go back into their own situations with
greater confidence and skill. We need to respect and take seriously learners'
experience and their potential input. We have to deconstruct the teacher as
expert.

What I am trying to do is to teach students that knowledge is not locked up in the
university; that if they really want to learn something, OK they may go to class,
but go outside where the actual work is being processed and then see what you
are working toward. I can't send them out there unless there are people who will
help to open their eyes. People who are actually outside of the university, and
who help them to be empowered and learn that these other experiences are just

as valid and that these students have something to learn from people outside institutions.

We mustn't create a myth around experiential learning. It can also be used in a very narrow perspective. Experiential learning can be used as a means of just making production more efficient. Institutions and productive structures are pushing towards experiential learning. Experiential learning is therefore not just something that goes against the grain of the system, but rather it increasingly *is* the direction of the system. We must remain aware of this.

22

Continuing the Dialogue: New Possibilities for Experiential Learning

Ian McGill and Susan Warner Weil

Introduction

In Chapter 1, we identified the four villages associated with the notion 'experiential learning'. We also sought to make the differences across the villages more explicit. Here, we consider some new possibilities that can evolve out of diversity and dialogue across the villages. This chapter builds on the ideas explored in Chapter 1, as well as on issues raised throughout the book in our introductory paragraphs to other contributions.

Our conviction is that experience drawn from across the villages provides the potential for new integrations. Encounters among different groups from all the villages can help us to 'think afresh about what we know so well'. The resulting dialogue can reduce the risk that in each village, as Griffin (1982) says, we become so complacent about working with experience that we cease to be surprised, informed and transformed by it.

We pose questions for each village that arise out of the wider dialogue and consider some of the implications of integrating alternative meanings and purposes into each of the villages. But first, we believe it is necessary to share some of the assumptions and meanings we bring to the notion 'experiential learning', and some of the ideas and theories we draw on to guide and make sense of our own practice and commitments in formal education and training, staff and organizational development, and social change.

Making connections with others' reflections on experiential learning

In our view, no one theory or model at present adequately accounts for the issues raised across the four villages. Experiential learning, for us, is simultaneously an educational philosophy, a range of methodologies, and a framework for being, seeing, thinking and acting, on individual and collective levels. It involves the active transformation and integration of different forms of experience. These processes lead to new understandings and the development of a wide range of capabilities to behave more effectively, in what Argyris and Schön (1974) refer to as 'situations of action'. Experiential learning enables us to engage with the interrelatedness of self and the social context, inner experience and outer experience, content and process, and different ways of knowing.

We see experiential learning as a means by which we cease to fragment our experience and our ways of knowing: for instance, intellectual, intuitive, social and behavioural. Through experiential learning cycles and processes, we learn to see underlying patterns and connections, and powerful central themes within larger wholes. Making sense of ourselves in relation to the world is at the centre of experiential learning.

We see engagements with any learning situation, and the meanings we construct out of it, as the product of what we bring to that situation, what happens within it, and what happens when the former and the latter impact upon each other.

There are a number of models and theories which assist our own reflections on our practice, and can guide the development of new ones. Kolb's (1984) theory is frequently cited as a means of explaining experiential learning processes. He speaks of learning 'as the process whereby knowledge is created through the transformation of experience'. His cycle addresses learning as a dialectic between 'grasping' what is happening on concrete and abstract levels, and actively transforming such experience, through reflection or observation, and the testing or application of learning outcomes (ibid.).

We feel that his is an important theoretical contribution, in that he highlights the imbalance in traditional Western educational systems. In other words, symbolic or abstract modes of experiencing and subject specialization continue to be emphasized at the expense of alternative modes of experiencing.

We also, however, agree with Jarvis (1987), who stresses the fact that:

> . . . learning always occurs within a social context and that the learner is also to some extent a social construct, so that learning should be regarded as a *social phenomenon as well as an individualistic one* [our emphasis].

Therefore, new models need to reflect this. Jarvis' own model, based on adult learners' accounts of their own learning processes, challenges Kolb's assumption that learning entails a cyclical sequence of stages. Instead, Jarvis charts nine different routes that can result from a 'potential learning situation', and may or may not result in learning. A potential learning situation occurs when individuals' 'stock of knowledge and/or their self-concept and the socio-cultural milieu in which experience occurs' are at odds in some way: what he refers to as 'disjuncture'. Each of the routes relate to 'different social situations, different forms of knowledge, and have different purposes' (ibid.).

There are others who are grappling with learning as more than merely an individualistic process. Taylor (1986), for example, suggests that learning is both a psychological and social process that cannot be divorced from the context of relationships. She has studied experience-based learning applied in particular towards self-direction. She has identified patterns in peoples' experience, and recurring phases, each of which embodies a change in perspective and therefore an important transformational point, with resulting implications for action. Relationships play a critical role in enabling the learner to move through a cycle. She suggests that this is sequential, and that learners move from disorientation and exploration, to reorientation and equilibrium. Ramsden (1987) also emphasizes the need to consider teaching and learning in higher education from a relational perspective to account for what happens in a learning situation.

Mezirow (1978, 1981, 1985) enables us to grapple with the notion of 'meaning' – something which is a key concern in our own consideration of possibilities for each village in the sections which follow. He speaks about an individual's 'meaning perspective' as:

. . . the structure of cultural and psychological assumptions within which new experience is assimilated to – and transformed by – one's past experience (Mezirow, 1978).

Mezirow suggests that our meaning perspectives guide our understanding of ourselves and our relationships. Experiential learning, for Mezirow, is often rooted in some disorientating dilemma. This leads to some form of assessment – of self, and of patterns in others' experience. Out of alienation (analogous to Taylor's 'disorientation') and struggle can come empowerment, and the commitment to exploring new forms of being and acting that are more in tune with new meaning perspectives (Mezirow, 1981). 'Perspective transformation' (Mezirow, 1978), by its very nature entails struggle, as individuals reassess former meaning perspectives and try to evolve new ones, to make sense of themselves and their past. It entails a critique of the sociopolitical forces which constrain perceptions and choice (Mezirow, 1981, 1985). New forms of being and relating emerge out of struggle. It is some time however, before we can feel a sense of integration between such learning and our actual transactions with the world.

Mezirow's emphasis on the interrelatedness of personal and social meaning, on struggle, and on how difficult it is to internalize and then act upon something that is clear in our heads has a great deal of relevance to our own experience. Readers will see the influence of these concerns in our consideration of new possibilities within the four villages.

We agree with Salmon (Chapter 21) that the experience of learning situations is mediated through the learner's personal stance (see also Salmon, 1988). This is shaped by personal biography, and the actions individuals have taken in their lives, as well as by particular historical, social, political and economic forces. The interaction of these give rise to assumptions, beliefs, perceptions and ways of construing and acting upon experience.

Freire's work provides another important dimension to our reflections on experiential learning that has relevance to our own experience. His cycle of experiential learning begins with problem-posing, which in turn provides the basis for increasing our critical consciousness of how the social context has shaped our interpretations and perceptions of that experience. Personal and collective action, aimed at changing the social structures and processes which maintain inequality, are the aims of this 'conscientisation process' (Freire, 1972a).

Finally, Dewey's classic statement on experience and education, remains a beacon of clear thinking. His work guides not only our own efforts to 'make sense' of experiential learning, but continues to influence many other Western educationalists whom we cite above. There are two gems in particular that we believe are of particular relevance to our considerations here. Firstly, Dewey wisely cautions us against setting 'traditional' education against 'progressive' education. This is as valid and valuable today as it was then. Secondly, we are as challenged as ever before by his commitment to thinking about education as the 'intelligently directed development of the possibilities inherent in ordinary experience' (1938).

These are some of the writers and theorists whom we have encountered within the limitations of our own cultural experiencing and who have helped us to reflect on our own practice. We suggest that they have validity only insofar as they have helped us to evolve and shape some of our meanings of experiential learning.

In summary, we currently interpret experiential learning as the process whereby people, individually and in association with others, engage in direct encounter and then *purposefully* reflect upon, validate, transform, give personal meaning to and seek to integrate their different ways of knowing. Experiential *learning* therefore enables the discovery of possibilities that may not be evident from direct experience alone.

Reflections on the role of the facilitator

Experiential learning can be self-managed, by individuals and groups, or facilitated by trainers or change agents outside post-school education. Within post-school education, it can be the basis for programmes of study, along a continuum running from learner-controlled study to taught courses.

When a facilitator is involved, such as to support independent study or to play a key role in a group, his or her role is critical. Whatever the degree of learner centredness operating in that situation, the facilitator is a critical participant in the 'transactional encounter' (Brookfield, 1986) that is at the heart of significant learning and quality education. We share concerns about the extent to which this role is being reduced to merely:

> 'a knee-jerk' satisfier of consumer needs [where education] thus becomes one giant department store in which facilitators are providers of whatever learners [consumers] believe will make them happy (Brookfield, 1986, pp. 97–8).

Facilitators can play a key role in enabling learners to reflect critically on their experience, to explore different perspectives, in serving as an important source of and guide towards knowledge and information and to consider how knowledge is rooted in personal and social circumstances.

In discussing the role of the facilitator, we recognize the value and need for more opportunities for learner-directed or independent study. But we share Wildemeersch's concern (Chapter 5) about the strictly technological and functional meanings currently being ascribed to 'self-direction' and 'autonomy'. For us, self-directed experiential learning is not just a matter of managing procedures and information in a vacuum; it entails making sense of, and transforming, personal meaning within the social context. Opportunities for support, challenge and dialogue on a whole variety of levels, in groups and through one-to-one relationships with different people who can serve as resources for learning, can make the difference between independent study being merely functional learning, and education.

In groups, the climate for experiential learning is critical and facilitators often play a key role in creating an environment that is conducive to working with and transforming experience. For example, we strive to replace a traditional educational emphasis on rights and wrongs, on certainty and prediction, with an emphasis on dialogue. Such dialogue can embrace a consideration of personal meanings as well as the wider influences which have helped to shape those meanings. Whether we are engaging with the paradoxes of current research in nuclear physics, or the disabling effects of a particular professional assumption or practice upon a community group, dialogue is essential. For us, experiential learning, even that which is essentially self-managed, is borne out of *dialogue* in some way. Through dialogue, we come to understand how our own personal stance as facilitators, maintains or challenges power relationships that dominate in the wider society. Freire (1972a), perhaps, best expresses what the latter means to us in practice (see also Wildemeersch and Keregero, Chs 5 and 18, this volume).

> . . . only through communication can human life hold meaning. The teacher's thinking is authenticated only by the authenticity of the students' thinking. The teacher cannot think for his [as originally written] students, nor can he impose his thought on them. Authentic thinking, thinking that is concerned with *reality*, does not take place in ivory-tower isolation, but only in communication.

Below, we explore some possibilities for experiential learning from the perspective of each village. These emerge out of reflections on our own practice, guided by some of the ideas above, and our own engagement in dialogue across the villages. We do not dismiss as immaterial ideological and attitudinal differences (conscious or not) within and across the villages. These, as Boud says in Chapter 3, obviously 'place some limits on transferability'. Nor is our aim either to effect a compromise or make an eclectic combination out of the various practices. Instead, we are striving to develop, in the words of Dewey, 'a new order of conceptions which can lead to new modes of practice' (1938). By sharing some of the ways we are trying to push the boundaries of our own thinking and practice, we aim to provoke critical reflection and further discussion about theory and meanings-in-practice.

Revisiting the assessment and accreditation of prior experiential learning from new perspectives

In this village (to which we shall continue to refer as 'APEL') the identification of learning outcomes, in the form of specific knowledge and skills, is the primary aim. As a vehicle for access to opportunity, APEL processes and procedures for identifying those outcomes have value in themselves. But they can also be used for other purposes. Below, we focus particularly on possibilities that might be considered at the point of entry to courses in higher education.

APEL as a basis for learning about learning

The procedures and practices associated with APEL (e.g. see literature from CAEL and LET, such as that cited in Chapter 1), can help learners to consider their experiences as 'learners learning' in different contexts. For example, an adult who left school with no qualifications, but has been involved in community development activity, consciousness-raising groups, and work-based learning, would benefit from reflecting not just on the learning outcomes, but also on what has it meant to be a learner in those situations.

Recent writing and research (e.g. Weil, 1988; Thomas and Harri-Augstein, 1985; Griffin, 1987; Usher, 1986) stress the value of helping students to develop a vocabulary for making sense of their experiences of learning:

> The construction of a 'theory' about learning enables students to recognise that they themselves are a legitimate source of knowledge about their own learning and through structured interaction with others can share this and make generalisations about the nature of the learning process. It contributes, therefore, to developing a reflexive awareness of learning (Usher, 1986, p. 31).

How can academic staff and employers who are committed to APEL help adults develop a deeper understanding of their own ways of 'knowing'. This entails more than an identification of dominant learning styles or a consideration of study skills. It includes exploring with others, for example, what it has meant to learn at different times in one's life; what factors have heightened their capacity and willingness to learn in different learning environments; what kinds of relationships in learning situations have enhanced their potential to engage in meaningful learning; what kinds of personal stances in others (as discussed by Salmon in Chapter 21) have enabled them to fully engage with the content and processes of learning. Reflection and analysis in relation to these aspects of experience can give learners a further resource for grappling with other meanings for learning they will encounter through a range of encounters within the learning environment to which they have gained access (see also Peterson, Chapter 16). Such reflections also enable academic staff to extend the boundaries of their own experience, and be constructively challenged in their assumptions and perceptions.

APEL as a basis for recognizing differences

These additional purposes for APEL relate to the ideas of Chickering (1981) and Weathersby (1981), who advocate the use of life-span research and theory, and an acknowledgement of wide-ranging life-cycle differences as the basis for educational planning and programme development. Much life-cycle theory and research:

> would undoubtedly differ in significant particulars from results which would be obtained in Latin America, Africa, or the Middle- or Far East. We should also recognize that these findings, with some important exceptions, come from studies of white, middle- and upper-class men. The patterns identified are probably off-target in some significant ways for farmers, factory and construction workers, truck drivers, and other blue-collar workers. No doubt they are also significantly off-target for many blacks, Orientials, native Americans, Chicanos, and other minorities. These findings would also be different for women, as the growing research . . . makes clear (Chickering and Havighurst, 1981).

Belenky *et al.* (1986) have researched the learning experiences of black and white women, from different socioeconomic backgrounds. They identify five categories of ways of knowing in relation to the image of a spiral. Women move forwards and back along this spiral, depending upon their interactions with others in particular learning environments, and the ways in which they have come to make sense of their experiences as learners:

> *silence*, a position in which women experience themselves as mindless and voiceless and subject to the whims of external authority; *received knowledge*, a perspective from which women conceive of themselves as capable of receiving, even reproducing, knowledge from the all-knowing external authorities but not capable of creating knowledge on their own; *subjective knowledge*, a perspective from which truth and knowledge are conceived of as personal, private, and subjectively known or intuited; *procedural knowledge*, a position in which women are invested in learning and applying objective procedures for obtaining and communicating knowledge; and *constructed knowledge*, a position in which women view all knowledge as contextual, experience themselves as creators of knowledge, and value both subjective and objective strategies for knowing (Belenky *et al.*, 1986).

This work both builds upon and contrasts with Perry's (1970, 1981) research with traditional-age, white, middle-class male students at Harvard, through which he identified nine stages of cognitive ethical growth. He suggests that students move from dualistic conceptions of the world, to those which acknowledge that all knowledge is relativistic and contextual. Griffin (1987) also writes about strategies to assist learners in 'naming' the processes of learning in which they are engaged, in order to make better sense, and better use, of them. These kinds of frameworks further enable adults to examine their own experience, as well as the patterns and differences that recur across the experience of individuals who identify with particular social groups.

We recognize the considerable value of APEL as a vehicle for access to opportunity. But, if staff who participate in the teaching of educational programmes had opportunities to participate in the use of APEL procedures and processes towards these wider ends, they may become able to use to greater effect the rich curricula provided by learners' experiences. We believe that the ideas of Redwine (Chapter 8), Horwitz (Chapter 7) and Steltenpohl and Shipton (1986) can help us to evolve programmes at entry. Broader uses of APEL are also relevant to 'access' courses, which are currently being developed in the UK. These are targeted at groups traditionally under-represented in higher education (see, e.g. the *Journal of Access Studies* for accounts and critiques of current practice). Such programmes may help to reduce the discontinuities adults can experience as they move across different learning contexts (Weil, 1986, 1988).

APEL in the social context

Currently, as discussed in Chapter 1, one experience is treated no differently than any other in this village, as long as skills and knowledge, matched to those required for the course or job, can be demonstrated. As Barkatoolah (Chapter 14) argues, our notions of what constitute legitimate competences are inextricably entwined with our particular experience of the social context. What kinds of people are being given access and what kinds of competences are being emphasized more than others? What competences for meeting the complex challenges of living in today's world are being identified and on the basis of what kinds of criteria?

Research is required to examine what kinds of learning and competences are kept outside the remit of current accreditation frameworks. Inquiry is needed into how dominant, often implicit, values and ideologies determine what experience, skills and qualities count as valid outcomes. We need to analyse the wider implications of competency frameworks that are predetermined by academic institutions and employers. For example, Wylde (Chapter 11) offers an account of experiential learning that we suggest would sit uncomfortably with many assumptions about valid learning and competences, but why is that, and at what cost to society as a whole? Hinman (1986, 1987), through her work in the UK in further education, is grappling with these issues.

To what extent have institutions using APEL procedures and practices, particularly higher education environments that are more traditional, been genuinely transformed by the experience of diverse learners? Does 'prior' simply become that learning gained, before gaining access, only to be fitted into conventional academic constructions of knowledge? To what extent is the complexity and richness of 'non-traditional' students' experience being compromised? What are the wider implications of this? To what degree have traditional disciplinary boundaries been redefined? What kinds of professional development strategies enable staff to work with APEL in less academically determined ways?

The increasingly widespread use of APEL as a basis for access provides a solid foundation for using its possibilities to greater effect. Reflection upon, and the analysis of, prior work and life-experience, opens up challenging ethical and social questions for teachers and learners alike. A wider focus than on narrowly defined academic or employer led criteria may address the concerns of those who find it difficult to reconcile some aspects of current practice with curriculum or social change objectives associated with this village (see Chapter 1). Can APEL provide a basis for not just economic, but also social, personal and institutional development objectives?

New possibilities for post-school education

One of the biggest challenges for post-school education systems in the USA and Europe is to change the participation patterns that still persist, (e.g. Schutze, 1987) despite years of supposed commitment to reversing them:

> . . . those who participate most actively are those who already have the greatest degree of education and training, those who have the highest incomes, those who are of the ethnic majority, and those who regard themselves as the educated classes (Keeton, 1987).

The section below focuses primarily on adults in higher education. We believe, however, that many of the issues we address have wider relevance.

Reversing current patterns of participation

Kolb (1984) argues:

> For many so-called nontraditional students – minorities, the poor, and mature students – experiential learning has become the method of choice for learning and personal development.

Chickering (1976) suggests that current approaches to and assumptions about teaching and learning generally tend to reinforce:

> . . . fearful-dependent, opportunistic, and conforming-to-persons levels of ego development and the obedience–punishment, instrumental egoism and exchange, and good-boy [as originally written] orientations of moral development (Chickering, 1976).

Students whose backgrounds are characterized by a high degree of conformity to the demands of traditional formal schooling may groan about the status quo in higher education institutions, but will none the less accommodate themselves to the system as they know it. For others, this may require major compromises. Fundamental issues of identity, and core values and beliefs, that have emerged *since* initial schooling, may be put at risk through a re-accommodation to the purposes and assumptions of the formal system (see, e.g. Weil, 1986, 1988; Peterson, Chapter 16).

To what extent is higher and continuing education currently *perceived* by *diverse* learners to offer quality learning opportunities of relevance, not only to the complexity of their own lives, but also to the problems they confront on a variety of levels in their communities and their society as a whole? We suggest that experiential learning as simultaneously a philosophy, a choice of methodologies, and a set of principles, leads to new experiences and 'potential learning situations' (Jarvis, 1987) that we can neither predict nor control. These experiences may enhance our capacity to engage genuinely with issues of access.

When we consider this village from the perspective of, for example, the APEL village, the concern is to develop a variety of strategies for recognizing what adults have gained from life and work experience. But, as Chickering (1976) asks:

How many curricula, courses, classes, seminars and examinations help students build knowledge from personal experiences and personally generated syntheses and paradigms? How many teachers in the natural sciences, the humanities, and the social and behavioural sciences help students not only to acquire basic concepts, competency, and knowledge, but also help them to use those learnings to make sense of life and of themselves, to generate personal insights through subjective and dialectical processes.

The social change village might ask: 'With what consequences is the wider context of experience and knowledge generation and use dismissed as irrelevant by formal education systems?' Equally, whose interests are being served by adopting an approach to education that focuses on the deficiencies of individuals, at the expense of deficiencies in the society as a whole? (Youngman, 1986). As Tumin (1976) argues, in his discussion of valid and invalid rationales for the assessment and accreditation of experiential learning:

Simple sociological analysis shows us, too, that you cannot significantly alter the educational certification system of society without large-scale social change in other institutional arrangements, and in the preceding values and supporting resources.

Finally, the personal growth and development village would argue that traditional higher and continuing education still perpetuates the illusion that people function as coherent, rational and objective human beings. The 'theory-in-use' evident at the level of action in our institutions and courses (Argyris and Schön, 1974, 1978) suggests that we are somehow immune from the effects of earlier experience, emotions, anxieties and fears. For example, intuitive knowing tends to be discredited, and the importance of understanding how our personal stance shapes our educational engagements is denied (see Salmon, Chapter 21). This village would argue that there need to be far more opportunities for individuals to become self-aware of themselves as learners, and as people.

Failure to address these dimensions of human and social development through experiential approaches may ensure that huge gaps persist between what we say we believe and our actions. Some have argued that educated individuals, and the organizations which they create, are becoming *increasingly* less able (1) to recognize such gaps, and (2) to know how to reduce them (Argyris and Schön, 1974, 1978).

Learning how to learn, and the need for diverse adults to have such opportunities, is an increasingly predominant concern in post-school learning contexts. But how can we develop and apply 'learning to learn capacities', not just to the demands of technological change and the 'knowledge explosion', but to other equally important concerns, that involve ourselves and the societies within which we live?

Experience provides the baseline against which reflection, reconceptualization and reframing, and the consideration of new integrations and applications can occur. We believe that students need varied learning experiences in post-compulsory education, through which they can become more capable of understanding and transforming their experience. Such experiences may include internships, projects, structured activity, opportunities for dialogue on a variety of levels, systematic reflection on prior learning and on group processes. These provide the 'meaning frameworks' within which theory and research, information and ideas can be made sense of, assessed from different perspectives, and applied. Recurring cycles of engagement and, as Bawden (1988) says, 'problem tackling', needs to involve the 'concrete and the abstract, reflection and action'. Each experiential engagement provides a vantage point for addressing the interrelatedness of intellectual, personal and social learning. Each cycle can engender new understandings for agency or action.

Untapped group learning possibilities

Group processes in higher education are a rich source for experiential learning, but we believe that they are seldom tapped to their full potential. When group learning involves reflection on the processes in which learners and group members engage, and the meanings they attribute to such processes, students can develop a language to make sense of their own experience as learners.

For example, Jaques (1984) speaks of the extrinsic and intrinsic aims and purposes of small-group teaching, and some of the task and socio-emotional capabilities to be derived from working in groups in post-school education. Others offer specific strategies for using group experience to increase self-awareness and awareness of self in relation to others (see, e.g. Miles, 1981; Johnson and Johnson, 1982). Griffin (1987) writes about how groups can help learners to 'name the processes' in which they are engaged, and develop a deeper understanding of new possibilities for learning – individually and in groups. Boud *et al.* (1985) cite strategies for facilitating reflection, as a basis for turning experience into learning.

When we make ourselves and our learning processes the focus of reflection and analysis, we can better learn to value alternative ways of knowing (e.g. Belenky *et al.* 1986; Gilligan, 1982). We can acknowledge those aspects of our experience and our understanding that remain incoherent, as O'Reilly has discussed (Chapter 9), and discover the validity of our intuitive learning, as discussed by Wylde (Chapter 11). The personal development village stresses the importance of noticing those aspects of experience which fortify defensive postures, and those which make us eager to engage in further learning. Through reflection, we can learn more about what our leanings or resistances say about our own personal stance (Salmon, Chapter 21).

But we suggest that group processes cannot be divorced from the social context of experiencing. Many of the assumptions that continue to permeate higher education systems, and its rhetoric, stem from the belief that if we change the individual, improvements in our institutions and our society will result. We question this basic premise, as does London (1972, p. 13):

> Much of the curriculum of formal education is developed for its value for the teacher and not the students. Far too many faculty members are elitists who mistrust students, and are more interested in producing imitations of themselves than active, involved, and dedicated citizens who are participating in community activities and taking an active part in helping determine the character of their society.

He goes on to suggest,

> . . . while we often assert that the schools should help their students to learn how to think critically, critical thinking in practice is restricted. Teachers infrequently assume the role of social critics, nor do they tolerate much criticism of themselves or of our major institutions (London, 1972).

Experiential learning and reflection in groups provides opportunities for enabling students to think beyond their own individual needs, to acknowledge the interrelatedness of their experiencing and their autonomy within the wider social system. In groups, students can consider patterns that recur in the experience of particular social groups, and the ways in which we are shaped through interactions with wider cultural norms and social structures. We can be helped to see how our leanings and resistances suggest clues to our relationship to, and positioning within, the wider social context (see, e.g. Brah and Hoy, Chapter 6). In such kinds of processes, new forms of individual and collective commitments and responsibilities may be nurtured. Reflection in groups on these levels can provide another means for making sense of experiences of field placements or internships. A range of facilitators, from a variety of backgrounds, can help us to become attuned to different kinds of experiencing and knowing. Such groups can be built into taught courses, and also provide forums within which students engaging in independent study can reflect on their own experiences from alternative perspectives (e.g. McGill *et al.*, Chapter 12).

Group learning that increases awareness and empowers on personal and social levels is no less relevant to the study of the social sciences than that of the natural or engineering sciences. Whether chemist, engineer, independent learner or psychologist, we all exist in relation to others, through work and living, in societies currently characterized by inequality of opportunity, diversity and problems of global concern.

New conceptions of learning and knowing

Descartes, often regarded as the 'father of modern philosophy' in the West, was a brilliant thinker whose influence is still pervasive within higher and continuing education. His influence, however, has helped to reinforce the academic tradition of perpetuating dichotomies between mind and matter, between thinking and doing, between intellect and emotion: 'I think, therefore I am.' The dominant image is a man, isolated from the contamination of everyday life. It is said that Descartes used to crawl into a stove to do his thinking, to ensure that he would not be disturbed. For us, from a current perspective, his intellectual brilliance is diminished by this image. How capable would Descartes be of working with diverse men and women today, the majority of whom need to cope with the complexities of the real world?

Higher education *still* overemphasizes cognitive learning of fixed content by the individual student. Academic theories and research remain largely the responsibility of people with particular perspectives and interests, representing a small band of social experience. Our view, and that of growing numbers of others, is that this can only be dysfunctional in today's complex society (we return to this in our conclusion).

New conceptions of knowing are now evolving. The authority traditionally ascribed to subject experts is being challenged:

> To truly know does not require that we separate ourselves from that which we wish to know, but that we become critically engaged with it with a view towards changing it. Indeed, to learn about something *is* to change it, for to learn is to appropriate, name, and use (Boston, 1972).

Lindquist is an American educator whose institution, Goddard, has for many years been at the forefront of developments in experiential learning in the USA. He has argued that competitive and meritocratic systems of traditional education, although helpful for some objectives, are not helpful for achieving the democratic ideals of freedom with responsibility, and independence with cooperation. He cites the challenge of experiential educators as that of bringing together the voices of 'inner' and 'connective' with those of 'others' and 'reason' (CAEL, 1987).

Kolb (1984, p. 225) speaks of integrated, experientially based knowing as:

> . . . essentially eclectic, if by the term is meant, 'not consistent with current forms.' It stands with one foot on the shore of the conventions of social knowledge and one foot in the canoe of an emergent future – a most uncomfortable and taxing position, one that positively demands commitment to either forging ahead or jumping back to safety.

New roles for educators

Academics' subject expertise is important but not sufficient for engaging with the implications of new conceptions of teaching and learning. They must learn how to become a different kind of resource for students' learning. For example, their understanding of particular disciplines can provide the basis for posing problems which will challenge students, and strengthen their capacity to seek and apply a wide range of resources in relation to it. (Hutton's framework, in Chapter 4, offers a useful guide in this respect, since it is based on a recognition of the complexity of issues entailed in 'problem solving'.) Educators can also use their understanding of particular areas of knowledge as the basis for designing sequences of activity for engaging learners through a range of learning modes (see, e.g. Packham *et al.*, Chapter 13; Järvinen, Chapter 15; Nelson, Chapter 10; Peterson, Chapter 16). The key challenge is to support learners in the development of personally grounded frameworks of meaning within which they can better assimilate new ideas and ways of seeing.

Educators need to become better attuned to the logic of the learner, and to allow this to have primacy over their own conception of the logic of the subject. Problems derived from the unartificial setting of life seldom fit neatly into the artificial boundaries around which our institutions still tend to be structured. Kirkwood (1976) says that if we can agree that:

> learning is what matters, and that setting, structure and process are the means to that end and not ends in themselves, it will be the best evidence of all that we [as academics] do, that we can indeed learn greatly from experience.

Educators can play a key role in setting up experiential opportunities whereby learners can be challenged to apply their learning, and engage with real complexities and consequences entailed in that application. The extensive body of research stemming from work at Lancaster University and at Gothenburg can also help to guide educators in coming to grips with what teaching and learning and assessment strategies promote deep learning, as opposed to surface learning (see, e.g. Entwistle and Ramsden, 1983; Marton *et al.*, 1984; Richardson *et al.*, 1987).

Boreham (1987) suggests that:

> Educators wishing to promote learning from experience . . . have to revive in their students learning styles which may have been discouraged since primary school – learning from experience depends on learning *how to learn* from experience.

This is no less true for students than it is for educators. As Whitaker (1978) says, academics are still trained:

> in content rather than process; we were trained to pursue research and writing activities rather than to interact effectively with other learners. Paradoxically, we have learned experientially how to teach traditionally. We now need to reverse the process.

Academics must be helped to use the full range of their expertise in new ways, while also being able to be a co-learner with students – tackling with them issues and problems that transcend traditional subject boundaries.

The capacity to structure experientially based learning cycles and to understand the notion of 'process' at the curriculum, interpersonal, group and social levels places new demands on academics who are accustomed to delivering lectures to passive, traditional students. Structures of promotion and reward should recognize the development entailed in endeavours that go against the mainstream; new forms of staff and organizational development thus become critical. Developments in continuing education and shifts in existing patterns of access will redraw subject, sector and staff role boundaries (Schuller *et al.*, 1988).

We believe that new roles and capabilities can only be learned experientially, through a wide range of professional development opportunities that in themselves model, and engage academics in, new conceptions of learning and knowing. Academics need opportunities to reflect, re-frame and transform their own experience in ways that help them to respond more effectively to new expectations and demands.

For example, McGill *et al.* (Chapter 12) offer one strategy that can be self-managed by staff, and can better attune them to what experiential learning, and working in problem and process-centred ways may mean. Packham *et al.* (Chapter 13) discuss others.

We believe it is critical to evolve new meanings-in-practice for teaching and learning within the more relevant terrains suggested by experiential learning theories and practices across the four villages. In our experience, there are grave consequences in the still predominant tendencies to transmit prepackaged, abstract knowledge at the expense of developing and recognizing other kinds of learning and knowing; to assume that individual development and learning, with no opportunity to reflect on the social context, will result in people who will challenge the ways in which current patterns of participation and inequality are maintained. In working with groups outside higher education, we have learned just how far and how deeply beyond the academy walls the consequences of these choices extend. Chickering (1981) say:

> Given the social forces and the cultural contexts to which we are subject, we seldom reach those developmental goals we value. Our becoming typically falls short of what we would become. But the striving is there in most of us.

Expanding notions of transforming and empowering

In the social change village, there are a number of subgroups, each of which interprets the relationship between theory and experience in a different way. When we examine our own experience in social change groups where an emphasis on particular ways of working and on theory predominate, we can identify influences that diminish our capacity and willingness to learn in that environment. For instance, the following can be disempowering rather than empowering: when any reference to subjective experience is seen as tangential or irrelevant; when the emphasis is on 'getting it right' and on analytical and intellectual critique at the expense of listening, exploring and creating personal meaning; when the language used makes us feel so disconnected from our own experience that we lose the ground from which we might speak; when intellectual posturing makes genuine dialogue and risk taking impossible; when the emphasis is on exclusion rather than engagement; when the intricate connections between task and process, and between thought and deed, are disregarded; when reflection on contradictions between rhetoric and reality is dismissed as unnecessary; when creativity is submerged by excessive critique. Many of these features of a learning environment operate in higher education, where we believe they can be equally disabling, and particularly for new kinds of adult learners.

Other groups in this village are genuinely struggling with what dialogue, personal and collective empowerment, participation, support, and learning from experience mean in practice in terms of their aims for social change (see, e.g. Keregero and Criticos, Chapters 18 and 19). Overall, however, this village provides a critique that helps us to consider, for instance, how dominant, 'taken for granted', or academic, conceptions of experience can constrict our own understandings of experience; how myths perpetrated as the reality for all may have only a limited range of applicability; how conciousness-raising in groups with others who share aspects of our experience can become a means of personal and collective empowerment (see Serrao and Jensen, Chapter 20).

In this village, no more or no less than any other, there is a need for reflection on the meanings and values associated with experiential learning, and to examine the extent to which practice may betray intentions.

'Real talk' vs 'Didactic talk'

Freire, an important figure for many groups in this village, speaks of the critical importance of 'dialogue', as discussed earlier in this chapter and in Chapter 1. However, he refers only to men through his images and his words in the books which have had the greatest impact (e.g. Freire 1972a,b, 1974).

Feminist theory and research provide an important analysis of these recurring features in our experience. At the level of the experiential learning process, the more recent work of people like Belenky *et al.* (1986) and Gilligan (1982) can help to consider the notion of dialogue from alternative perspectives. New ways of seeing, of knowing and of relating, need to take account of gender-related patterns. For example, Gilligan identifies the different ways in which women in her study spoke about ethical issues. Motions like 'equality', 'truth' and 'justice' had little meaning when interpreted out of the context of relationships. In other words, the interrelatedness of moral choice and the social context was what gave meaning to moral issues and, therefore, their consideration was grounded in actual experience.

Belenky *et al.* (1986) explore how the different ways of knowing, introduced earlier in this chapter (p. 251), each interpret dialogue and the use of experience for learning in different ways. For example, their study suggests that women who come to see knowing and learning from a constructed position, may find it difficult, if not impossible, to learn in a group where intellectual posturing predominates:

Constructivists make a distinction between 'really talking' and what they consider to be didactic talk in which the speaker's intention is to hold forth rather than to share ideas. In didactic talk, each participant may report experience, but there is no attempt among participants to join together to arrive at some new understanding. 'Really talking' requires careful listening; it implies a mutually shared agreement that together you are creating the optimum setting so that half-baked ideas can grow. 'Real talk' reaches deep into the experience of each participant; it also draws on the analytical abilities of each (Belenky *et al.*, 1986, p. 144).

Such issues have particular relevance to social change and formal education contexts where didactic talk is the norm. The work of these writers enables us to re-examine the role of dialogue from an alternative grounding in reality. This alternative reality is borne out of a particular form of socialization and oppression. Different meanings-in-practice are suggested, emerging out of a different experience (see Serrao and Jensen, Chapter 20).

Freire's writing and work in social change yields additional issues of wider relevance – to this and other villages. We share Boston's (1972, p. 87) view, who, a 'loving critic' of Freire, questions the contradiction between Freire's:

> career in which the causes of clarity, demythologizing, demystifying, and de-obfuscation have been pursued at great personal cost and the leaden philosophical prose which Freire inflicts on his readers.

Boston applauds the ways in which Freire describes how he always works back to the experience of the concrete situation. But in his writing:

> . . . he makes experience subservient to philosophy; separates knowing from intentionality and the knower *in situ*. The effect is that the explanation of a new educational approach is at odds with the approach itself. We are invited to a parade of concepts before we share an experience, or before we are even told a story (ibid.).

(We are all too well aware of our own struggles with these issues, by virtue of doing a book on experiential learning.)

Social change groups and movements that espouse empowerment and transformation objectives may inadvertently under-rate the significance of enabling people to make personal sense and meaning of those social change objectives. In failing to recognize the importance of this, advocates of social change can undermine their objectives. Experiential learning can enable those connections.

Ideology, experience and personal meaning

Many people in social change movements are motivated by commitments to eliminating oppression in its many forms. They are highly critical of top-down, economically driven national agendas that stress individualism and utilitarian objectives for maintaining the social order. But in our experience, there are also social change movements within this village that operate in ways that are no less functional and autocratic. For example, Griffith (1972) critiques Freire's assumption that the ideals which he espouses as the means of transformation can legitimately be thrown to the wind, once the 'revolution has come to power'.

An experiential learning philosophy helps to clarify when ideology constrains and when it empowers. Griffin's essay points out how ideology is borne out of reflection upon experience, but may get to a point where it fails to recognize experience as a transformative force:

> Originally borne of feeling, it pretends to float about and around feeling . . .
> It organizes experience according to itself, without touching experience . . .
> No one can tell it anything new. Experience ceases to surprise it, inform it, transform it. It is annoyed by any detail which does not fit into its world view. Begun as a cry against the denial of truth, now it denies any truth which does not fit into its scheme. Begun as a way to restore one's sense of reality, now it attempts to discipline real people, to remake natural beings after its own image . . . All that makes it question, it regards as the enemy. Begun as a theory of liberation, it is threatened by new theories of liberation (Griffin, 1982, p. 168).

We believe that looking at experiential learning in the context of the social change village can clarify the ideologies operating with respect to experiential learning and change processes – often implicity – in other villages. Experiential learning in this context (to review some of the issues we addressed at the beginning of this chapter) concerns the process and content of experiencing, reflecting on experience, making sense of experience (on personal, group, institutional and social levels), perspective transformation and, in turn, translating the outcomes of these processes into personal, institutional and social action. Only through recurring cycles, starting with many different sources of experience, can what Argyris and Schön (1974) call 'double loop learning' be achieved, whereby the contradictions between what is espoused and what is done become clearer.

We suggest that this village can learn from some of the processes and practice associated with the personal growth and development village. For example, the 'learning climate' and the process of dialogue needs to enable, rather than disable – as discussed earlier in this chapter. Equally, many of the experiential learning approaches used in post-school education, as described in the previous section and Chapter 1, tend to be dismissed by some in this village as mere 'methodology' or 'technique'. But such approaches may help people to make the analysis of the social context more relevant and accessible. Experiential learning for social change needs to have at its heart a constant emphasis on personal and social struggle, on personal and social experience, as discussed by Salmon (Chapter 21). How can people avoid ossifying the processes of learning into a product to be thrust upon others, who have had little opportunity to make sense of an alternative analysis from the framework of their own experience. Group support, personal and collective empowerment, and dialogue are all critical aspects of any transformative process, in which perspective transformation and individual and social change are at issue.

A radical social change movement may:

> sing the songs of collectivity with great passion, but how do those involved learn deep in their bones the meanings of those words through living practice. To read about equality may warm the heart and nourish the intellect, but what do the words mean in terms of 'being' and 'doing' in everyday life? What does it mean to genuinely translate espoused values into daily words, gestures, nuance and deed? (McGill, 1988).

How do they ensure that the critique does not paralyse but empowers people to create alternatives and concrete learning outcomes?

In our experience, there are as many community-based groups within this village that are enabling, as there are those that are disabling. The former help us to see how dialogue, group support, equality, personal and collective empowerment, and social change can be at the centre of experiential learning processes. They can help people in other villages to engage with, rather than avoid, sources of learning located in the social context of experience. This village can bring new meanings to the implications of broadening access and generating responsibility and commitment in higher education, and to current notions of personal growth and development.

Broadening notions of personal growth and development

This village provides opportunities to explore aspects of ourselves that inhibit our potential to be as we wish to be. Our motivation to become involved in such groups may come from the awareness that there are immense contradictions between how we want to be and what we say we do, between our stated values and beliefs, and how we tend to be experienced by others. But we suggest that personal growth and development groups often get stuck, and seldom go beyond the individual level to examine how the social context may also shape our personal experiencing. Many in the social change village would also argue that much of the practice in this village only helps people to adjust to the status quo. A disproportionate emphasis on individual responsibility and autonomy, at the expense of consciousness raising as a basis for personal and collective empowerment, can undermine stated aims of social change in this village (see, e.g. Walter and Marks, 1981).

Addressing the social context

An example from a 'personal growth' learning environment
Taking an example from a therapeutically oriented group, someone might begin to recognize the disabling influence of an early relationship with a parent and ways in which that may be at the source of a great deal of personal anger. She or he may work very hard to understand that damage on a personal level, and to see how it has perhaps affected current relationships. A skilled facilitator may help the person to role-play, or explore psychodramatically, ways of dealing

with similar situations in their everyday life that seem linked to that early childhood experience.

If, however, a number of men in the group speak of tremendous resentment and anger towards their mothers for not standing up to their fathers, that pattern can serve equally as a focal point for experiential learning. Questions to guide such learning beyond the level of mere self-awareness and understanding could address the institutional and public arenas for our experiencing. They might include: What might be the consequences of such anger in the organization or community where we work or live? How might anger towards women be reinforced by cultural and institutional norms? What policies and practices work to maintain inequality and oppression? How are men encouraged to collude with these? What does the fact that so many men feel that way towards women, say about gender relations in this society? What wider social forces make it difficult for us to change existing patterns of power and dominance? What can individuals do? What can men do to challenge and change these, in our own lives and in the spheres within which we live and work? Small-group work can enable men and women, or black and white people, to reflect initially on their experience in the social context separately, and then together.

An example from education or organizational training/consultancy
Alternatively, someone working with groups on issues of teamwork might stress the importance of effective group functioning, and processes such as constructive feedback and mutual support. She or he may use experiential activities designed to foster the development of interpersonal and communication skills. Imagine, however, that within that learning group, there are men and women, black and white, from different social backgrounds, with experience of how themes related to race and gender oppression become reinforced by group processes and organizational functioning. They may be all too aware of just how irrational the behaviour of certain individuals might be within that particular organizational culture, and how power and prejudice combine to ensure that the status quo remains little changed (see, e.g. Weil *et al.*, 1985).

The objectives for personal development activity in work or educational groups may be undermined if the social dimensions of experience are kept invisible, as if they were not at issue. Some dimensions may *feel* more at issue for some rather than others; but certain norms may make it difficult, nigh impossible, to raise them. These issues might, therefore, not be the object of group reflection and exploration, although these aspects of experiential learning are as relevant as any other. The onus for raising such issues is also often put upon those who have the most to lose. For example, in largely male or white groups, it is common for members of oppressed groups to be seen as 'the problem', or as 'having a problem' that is not 'the group's' concern, as discussed in Chapter 1. Equally, when women or black people try to highlight aspects of their own experience, which may differ from that of others in the group, they can be seen as disrupting the status quo.

We have come to realize just how much prior educational and social experience has conditioned us to see engagement with such issues as 'disruptive' or 'divisive' and as somehow separate from the realm of experience considered 'legitimate' within personal growth and development contexts. The perspective from the social change village enables us to ask: 'Disruptive to whom? Divisive for whom? Legitimate on whose experiential terms?'

When such issues are not regarded as integral to personal growth and development, the realities of divisiveness as persistently manifested across our cultures and social structures, and its origins in our personal and collective experience, can be denied (see McGill *et al.*, Chapter 12).

Responding as facilitators

Facilitators in these contexts can have a key influence on the extent to which such explorations are seen as legitimate and relevant to personal growth and development as any other aspects of our experience. So, for example, returning to the example of 'teamwork', enabling different groups to reflect on their experience of a particular organization becomes an important source of further learning. The identification of patterns in the informal culture, such as white men socializing most nights, to the exclusion of others in the team, can help work-based groups to examine how a great deal of information may be kept from certain team members – no matter how adept they are at teamwork 'skills'. The experience of different groups can also be used to examine how particular structures, policies and practices in the organization may undermine stated aims and values about responsiveness to the community, in all its diversity.

In offering such an analysis, it is important to acknowledge the irrationality and the uses and abuses of power that are so much a part of our social experience and social structures. But, increasingly, people working as facilitators in this village are confronting participants who are concerned with challenging the many complex ways in which dominant perceptions and assumptions, and patterns of inequality, are maintained. Such participants may have had considerable experience of groups where learning from experience, and the development of a deeper understanding of and challenge to the social context of experience, have been central. Their experience of such groups may have helped them to see patterns in the wider reality more clearly. They may also have had opportunities to reflect on their prior experience with others from similar backgrounds, and to identify the themes that recur despite individual diversity. They may have realized, however, that although some aspects of their development are explicable in terms of the social context, others are explicable only in terms of themselves. Untangling those interactions, between self and society, is a process of experiential learning that becomes critical to their personal meanings for individual growth and development.

In placing new demands on facilitators working in this village, there is a need to develop competence, confidence and creativity in legitimating individuals' social experiential learning, as a basis for development and change. Facilitators and trainers need opportunities to consider how they may inadvertently be colluding with assumptions and perceptions that contradict their very purposes, and cause particular social groups to conclude that they have little to gain here.

This village provides a forum for a great deal of learning and development in Western society. We believe, therefore, that it is important that it considers how its dominant values and assumptions may be subtly undermining progress towards equality, and legitimating certain aspects of experience at the expense of others – equally valid. In this way, what this village has to offer may become available to a wider range of social groups who are committed to understanding how the personal is also political.

Conclusion

Is there a larger 'story' that provides a more coherent conceptual framework that can guide the development of new possibilities for experiential learning? Henry (Chapter 2) poses a similar question. We believe that there is.

The 'story' that helps us to ground our experience and understanding of the breadth and diversity of the field is offered by the notion of 'paradigm shift'. This is described by Capra as referring to:

> . . . a profound change in the thoughts, perceptions, and values that form a particular vision of reality. The paradigm that is now shifting has dominated our culture for several hundred years, during which it has shaped our Western society and has significantly influenced the rest of the world. This paradigm comprises a number of ideas and values that differ sharply from those of the Middle Ages; values that have been associated with various streams of Western culture, among them the Scientific Revolution, the Enlightenment, and the Industrial Revolution. They include the belief in the scientific method as the only valid approach to knowledge; the view of the universe as a mechanical system comprised of elementary material building blocks; the view of life in society as a competitive struggle for existence; and the belief in unlimited material progress to be achieved through economic and technological growth. During the past decade all these ideas and values have been found severely limited and in need of radical revision (Capra, 1982, pp. 11–12).

The notion of 'paradigm', therefore, refers to patterns of assumptions, values, concepts, and propositions that underpin a particular world view. As Patton (1978, p. 203) says: 'paradigms tell [people] what is important, legitimate, and reasonable'.

The notion of 'paradigm shift' is supported by evidence from three major sources of experience that challenge dominant assumptions about the nature of reality and truth, and how learning and change is best brought about. The first of these emerges from research taking place at the frontiers of all disciplines but, in particular, nuclear physics. Such research undermines fundamental premises of traditional science (Bohm, 1980; Heisenberg, 1962; Capra, 1982). The second comes from the world around us. The evidence of our senses causes us to question the traditional authority of professional and academic institutions, and pervasive assumptions about the key role they play in ensuring social and technological progress. Finally, there is the growing influence of social movements, through which common sense and institutionalized views of the world that have held sway for many years, and the power of a few, are being challenged. Capra (1982) cites the example of patriarchy:

> [This] has been extremely difficult to understand because it is all-pervasive. It has influenced our most basic ideas about human nature and about our relation to the universe – man's nature and 'his' relation to the universe, in patriarchal language. It is the one system which, until recently, had never in recorded history been openly challenged, and whose doctrines were so universally accepted that they seemed to be laws of nature; indeed, they were usually presented as such. Today, however, the disintegration of patriarchy is in sight. The feminist movement is one of the strongest cultural currents of our time and will have a profound effect on our further evolution.

The assumptions of the old paradigm bar subjective experience from the realm of scientific discourse. In the new, the validity of such experience is upheld, and the capacity to reflect critically and objectively on subjective experience becomes essential (e.g. Rowan, 1981). In the framework of the old, intuitive and emotional knowledge tend to be seen as a threat to 'man's reason and civilization'. Francis Bacon spoke of putting nature 'on the rack and wresting her secrets from her' (Merchant, 1980). The new exposes these assumptions and fears as borne out of commitments to maintain the dominance and power of patriarchy. From the perspective of the old paradigm, detachment is seen as possible, and the scientist 'arranges the data to speak for itself' (Lincoln and Guba, 1983). Bakan (1967) argues that this has caused verification and measurement to take precedence over discovery and openness to new experience in the natural and human sciences. In the new, the mutual interaction of observer and observed is actively acknowledged. In the old, there was no room for paradoxes, only for certainty and prediction. In the new, paradoxes are the essence of experiencing, and our challenge is to discover patterns in the rich fabric of our experience. Tentativeness is valued. In the old, linear logic was the foundation of reason and we relegated alternative channels for knowing to a subsidiary position in the hierarchy, in which cognitive knowing was dominant. In the new, lateral thinking, right and left brain thinking, and new metaphors for wisdom emerge; images of webs, tapestries, and spirals predominate. In the old, the power of particular groups to define the ways in which experience is interpreted tends to be taken for granted; in the new, such power, and its consequences, is questioned and challenged. The old paradigm was founded on the belief that knowledge could be built up, piece by piece, through fragmenting it down into its component parts. This belief is reflected in the current structures and assumptions of academic institutions. The new paradigm stresses wholeness through interconnectedness and interdependence of biological, psychological, social and environmental phenomena and the ways in which they impact upon our experience – at individual, community, social and global levels. (For further discussion of these issues, see Heinsenberg, 1962; Bohm,

1980; Reason and Rowan, 1981; Capra, 1982; Wilbur, 1982; Harding, 1987; and Reason, 1988.)

We have focused on the above as dichotomies. From the perspective of the new paradigm, we would ideally like to avoid such polarized distinctions. But from the perspective of the old paradigm, this is how the world can be seen. We are concerned to present the dichotomies in order to help establish the legitimacy of the new. This is necessary if only because there is still so much power in the old ways of seeing and interpreting the world.

The challenges of taking on board the implications of 'paradigm shift' are immense:

> Like the choice between competing political institutions, that between competing paradigms proves to be a choice between incompatible modes of community life (Kuhn, 1970).

Lather argues that paradigm shift may be in evidence, but a single group conversion to the assumptions of the new is rare. Instead, there is an 'increasing shift in the distribution of professional alliances' as practitioners of the new paradigm: 'improve it, explore its possibilities, and show what it would be like to belong to the community guided by it' (Lather, 1986).

We suggest that this is exactly what is currently happening in each village where a particular emphasis for experiential learning predominates. Some interpretations and practices still uphold norms and assumptions of the former paradigm. For example, when APEL is interpreted in practice as strictly a functional means to an end, and as a process of fragmenting experience into competences that are predetermined by traditional academic- and employer-based criteria, the assumptions of the old paradigm can be reinforced. The same occurs in social change movements that deny or subordinate personal experience, and refute the possibility of a ruling theory being challenged and transformed by new experience.

In such examples, we would question the extent to which their aims for change are undermined by the underlying paradigmatic stance. To what extent do their applications of experiential learning jeopardise their stated aims and values, and delimit their potential for addressing the complexities of a changing world? (But look at what happens when we broaden the possibilities for APEL.)

Equally, we see others, in each village, struggling to make sense of what it might mean to be part of communities and social structures within which the assumptions of the new paradigm are as pervasive as the old. We ourselves are struggling with these conceptions, and have traced some of their outlines in this chapter. As Piercy (1979) writes, through the character of Jackrabbit, in her novel offering a Utopian vision of a society where people struggle to translate what the implications of the new paradigm may mean in practice:

> 'A powerful image says more than can be listed. It cannot be wholly explained rationally,' Jackrabbit said. 'What does a melody mean?'

We believe that developments in experiential learning still tend to be caught between two paradigms of practice. We see aggressive retreats to the values and assumptions of the old as an inevitable part of the process of paradigm shift.

Making sense of the implications of what it means to live in a community where the assumptions of the new paradigm are equally pervasive has to be largely intuitive and incoherent. As O'Reilly argues, we need to affirm the validity of such knowing. It may become the basis for experiential learning out of which new understandings and strivings will emerge.

To take on board the implications and challenges of the new paradigm requires fundamental 'perspective transformation' (Mezirow, 1978), and new capabilities for application. Such transformations can be sudden. They can also proceed more slowly:

> . . . by a series of transitions which permit one to revise specific assumptions about oneself and others until a stage occurs in which the assumptions become transformed (Mezirow, 1985).

Our argument in this chapter is that we now need to push the boundaries of our visions and our villages to acknowledge the interconnectedness of the whole:

> Without a sense of the whole, we have no way of evaluating the parts, no ways of appraising the importance of the expert, no way of seeing that the fragmentation and violence we lament in the world around is but the mirror image of our own cluttered and frenetic psyches (Bailey, 1977).

Our purpose in this chapter, and the book as a whole, has been to identify the key features of each village, and some new possibilities for them deriving from the perspective of other villages. We must try not to be complacent about what we seek to change, and the ways in which we go about it. Our values and commitments in each village can become impoverished through a lack of dialogue.

Keeton (1987) argues that the future challenges for those of us committed to experiential learning will take us into arenas where it will become necessary to confront 'strange and previously neglected questions'. The vantage point offered by the contrasting assumptions of the old and new paradigm, as currently envisaged, may help us to reflect on and take risks in our own experiential learning. The resulting struggles may make us better able to discover the questions we need to ask, and new ways in which we can act upon their implications.

References

Argyris, C. and Schön, D. (1974). *Theory in Practice: Increasing Professional Effectiveness*. San Francisco: Jossey-Bass.

Argyris, C. and Schön, D. (1978). *Organisational Learning: A Theory of Action Perspective*. New York: Addison-Wesley.

Bailey, S. K. (1977). Needed changes in liberal education. *Educational Record*, **58**, 250–8.

Bakan, D. (1967). *On Method: Toward a Reconstruction of Psychological Investigations*. San Francisco: Jossey-Bass.

Bawden, R. (1988). On leadership, change and autonomy. In Boud, D. (Ed.), *Developing Student Autonomy in Learning*. London: Kogan Page.

Belenky, M. F., Clinchy, B. M., Goldberger, N. R. and Tarule, J. M. (1986). *Women's Ways of Knowing: The Development of Self, Voice and Mind*. New York: Basic Books.

Bohm, D. (1980). *Wholeness and the Implicate Order*. London: Routledge and Kegan Paul.

Boreham, N. C. (1987). Learning from experience in diagnostic problem solving. In Richardson, J. T., Eysenck, M. W. and Piper, D. W. (Eds), *Student Learning*. Milton Keynes: SRHE and Open University Press.

Boston, B. O. (1972). Paulo Freire: Notes of a loving critic. In Grabowski, S. (Ed.), *Paulo Freire: A Revolutionary Dilemma for the Adult Educator*. Syracuse, N.Y.: Publications in Continuing Education and ERIC Clearinghouse in Adult Education.

Boud, D., Keogh, R. and Walker, D. (1985). *Reflection: Turning Experience into Learning*. London: Kogan Page.

Brookfield, S. (1986). *Understanding and Facilitating Adult Learning*. Milton Keynes: Open University Press.

CAEL (1987). Lindquist seeks principles for 'Democracy's College'. *CAEL News*, 11(2), 1.

Capra, F. (1982). *The Turning Point: Science, Society and the Rising Culture*. London: Fontana.

Chickering, A. W. (1976). Developmental change as a major outcome. In Keeton, M. T. (Ed.), *Experiential Learning: Rationale, Characteristics and Assessment*. San Francisco: Jossey-Bass.

Chickering, A. (Ed.) (1981). *The Modern American College*. San Francisco: Jossey-Bass.

Chickering, A. W. (1986). *Principles of Good Practice in Assessing Experiential Learning*. Columbia, MD.: CAEL.

Chickering, A. W. and Havighurst, R. J. (1981). The life cycle. In Chickering A. (Ed.), *The Modern American College*. San Francisco: Jossey-Bass.

Dewey, J. (1938). *Experience and Education*. New York: Collier and Kappa Delta Pi.

Entwistle, N. and Ramsden, P. (1983). *Understanding Student Learning*. Beckenham, Kent: Croom Helm.

Freire, P. (1972a). *Pedagogy of the Oppressed*. Harmondsworth: Penguin.

Freire, P. (1972b). *Cultural Action for Freedom*. Harmondsworth: Penguin.

Freire, P. (1974). *Education: The Practice of Freedom*. London: Writers and Readers Cooperative.

Gilligan, C. (1982). *In a Different Voice*. Cambridge, Mass.: Harvard University Press.

Griffin, S. (1982). The way of all ideology. In *Made from this Earth*. London: Women's Press Ltd.

Griffin, V. (1987). Naming the processes. In Boud, D. and Griffin, V. (Eds), *Appreciating Adults Learning: From the Learner's Perspective*. London: Kogan Page.

Griffith, W. S. (1972). Paulo Freire: Utopian perspectives on literacy education for revolution in Grabowski, S. (Ed.) *Paulo Freire: A Revolutionary Dilemma for the Adult Educator*. Syracuse, N.Y.: Publications in Continuing Education and ERIC Clearinghouse in Adult Education.

Harding, S. (1987). *Feminism and Methodology*. Milton Keynes: Open University Press.

Heisenberg, W. (1962). *Physics and Philosophy*. New York: Harper and Row (London: Allen and Unwin, 1963).

Hinman, J. (1986). Access intentions: A practitioner view. *Journal of Access Studies*, 1(2), 72–6.

Hinman, J. (1987). From assessment to accreditation: Reflections on the use of prior learning in further education. In *Assessing Prior Learning: Progress and Practices*. London: Learning from Experience Trust.

Jaques, D. (1984). *Learning in Groups*. London: Croom Helm.

Jarvis, P. (1987). *Adult Learning in the Social Context*. London: Croom Helm.

Johnson, D. W. and Johnson, F. P. (1982). *Joining Together: Group Theory and Group Skills*. Englewood Cliffs, N. J.: Prentice-Hall.

Keeton, M. (1987). *Learning from Experience: A Requirement of Technological Change*. London: Learning from Experience Trust.

Kirkwood, R. (1976). The importance of assessing learning. In Keeton M. T. (Ed.), *Experiential Learning: Rationale, Characteristics, Assessment*. San Francisco: Jossey-Bass.

Kolb, D. A. (1984). *Experiential Learning*. Englewood Cliffs, N.J.: Prentice-Hall.

Kuhn, T. S. (1970). *The Structure of Scientific Revolutions*, 2nd edition (enlarged). Chicago: University of Chicago Press.

Lather, P. (1986). Issues of validity in openly ideological research: Between a rock and a soft place. *Interchange*, **17**(4), 63–84.

Lincoln, Y. and Guba, E. (1983). *Naturalistic Inquiry*. London: Sage.

London, J. (1972). Reflections upon the relevance of Paulo Freire for American adult education. In Grabowski, S. (Ed.), *Paulo Freire: A Revolutionary Dilemma for the Adult Educator*. Syracuse, N.Y.: Publications in Continuing Education and ERIC Clearinghouse in Adult Education.

Marton, F., Hounsell, D. and Entwistle, N. (1984). *The Experience of Learning*. Edinburgh: Scottish Academic Press.

McGill, I. (1988). *Restructuring the Organisation of the Local State: Socialism and Bureaucracy Within the GLC*. University of Bristol: Ph.D. in progress.

Merchant, C. (1980). *The Death of Nature*. New York: Harper and Row.

Mezirow, J. (1978). Perspective transformation. *Adult Education*, **28**(2), 100–10.

Mezirow, J. (1981). A critical theory of adult learning and education. *Adult Education*, **32**, 3–24.

Mezirow, J. (1985). Concept and action in adult education. *Adult Education Quarterly*, **35**(3), 142–51.

Miles, M. (1981). *Learning to Work in Groups*, 2nd edition. New York: Teachers College Press.

Patton, M. Q. (1978). *Utilization-focused Evaluation*. Beverly Hills, Calif.: Sage.

Perry, W. G. (1970). *Forms of Intellectual and Ethical Development During the College Years: A Scheme*. New York: Holt, Rinehart and Winston.

Perry, W. G. (1981). Cognitive and ethical growth: The making of meaning. In Chickering, A. (Ed.), *The Modern American College*. San Francisco: Jossey-Bass.

Piercy, M. (1979). *Woman on the Edge of Time*. London: Women's Press.

Ramsden, P. (1987). Improving teaching and learning in higher education: The case for a relational perspective. *Studies in Higher Education*, **12**(3), 275–86.

Reason, P. (Ed.) (1988). *Human Inquiry in Action*. London: Sage.

Reason, P. and Rowan, J. (Eds) (1981). *Human Inquiry: A Sourcebook for New Paradigm Research*. Chichester: John Wiley.

Richardson, J. T., Eysenck, M. W. and Piper, D. W. (1987). *Student Learning*. Milton Keynes: Society for Research into Higher Education and Open University Press.

Rowan, J. (1981). A dialectical paradigm for research. In Reason, P. and Rowan, J. (Eds), *Human Inquiry: A Sourcebook for New Paradigm Research*, pp. 93–112. Chichester. John Wiley.

Salmon, P. (1988). *Psychology for Teachers: An Alternative Approach*. London: Hutchinson.

Schuller, T., Tight, M. and Weil, S. (1988). Continuing education and the redrawing of boundaries. *Higher Education Quarterly*. **42**(4), 335–52.

Schutze, H. G. (Ed.) (1987). *Adults in Higher Education: Policies and Practice in Great Britain and North America*. Stockholm: Almquist and Wiksell International with OECD.

Steltenpohl, E. and Shipton, J. (1986). Facilitating a successful transition to college for adults. *Journal of Higher Education*, **57**(6), 637–55.

Taylor, M. (1986). Learning for self-direction: The pattern of a transition process. *Studies in Higher Education*, **11**(1), 55–72.

Thomas, L. G. and Harri-Augstein, S. (1985). *Self-organized Learning*. London: Routledge and Kegan Paul.

Tumin, M. (1976). Valid and invalid rationales. In Keeton, M. T. (Ed.), *Experiential Learning: Rationale, Characteristics and Assessment*. San Francisco: Jossey-Bass.

Usher, R. S. (1986). Adult students and their experience: Developing a resource for learning. *Studies in the Education of Adults*, **18**(1), 24–34.

Walter, G. A. and Marks, S. E. (1981). *Experiential Learning and Change: Theory, Design and Practice*. New York: John Wiley.

Weathersby, R. (1981). Ego development in Chickering, A. (Ed.), *The Modern American College*. San Francisco: Jossey-Bass.

Weil, S. W. (1986). Non-traditional learners within traditional higher education: Discovery and disappointment. *Studies in Higher Education*, **11**(3), 219–35.

Weil, S. W. (1988). Moving from a language of observation to a language of experience: Studying the perspectives of diverse adult learners in higher education. *Journal Access Studies*, **3**(1), 14–43.

Weil, S., Annamanthodo, P., Brandt, G., Chung, D., Douglas, C., Gunning, M. and Phoenix, A. (1985). *Through a Hundred Pairs of Eyes*. London: Institute of Education.

Whitaker, U. G. (1978). Equipping faculty for their emerging role as experiential educators. In Keeton, M. T. and Tate, P. J. (Eds), *Learning by Experience: What, Why, How*. San Francisco: Jossey-Bass and CAEL.

Wilbur, K. (Ed.) (1982). The *Holographic Paradigm and other Paradoxes*. London: New Science Library.

Youngman, F. (1986). *Adult Education and Socialist Pedagogy*. London: Croom Helm.

Index

The Society for Research Into Higher Education

The Society exists both to encourage and to co-ordinate research and development into all aspects of higher education, including academic, organizational and policy issues; and also to provide a forum for debate, verbal and printed. Through its activities, it draws attention to the significance of research into, and development in, higher education and to the needs of scholars in this field. (It is not concerned with research generally, except, for instance, as a subject of study or in its relation to teaching.)

The Society's income is derived from its subscriptions, book sales, conferences and specific grants. It is wholly independent. Its corporate members are universities, polytechnics, institutes of higher education, research institutions and professional and governmental bodies. Its individual members include teachers and researchers, administrators and students. Members are found in all parts of the world and the Society regards its international work as among its most important activities.

The Society discusses and comments on policy, organizes conferences and encourages research. Under the imprint SRHE & OPEN UNIVERSITY PRESS it is a specialist publisher of research, having some 40 titles in print. It also publishes *Studies in Higher Education* (three times a year), which is mainly concerned with academic issues, *Higher Education Quarterly* (formerly *Universities Quarterly*) which will be mainly concerned with policy issues, *Research into Higher Education Abstracts* (three times a year), and a *Bulletin* (six times a year).

The Society's committees, study groups and branches are run by members (with help from a small staff at Guildford), and aim to provide a forum for discussion. The groups at present include a Teacher Education Study Group, a Staff Development Group, a Women in Higher Education Group and a Continuing Education Group which may have had their own organization, subscriptions or publications; (e.g. the *Staff Development Newsletter*). The Governing Council, elected by members, comments on current issues; and discusses policies with leading figures, notably at its evening Forums. The Society organizes seminars on current research for officials of DES and other ministries, an Anglo-American series on standards, and is in touch with bodies in the UK such as the NAB, CVCP, UGC, CNAA and the British Council, and with sister-bodies overseas. Its current research projects include one on the relationship between entry qualifications and degree results, directed by Prof. W. D. Furneaux (Brunel) and one on questions of quality directed by Prof. G. C. Moodie (York). A project on the evaluation of the research standing of university departments is in preparation. The Society's conferences are often held jointly. Annual Conferences have considered 'Professional Education' (1984), 'Continuing Education' (1985, with Goldsmiths' College) 'Standards and

Criteria in Higher Education' (1986, with Bulmershe CHE), 'Restructuring' (1987, with the City of Birmingham Polytechnic) and 'Academic Freedom' (1988, the University of Surrey). Other conferences have considered the DES 'Green Paper' (1985, with the Times Higher Education Supplement), and 'The First-Year Experience' (1986, with the University of South Carolina and Newcastle Polytechnic). For some of the Society's conferences, special studies are commissioned in advance, as 'Precedings'.

Members receive free of charge the Society's *Abstracts*, annual conference Proceedings (or 'Precedings'), *Bulletin and International Newsletter* and may buy SRHE & OPEN UNVERSITY PRESS books at booksellers' discount. Corporate members also receive the Society's journal *Studies in Higher Education* free (individuals at a heavy discount). They may also obtain *Evaluation Newsletter* and certain other journals at a discount, including the NFER *Register of Educational Research*. There is a substantial discount to members, and to staff of corporate members, on annual and some other conference fees.